Global Norms, American Sponsorship and
the Emerging Patterns of World Politics

Palgrave Studies in International Relations Series

General Editors:
Knud Erik Jørgensen, Department of Political Science, University of Aarhus, Denmark

Audie Klotz, Department of Political Science, Maxwell School of Citizenship and Public Affairs, Syracuse University, USA

Palgrave Studies in International Relations, produced in association with the ECPR Standing Group for International Relations, will provide students and scholars with the best theoretically informed scholarship on the global issues of our time. Edited by Knud Erik Jørgensen and Audie Klotz, this new book series will comprise cutting-edge monographs and edited collections which bridge schools of thought and cross the boundaries of conventional fields of study.

Titles include:

Mathias Albert, Lars-Erik Cederman and Alexander Wendt (editors)
NEW SYSTEMS THEORIES OF WORLD POLITICS

Barry Buzan and Ana Gonzalez-Pelaez (editors)
INTERNATIONAL SOCIETY AND THE MIDDLE EAST
English School Theory at the Regional Level

Cornelia Navari (editor)
THEORISING INTERNATIONAL SOCIETY
English School Methods

Dirk Peters
CONSTRAINED BALANCING: THE EU'S SECURITY POLICY

Simon Reich
GLOBAL NORMS, AMERICAN SPONSORSHIP AND THE EMERGING PATTERNS OF WORLD POLITICS

Robbie Shilliam
GERMAN THOUGHT AND INTERNATIONAL RELATIONS
The Rise and Fall of a Liberal Project

Rens van Munster
SECURITIZING IMMIGRATION
The Politics of Risk in the EU

Palgrave Studies In International Relations Series
Series Standing Order ISBN 978–0230–20063–0

You can receive future titles in this series as they are published by placing a standing order. Please contact your bookseller or, in case of difficulty, write to us at the address below with your name and address, the title of the series and the ISBN quoted above.

Customer Services Department, Macmillan Distribution Ltd, Houndmills, Basingstoke, Hampshire RG21 6XS, England

Global Norms, American Sponsorship and the Emerging Patterns of World Politics

Simon Reich
Professor, Division of Global Affairs, Rutgers Newark, the State University of New Jersey, USA

First published 2010 by
PALGRAVE MACMILLAN

Palgrave Macmillan in the UK is an imprint of Macmillan Publishers Limited, registered in England, company number 785998, of Houndmills, Basingstoke, Hampshire RG21 6XS.

Palgrave Macmillan in the US is a division of St Martin's Press LLC, 175 Fifth Avenue, New York, NY 10010.

Palgrave Macmillan is the global academic imprint of the above companies and has companies and representatives throughout the world.

Palgrave® and Macmillan® are registered trademarks in the United States, the United Kingdom, Europe and other countries.

ISBN: 978–0–230–20593–2 hardback
ISBN: 978–0–230–24116–9 paperback

This book is printed on paper suitable for recycling and made from fully managed and sustained forest sources. Logging, pulping and manufacturing processes are expected to conform to the environmental regulations of the country of origin.

A catalogue record for this book is available from the British Library.

A catalog record for this book is available from the Library of Congress.

10   9   8   7   6   5   4   3   2   1
19 18 17 16 15 14 13 12 11 10

Printed and bound in Great Britain by
CPI Antony Rowe, Chippenham and Eastbourne

For Ariane
"Sail away with me, what will be will be"

Contents

Abbreviations

ACI	Airports Council International
AGETIP	Agency for the Execution of Works in the Public Interest to Combat Unemployment Program
AOR	Area of Responsibility
CAS	Country Assistance Strategies
ccTLD	Country Code Top-Level Domain
CCW	Convention on Conventional Weapons
CD	Conference on Disarmament
CDF	Comprehensive Development Framework
CIA	Central Intelligence Agency
CMI	Chr. Michelsen Institute
COE	Council of Europe
CPIA	Country Policy and Institutional Assessment
CSG	Carrier Strike Groups
CSUCS	Coalition to Stop the Use of Child Soldiers
CTF	Combined Task Force
DHS	Department of Homeland Security
DII	Department of Institutional Integrity
DNS	Domain Name System
DOD	Department of Defense
DOT	Department of Transportation
ECLAC	Economic Commission for Latin America and the Caribbean
EDI	Economic Development Institute
EITI	Extractive Industries Transparency Initiative
ETA	Euskadi Ta Askatasuna
EU	European Union
FAA	Federal Aviation Administration
FIS	Islamic Salvation Front/ Front Islamique du Salut
FY	Financial Year
GA	General Assembly (United Nations General Assembly)
GAATW	Global Alliance Against Trafficking in Women
GNP	Gross National Product
GSMs	Global Social Movements
HIPC	Heavily Indebted Poor Countries
HLEG	High Level Experts Group

HMTC	Human Smuggling and Trafficking Center
HRW	Human Rights Watch
IASA	International Aviation Safety Assessments
IATA	International Air Transport Association
IBM	International Maritime Bureau
ICANN	Internet Corporation for Assigned Names and Numbers
ICAO	International Civil Aviation Organization
ICBL	International Campaign to Ban Landmines
ICC	International Criminal Court
ICRC	International Committee of the Red Cross
ICT	Information and Communication Technologies
ICTY	International Criminal Tribunal for the former Yugoslavia
IDA	International Development Agency
IFALPA	International Federation of Airlines Pilots Association
IFIs	International Financial Institutions
IGOs	International Governmental Organizations
IMF	International Monetary Fund
IMO	International Maritime Organization
IMPACT	International Multilateral Partnership against Cyber Crime Threats
INFID	International NGO Forum on Indonesian Development
INTERPOL	International Criminal Police Organization
IO	International Organizations
IP	Internet Protocol
IRA	Irish Republican Army
ITU	International Telecommunications Union
JWC	Joint War Committee
MCA	Military Commissions Act
NATO	North Atlantic Treaty Organization
NGOs	Nongovernmental Organizations
NTIA	National Telecommunications and Information Administration
OECD	Organization for Economic Cooperation and Development
OSCE	Organization for Security and Cooperation in Europe
P3	Private–public partnerships
PhD	Doctor of Philosophy
PICW	President Interagency Council on Women
PIPA	Program on International Policy Attitudes
PRC	People's Republic of China

PrepCom	Preparatory phases for the Information Society at the World Summit on Information Systems
PROTECT	Prosecutorial Remedies and Other Tools to End the Exploitation of Children Today
SCADA	Supervisory Control and Data Acquisition
SECI	Southeast European Cooperative Initiative
TFG	Transitional Federal Government
Three P	Protection, punishment and prevention
TI	Transparency International
TIP	Trafficking in Persons
TSA	Transportation Security Administration
TVPA	Trafficking Victims Protection Act (Victims of Trafficking and Violence Protection Act)
TVPRA	Trafficking Victims Protection Reauthorization Act of 2008
UK	United Kingdom
UN	United Nations
UNESCO	United Nations Educational, Scientific and Cultural Organization
UNGA	United Nations General Assembly
URLs	Uniform Resource Locators
US	United States of America
USAID	United States Agency for International Development
USS	United States Ship
VDP	Voluntary Disclosure Program
WGIG	Working Group on Internet Governance
WMDs	Weapons of Mass Destruction
WSIS	World Summit on the Information Society

Acknowledgments

This book took almost a decade to write. In that time, US administrations came and went; America descended from a supposed "unipolar moment" to purported hegemonic decline. During that time, I wrote and discarded nine drafts of each of the first two chapters, set up a research institute and then changed jobs. As things changed in both dimensions, I tried to encapsulate what was changing in the pattern of global politics, what remained the same, and where the combustible and fragile combination of the two is likely to take us.

The result of this effort is outlined in the pages that follow. I attempt to address a series of arguments about the roles of key actors and the nature of power that seek both to reconcile different positions and simultaneously to synthesize them in a way that identifies a new pattern in global politics. That pattern may be temporary or enduring. It is certainly not static, because US power waxes and wanes and – potentially – with it the American propensity for leadership and for what I describe as sponsorship. But until a suitable and willing replacement comes along, such as the People's Republic of China, the US is the only candidate that can enforce global norms. What is perhaps most surprising is the continued willingness of the US to do so in the face of economic decline, domestic antipathy and foreign hostility.

Honesty requires me to confess that I am more painfully aware of the limits of my argument than even my fiercest critics are likely to identify. But this book is an example of what I was told as a graduate student: "in the case of some books, you just have to stop redrafting, let it go, try and catch the moment, and hope that the readers will be generous." In that spirit, the case studies are therefore meant simply as a heuristic device – to illustrate the argument and, ideally, spark a debate. They do not constitute a definitive test. The conceptualization of a global norm is offered so that someone else generates a better version; the analytic and policy frameworks are presented in the hope that others will improve upon them; and the discussion of the relationship between material and social power is formulated transparently so that others will come up with a better term than "fused."

Prior versions of this work were presented at conferences, lectures, and workshops held at the International Studies Association meeting in New Orleans, Bilkent University in Ankara, Sciences Po (Paris), the University of Toronto, the Zentrum für Entwicklungforschung in Bonn, and the Institute of Social Studies at The Hague. I am grateful for the comments and suggestions of participants at all these places. The errors are all mine.

I have spent most of the last decade trying to be a scholar and an administrator at the same time. I have discovered what others already knew; the two are not easily reconciled. I could not have completed this manuscript without the help of Panayotis A. Yannakogeorgos. Pano helped me complete the research on three of the case study chapters and the conclusion, and is the author of the fifth chapter, on cybersecurity. He has learned that everything takes twice as long as he anticipates, but in doing so he pushed me over the finish line – and for that I am truly grateful.

I also wish to thank Tanu Kohli for all her heroic assistance with epigraphs, footnotes and research at Rutgers Newark; Ali Ashraf for his early assistance at the University of Pittsburgh; Alexandra Webster and Steven Kennedy at Palgrave for constantly harassing me to get this book finished; and to Audie Klotz – the only person brave enough to read the entire manuscript. Audie proved to be the best of critics, both cajoling and encouraging. I have known her for over two decades. My admiration of her has never been greater than it is now.

On a personal note, I wish to thank Richard Friman, Bill Keller, Louis Pauly, Ilya Prizel and Nita Rudra for their enduring friendship across the decades, and Steve Diner, Chancellor of Rutgers Newark, for his support since my arrival there.

In the last decade, while I grew older and stewed over this manuscript, my three daughters – Jamie, Melissa, and Amanda – grew up and became independent, reflective, and lovely young women. My sister, Ruth, became ever more lovable – if that is possible – even as she was stricken by illness. Above all else, however, I had the greatest stroke of luck. I met Ariane Chebel d'Appollonia: spouse, lover, friend, critic, and co-author. Truly, I could not have asked for more. This book is dedicated to her with my love, my gratitude and my deepest respect.

South Orange, NJ, March 2010

1
Old Hegemons, New Challenges and the Limits of Traditional Responses

> We do not seek to impose any system of government on any other nation, but we also don't believe that the principles we stand for are unique to our nation … These freedoms of expression and worship, of access to information and political participation – we believe are universal rights.
>
> Barack Obama, 16 November 2009[1]

Living in a world of "isms"

Policymakers and academics live in a world of foreign policy "isms:" isolationism, unilateralism, bilateralism, imperialism and multilateralism are regarded as the menu from which states choose as they attempt to effect foreign relations. For the United States, while the options have varied, each choice has been conditioned by the assumption that it must act decisively and lead, even when collaborating with other states. According to realist scholars, hegemony implies dominance – expressed through a unilateral or imperialist foreign policy; for liberals who prefer a multilateralist approach, it entails leadership – albeit a "first among equals."

These academic distinctions are then commonly translated into the language of policy debates. Politicians, aware of the popularity of (or at

---

[1] President Barack Obama (2009), "Remarks by President Obama at Town Hall Meeting with Future Chinese Leaders", *The White House Office of Press Secretary*, 16 November 2009, http://www.whitehouse.gov/blog/2009/11/16/full-video-and-photos-presidents-town-hall-shanghai

least the appearance of) a decisive foreign policy, and, conversely, ever fearful of appearing weak or indecisive, have reinforced the idea that the US must "act" to preempt threats to national security. Hard power must be brought to bear on potential opponents, with little patience for the time-consuming processes of negotiation and bargaining, let alone the idea that America might be better off avoiding a commitment to leadership altogether.

In this book, I argue that, in a world of emergent transnational threats, neither traditional academic formulations nor those employed by policy experts are always useful. We no longer live in a world where "isms" inevitably have the utility that they used to have. This is because that world was one exclusively dominated by state actors: where American dominance was predicated on unprecedented superiority, both economic and military; where the threat to security was geographically focused (the Soviet bloc); and where America's closest allies were essentially forced to cooperate with America due to lack of an alternative. Even America's enemies cooperated, in the sense that spheres of influence were implicitly established, treaties were signed (such as the Anti-Ballistic Missile Treaty) and limited amounts of goods, services, and even people were exchanged.

Accompanying this change, we have witnessed the emergence of new actors, notably nongovernmental organizations (NGOs), which have emerged in large part as a result of the proposed shrinkage in government functions (if not in their actual size) advocated by the new public management philosophy of Ronald Reagan and Margaret Thatcher. The governance of stakeholders has replaced government by states. The importance of NGOs is often overstated by their proponents, notably academics who focus on the capacity of NGOs to "get issues on the policy agenda" rather than on the actual enforcement of new policy. Yet their emergence is significant because they do not coexist comfortably with the world of "isms," the latter largely being predicated on the existence of a global system in which states monopolize deliberations, accords, and enforcement. Most importantly, in terms of the argument laid out in this book, NGOs intrude on that traditional structure because they increasingly legitimate policy demands. States, conversely, especially the most powerful states, have become decreasingly legitimate as advocates of specific policies.

This decline in state legitimacy is partially the product of a self-inflicted wound, as politicians of a variety of political hues have demanded a smaller and more efficient government even as the actual size of those on the government payroll has expanded through the process of subcontracting.[2] It is also, however, the product of decreasing capacity of states to meet transnational challenges while officials make promises they cannot keep in order to get themselves elected. Stopping immigration flows, adequately addressing transnational crime, thwarting terrorism and ensuring the preservation of economic and cultural rights all provide examples of political overpromising coupled with inevitable under delivery.

In contrast, I suggest that neither the traditional assortment of "isms" nor sole reliance on the assumption of leadership is effective or politically required by the electorate. The obverse of "leadership," critics might contend, is "followership" – an idea politically unpalatable in the United States. A third option, however, exists – that of "sponsorship." The concept of sponsorship, as used in this book, entails a willingness to enforce or underwrite the costs of enforcing a policy without necessarily taking the lead in placing it on an agenda. Sponsorship certainly entails relinquishing the appearance of acting decisively in the traditional sense. When used selectively, however, its effectiveness in achieving foreign policy outcomes might outweigh considerations of the political importance of "setting the agenda."

Sponsorship, however, is incompatible with a menu only consisting of "isms" – at least for a country like the United States that still seeks to assert its dominance while simultaneously recognizing its own increasing fallibility and the rise of a prospective challenger in the form of the People's Republic of China (PRC). Distinct from an exclusive menu of "isms," I offer an alternative formulation, that of "the global norm." This formulation has, I argue in the pages that follow, several theoretical and policy advantages.

First, it explicitly recognizes that new actors have emerged in world politics and with them a new pattern of global governance. I therefore seek to describe how a new configuration of relations is emerging between nongovernmental organizations (NGOs), global institutions and the most powerful states (notably the United States). This introduction of new actors, and the corresponding shift in the basis for legitimacy, has created a dilemma: while states generally lack the legitimacy to promote policy agendas, NGOs lack the resources (and more particularly the coercive capacity) to enforce them. Under specific conditions, as I shall elaborate in the pages that follow, the advent of global norms

---

[2] For a detailed discussion of this point see Janine Wedel (2009), *The Shadow Elite: How the World's New Power Brokers Undermine Democracy, Government, and the Free Market* (NY: Basic Books).

helps resolve this dilemma. Sponsorship entails the selective enforcement, by the United States, of policy initiatives promoted by NGOs and codified by global organizations. Where such conditions exist, global norms take root and influence behavior.

Second, my focus on global norms attempts to systematically address an issue at the heart of both academic and policy debates – the relationship between what academics term "social" and "material" power and what policymakers term "hard" and "soft" power. In these parallel sets of debates, two tendencies exist: the first is to focus *exclusively* on the importance of one form of power or the other; and the second is to acknowledge that both are important, without showing either how or why they are important or how they are related. In the following pages, I seek to show that both hard and soft power play particular and explicit roles in the formation of global norms. An illustrative set of case studies will show that, when they are alternatively configured in accordance with the old "isms," relying on US leadership, the end product is a predictable policy failure.

Third, the concept of norms has gained widespread usage. As a result, the term "norms" is often potentially misapplied. Everything has become a norm – even when it is not enforced. The concept of a global norm has been more selectively used and is vaguer in its operational application. My formulation, I believe, specifies distinctly both what a global norm is and when it is being applied. In that sense, it potentially adds to the literature by providing a degree of clarity while, I hope, avoiding the problem of overgeneralization.

In the remainder of this chapter and the one that follows, I seek to elaborate upon these claims. My goal is to demonstrate the theoretical and policy limitations of debates that focus on "isms" in view of the new policy challenges; to both define a global norm and substantiate why it differs from other formulations and offers potential new insights; and to lay out a schematic framework that shows how the new configuration of actors and institutions has led to a corresponding new pattern of global politics.

I argue that three conditions must be met for the creation of a global norm – broad-based NGO support, global institutional codification, and American sponsorship through enforcement. States must be willing and able to enforce global norms. Only the US, even if it is a hegemon in decline, currently meets both these conditions.

Chapters three to six of the book then examine four case studies. Each of the four chapters illustrates the varied fates of a potential global norm. One chapter examines a successful case in which all three conditions are met – that of the creation of the anti-human trafficking norm. The remaining three chapters examine cases in which only two of the three conditions are met in different configurations. In each of these cases, I argue, the result is predictable. American attempts at leadership rather than sponsorship, whether pursued through a multilateral (cybersecurity), imperial (anticorruption), or effectively unilateral (preemptive intervention) foreign policy, in attempting to address transnational problems all return to the world of "isms" – and result in policy failure.

The first paradox of power: failure in Iraq and Afghanistan

In the fall of 2000, with American power seemingly at its zenith, a group of academics drawn from America's leading schools of public policy and international affairs gathered in Paris to hear Hubert Védrine, then French foreign minister, deliberate on the global distribution of power. Védrine reflected the popular view from Paris – whether from the perspective of the media, the public, intellectuals, or the halls of politics – that America was not only the last superpower but had now become a "*hyper-power.*"[3] America was, he suggested, able to project power without boundaries, and would do so when it was considered to be in its interest. Such capacity of force projection, Védrine suggested, generated arrogance, the kind epitomized later that decade by Donald Rumsfeld's suggestion that Europe was "old" and America "new."[4] Rumsfeld's disparaging view subsequently gained intellectual ardor in the US through the type of analysis that contrasted a European focus on diplomacy because of its relative "weakness" with an American emphasis on military options because of its contrasting strength.[5]

---

[3] Hubert Védrine, private meeting with the deans of the American Policy Schools of International Affairs, held at the French Foreign Ministry, 26 November 2000. For press articles see also Hubert Védrine (2003), "Face à George W. Bush, trios Propositions", *Le Monde*, 22 May; Hubert Védrine (2003), "Inquiétudes et divergences occidentales", *Le Monde*, 24 December.

[4] See "Outrage at 'old Europe' remarks", BBC News, 23 January 2003, http://news.bbc.co.uk/2/hi/europe/2687403.stm.

[5] For the popularized version of this type of argument see Robert Kagan (2002), "The Power Divide", *Prospect Magazine*, 77, 20 August, http://www.prospectmagazine.co.uk/2002/08/thepowerdivide/. For the elaborated version see Robert Kagan (2003), *Paradise and Power: America and Europe in the New World Order* (New York: Alfred A. Knopf). For ripostes positing a less than sanguine view of the US relative to Europe, see Timothy Garton Ash (2004), *Free World: America,*

Védrine's comments could be accused of exaggeration, but only echoed the sentiment expressed a decade earlier by Charles Krauthammer with his celebrated proclamation of America's "unipolar moment."[6]

Events since 2001 should have served to generate a degree of humility in those who proposed the notion on both sides of the Atlantic.[7] The events of 9/11, and the subsequent wars in Afghanistan and Iraq, demonstrated both the extent and the limits of American power. America projected massive military power and failed to achieve its prescribed goals. The failure of this policy is a matter of public record. War and the insurgency that followed subsequently created broader regional instability; a vortex of resource commitment and massive violence in Iraq; a deepening chasm between the United States and two of its European partners, France and Germany, that lasted for the duration of the Bush Administration; a renewed commitment by terrorists to launching attacks on domestic and global American targets; an unresolved war in Afghanistan despite a renewed commitment to a war described as one "of necessity;" and, arguably, the greater hostility of much of the Islamic world, stretching from the Middle East to South East Asia. Little of this was anticipated, and few benefits from this policy are apparent today. The election of Barack Obama, supposedly more reliant on the tools of "soft power" (as reflected in the quote at the beginning of this chapter) and willing to close the prison on Guantanamo Bay on his first day in office, did little to assuage hostility at home or abroad. Iranian hardliners reiterated their determination to create a nuclear capacity, while North Korea's elite expressed their willingness to use theirs. America's military advantage had been frittered away, with few of its policy goals achieved. Indeed, by the end

---

Europe, and the Surprising Future of the West (New York: Random House); T. R. Reid (2004), *The United States of Europe: The New Superpower and the End of American Supremacy* (New York: Penguin Books); and Jeremy Rifkin (2004), *The European Dream: How Europe's Vision of the Future is Quietly Eclipsing the American Dream* (New York: Tarcher/Penguin).

[6] Charles Krauthammer (1991), "The Unipolar Moment", *Foreign Affairs*, 70:1, 23–33.

[7] For the European version of this argument see Hubert Vérdrine (2003), "Face à George W. Bush, trios Propositions", *Le Monde*, 22 May; Hubert Vérdrine (2003), "Inquiétudes et divergences occidentales", *Le Monde*, 24 December. The fullest expression of his views is to be found in Hubert Védrine (with Dominique Moisi and Philip Gordon, translator) (2001), *France in an Age of Globalization* (Washington DC: Brookings Institution Press). For a commentary on these views of American power see Ezra Suleiman (1998), "Entre la France et les Etats-Unis, le fosse se creuse", *Le Monde*, 10 May; and Ezra Suleiman (2001), "Quel modele américain?", *Le Monde*, 13 September.

of the decade, the huge debts incurred by the Obama Administration as a result of the global financial crisis made the prospect of sustaining US economic advantage unlikely. Once again, American leaders began to talk of burden-sharing, diplomatic solutions and (implicitly) multi-lateralist approaches rather than the (thinly disguised) unilateralism of the Bush era.

What can we conclude from this cycle? Clearly, the exercise of power by a state with vastly more hard power, although consequential for the target, is not synonymous with achieving stated goals.[8] Whether measured in terms of speed, scope, or scale, America demonstrated a historically unprecedented ability to wield force across the globe in the first decade of the new century. Yet in Afghanistan and Iraq, the purported American *hyperpower*, like the major empires before it, from the Athenians and Romans to the British, lacked precisely the capacity to achieve its prescribed, articulated policy goals. The British could not conquer Afghanistan in a century, and Iraq presented them with continuing problems throughout its period of imperial rule.

Likewise, the Americans were unable to achieve their expressly defined objectives in either country. American casualties in Iraq mounted, with Dick Cheney's assertion that the resistance would be defeated by the end of Bush's second term quickly being questioned even by senior members of his own Republican party in the US Senate, and contradicted by Rumsfeld himself within weeks of the claim being made.[9] Even President Bush, in a major foreign policy speech delivered within a month of Cheney's comments, would not commit himself to a timetable of withdrawal.[10] Proponents ultimately suggested that "the surge" in Iraq vindicated the overwhelming use of force. Any claims of vindication, however, should be measured against the ambitious goals specified by the Bush Administration at the outset of the invasion of Iraq, not the low threshold of relatively reduced violence they sought

---

[8] For an important critique of the contemporary realist approach on the grounds that it fails to link power to influence, see Richard Ned Lebow (2005), "Power, Persuasion and Justice", *Millennium: Journal of International Studies*, 33:3, 551–81.

[9] For reports of Cheney's original comments see CNN (2005) "Iraq insurgency in 'last throes,' Cheney says", 31 May, http://www.cnn.com/2005/US/05/30/cheney.iraq/index.html. For a response see CNN (2005), "McCain disputes Cheney on Iraq: Senator calls on White House to stop predicting successes", 20 June, http://www.cnn.com/2005/POLITICS/06/19/mccain/index.html

[10] CNN (2005), "Bush: As the Iraqis stand up, we will stand down", 28 June, http://www.cnn.com/2005/POLITICS/06/28/bush.excerpts/index.html

as their goal by the time of their departure from office. It took half a dozen years to quell insurgents in Iraq, but this was not enough to allow the new Obama Administration the luxury of complete confidence in declaring a definitive withdrawal. Events in Afghanistan proved even more sobering. Although they initially defeated the reigning Taliban regime, American forces failed to capture Osama Bin Laden, instill law and order, or centralize the government in Afghanistan. As the wind-down in Iraq began, American efforts became reinvigorated in Afghanistan, even as American leaders talked of shared responsibilities and renewed commitments.

In the language of policy pundits, America had progressed through a familiar cycle – from a messianic phase in which it claimed self-righteous leadership to a trough of self-doubt; expressed by proponents and opponents alike as the decline of the American empire. To academics, the shift was from hegemony to a narrower reliance on soft power. To policymakers it was a switch away from unilateral to multilateral approaches. In the language of all three approaches, American efforts to project power had resulted in policy failure.

These assessments may have elements of truth, although they may yet prove premature. Clearly, pronouncing any foreign policy action a success or failure is always a risky business, depending on the historical lens adopted. After five decades of military commitment, financial aid and investment, Americans ultimately claim to have "won" the Cold War – an outcome that could, at an admitted stretch, even justify the costs of the Vietnam War. Echoing such a perspective, George W. Bush claimed in June 2005 that, "when the history of this period is written, the liberation of Afghanistan and the liberation of Iraq will be remembered as great turning points in the story of freedom."[11] Proponents of this view focus on the long-term benefits of American participation, such as the possible spread of democracy and stabilization of political power in the Middle East; the effect of the war against Al Qaeda on homeland security; and an explicit awareness on the part of Iraq's neighbors that the threat of American military engagement – in the event that they engage in nuclear proliferation or provide support for global terrorism – is no mere bluff. One further, generally unarticulated benefit is that engagement in Iraq and Afghanistan may provide Americans with friendly regional powers (if not puppet governments) and thus a greater guarantee of access to natural resource markets in countries that form

---

[11] CNN (2005), "Bush: As the Iraqis stand up, we will stand down", 28 June, http://www.cnn.com/2005/POLITICS/06/28/bush.excerpts/index.html.

the geographic fulcrums of Central Asia and the Middle East. All these benefits are possible, however, rather than realized.

Rhetoric aside, the truth is rather more sobering. Even hegemony has its limits. Military commentators agree, in contrast, that with the "surge" in Iraq the US was incapable of fighting a war on a second front;[12] the budgetary costs of the conflict rapidly escalated, which undermined the long-term prospects of the US economy and undoubtedly hindered the recovery from the global financial crisis; and the US found it increasingly difficult in the second term of the Bush Presidency to gain the cooperation of its allies over a number of seemingly unrelated issues.[13]

In fact, the battle against terrorism is highly unlikely to be determined by the eventual outcome of events in Iraq; and it is foolhardy at this point to suggest that the invasions of Afghanistan and Iraq have been anything other than policy failures, given the economic and geostrategic costs incurred by the United States. Perhaps more emphatically, it is hard, given the present strategy, to imagine how a war on terrorism can even be "won" – certainly not overwhelmingly by military means. Terrorist attacks – devastating in terms of human life, psychological scars, and civil liberties – have spread in the last decade from East Africa to Southeast Asia; from the United States to Southern Russia; and from the Middle East to the Iberian Peninsula and on to London. No policy solution is in sight as the ranks of those willing to fight an Islamic Jihad swell. Neither a policy of containment nor one of "seek and destroy" offers a definitive solution to the problem of American security. The rejection of unilateralism in favor of a return to multilateralism may be more politically and intellectually palatable to liberals, but it may be just as ineffective in achieving the prescribed policy goals in the present context.

So is the problem too much use of power, too little use of it, or its misapplication? Continued proponents of the US decision to intervene in Iraq claim, in retrospect, that any policy failure was due to the fact that not enough "hard power" was used at the outset; mostly, too few

---

[12] For troop figures see Global Security, US Forces Order of Battle, http://www.globalsecurity.org/military/ops/iraq_orbat.htm.

[13] Such as then secretary of state Colin Powell's subsequent implicit call for collaborative diplomatic pressure to be exerted on the Sudanese government regarding their (reputedly genocidal) behavior in the Darfur region of Sudan. See Secretary Colin L. Powell, "The Crisis in Darfur", Written Remarks Before the Senate Foreign Relations Committee, Washington DC, 9 September 2004, http://2001-2009.state.gov/secretary/former/powell/remarks/36042.htm

troops were used prior to the surge.[14] Opponents of the "blunt force" version of realism in academia, in contrast, have pointed to the inability of the US to achieve its prescribed goals in each case as an evidence of, alternatively, the significance of asymmetric sources of material power on the one hand,[15] or the importance of "soft" or "social" power (as opposed to material power) on the other.[16] In this book, I reject all three formulations. Rather, arguably, America failed because its leadership was unable to establish the legitimacy of its version of the global norm of preventive intervention to justify its invasion of Iraq, a variant rejected in both the General Assembly and the Security Council of the United Nations.

In more general terms, at least three things have changed in the emergent global context, much of which has been generally recognized by academics, policy commentators, and politicians alike. First, new political stakeholders such as NGOs have assumed a degree of legitimacy in setting the agenda of policymaking. Second, dynamic and evolving global institutions – sometimes called regimes by academics, other times simply referred to as organizations by lay audiences – have attempted to address a series of transnational ecological, economic, and security threats. Third, new asymmetric drivers (such as technological and organizational innovations) have made traditional distinctions between power-holders increasingly blurred.

One option is to discount the importance of these changes; another is to discount the power of states. A third option, often stressed but largely

---

[14] For troop figures see Global Security, US Forces Order of Battle, op. cit.

[15] For the popularized version of the "blunt force" argument see Robert Kagan (2005), "The Power Divide", op. cit. For the elaborated version see Robert Kagan (2003), *Paradise and Power: America and Europe in the New World Order*, op. cit. For ripostes positing a less than sanguine view of the US relative to Europe, see Timothy Garton Ash (2004), *Free World: America, Europe, and the Surprising Future of the West*, op. cit.

[16] For popularized versions of this asymmetric argument, emphasizing European sources of soft or social power, see T. R. Reid (2004) *The United States of Europe: The New Superpower and the End of American Supremacy*, op. cit.; Jeremy Rifkin (2004), *The European Dream: How Europe's Vision of the Future is Quietly Eclipsing the American Dream*, op. cit. For an early discussion of soft power see Joseph S. Nye Jr (2004), *Soft Power: the Means to Success in World Politics* (New York: Public Affairs); and Joseph S. Nye Jr (1990) *Bound to Lead: the Changing Nature of American Power* (New York: Basic Books). For a seminal piece on norms see Martha Finnemore and Kathryn Sikkink (1998), "International Norm Dynamics and Political Change", *International Organization*, 52:4, 887–917.

left unaddressed, is to acknowledge these shifts and investigate how they work interactively to influence effective policy outcomes.

Examining the utility of these different traditional formulations in the context of explaining American policy failure offers insights into their qualities and limits. The multilateralist position emphasizes the importance of legitimacy as a source of influence, and with it a claim that multilateralism is more functional than the widely criticized unilateralism (for which one can substitute the term "realism" in academic parlance) of the Bush Administration. Power, arguably, was expended by the US to little positive effect and with a loss of international support. Policy-oriented scholars and commentators thus pointed to this apparent failure of US foreign policy in emphasizing the dysfunctional nature of unilateralism.

More theoretically oriented academics have engaged in an extended debate from both of the two perspectives. Liberal theorists have argued that the composition of the coalition in Iraq was too limited. More states had to be involved, a decision made through global or regional coalitions in a transparent, consensual process. Those from the constructivist perspective (pre-dating but including the US military intervention), taking a differing approach, focused on the significance of civil society actors as agents of social power in framing debates. From both the perspectives, the US action lacked legitimacy, and this – to varying degrees – explains its failure. *Efforts to generate a consensus, built around the version of the principles of preventive intervention favored by the Bush Administration, failed.* If so, the question remains unresolved as to why it failed, and whether a consensus built among states through traditional multilateral avenues would have worked to better achieve the stated goal of a stable, violence-free and democratic Iraq.

The second paradox of power: the spread of democracy

The first prong of the Bush Administration's oft-noted National Security Strategy document, issued in 2002, was preventive intervention. Yet what both the policy community and more theoretically oriented scholars have largely ignored is the comparative success of the US in support of another goal discussed in that same document – the promotion of democracy.

Arguably, despite the lack of progress in Pakistan, Uzbekistan, and parts of the Middle East, successful "Velvet" revolutions took place after 2000 in Europe, the Caucasus, and Africa without direct American military intervention, with limited violence and relatively little social instability. In many cases, illegitimate regimes fell with surprising ease. Even states resolutely opposed to the United States and its allies held elections embracing elements of democracy (even if they have not accepted all aspects of civil and political rights, and the outcome has been the election of regimes expressly hostile to the US and its allies) as in the case of Iran or the Palestinian Authority – and the refusal of Iranians to sit idly by when they felt an election was stolen from them.

Critics could suggest that not all of these cases constituted elections in the full democratic sense of the term. Women were excluded from the electorate in some places; candidates were prescreened so that they represented only a small proportion of the political continuum in others. Nonetheless, progress was made in the spreading of democracy. Only one authoritarian regime, in Belarus, remained in power in Europe by 2005. The Syrians left Lebanon and elections soon followed. By 2009, Lebanon elected a government openly supported by the US. Even in Togo, part of the African continent routinely described as a "basket case" by casual Western commentators, citizens rejected a coup and elections were soon scheduled. The same was true of Liberia, a country wracked by civil wars over the last two decades. Certainly, there were setbacks. Hamas' victory led to a civil war in Gaza; Ukraine's velvet revolution was followed by domestic turmoil; and the promised election in the Ivory Coast failed to materialize. Russia, under Putin, clearly regressed towards authoritarianism. Nonetheless, the progress towards the spread of democratic regimes was evident.

These numbers are quantifiable. According to one influential report, there were 23 democratic regimes in 1950 and 35 by 1977, and their number nearly doubled in the late 1980s and 1990s. By 2005, the number had increased to a total of 88.[17]

Of course, not all of these shifts towards democracy were directly American-inspired. Many, presumably, had indigenous roots. But the fact that they were seen as domestically inspired, and not as the product of American direct intervention, added to their strength.

---

[17] Monty G. Marshall and Ted Robert Gurr (2005), "A Global Survey of Armed Conflicts, Self-Determination Movements, and Democracy", *Peace and Conflict, 2005* (College Park, Maryland: Center for International Development and Conflict Management). In their large-scale report they define and measure democracies (on a 1–10 scale) as having institutionalized procedures for open, competitive political participation; choosing and replacing chief executives in open, competitive elections; and imposing substantial checks and balances on the powers of the chief executive. For both figures and measures see page 17.

Material support was often provided from external sources through aid, trade, and even, occasionally, coercive capability. It was coupled, however, with what was widely regarded as a moral imperative (through an appeal to human rights) consistent – where democracy took root – with the claims of both domestic and transnational NGOs.

We can thus place these recent developments in some context. Since the end of the Cold War, American efforts to promote civil and political rights, and to encourage a more transparent form of capitalism and governance, have been remarkably successful. The language of "good governance, transparency, and accountability" promoted aggressively by the US has become a part of the common lexicon, not just of the ruled but also of the rulers themselves. American administrations and civil society organizations have poured material resources into the promotion of democracy and capitalism, to clear effect. Although the exceptions remain numerous and significant, there is evidence of the development of a global norm towards democracy, which is an example of an American foreign policy success.

Reconciling the two paradoxes: the forms and substance of US foreign policy

So we are left with an apparent quandary; the *hyperpower* (or hegemon, in the language of international relations) failed to achieve its goal in the most critical of circumstances and with an extensive use of force. Yet the same power has achieved its other stated goal with a more modest use of resources – even in places where it routinely encounters fervent opposition – and in the absence of demonstrating such aggressive "leadership." Furthermore, there is little more than circumstantial evidence that the vibrant spread of democracy cannot be explained by the adoption of a multilateral approach or that states explicitly orchestrated the ensuing changes despite their evident involvement. Certainly, global and regional organizations were formed and a "human rights regime" emerged.[18] Yet it is hard to support the contention that states, let alone the hegemon acting unilaterally, were responsible for the spread of democracy.[19]

---

[18] See, for example, Jack Donnelly (1986), "International Human Rights: A Regime Analysis", *International Organization*, 40:3, 599–642.

[19] Indeed, a critic might argue that the momentum behind the spread of democracy began to suffer when the Bush Administration announced that this was its primary objective in Iraq.

There are several possible ways out of this apparent quandary. One is to suggest that the spread of democracy had little to do with American support: that the spread of human rights long pre-dated American engagement and developed along a quite distinct path. It was the product of social forces in a period when state power had declined. This type of approach focuses on the role of NGOs in influencing the dynamics of politics through a new process of global governance. Alternatively, one could conclude that force is not the key determinant in achieving foreign policy goals, or that American authority in the advocacy and material support of the spread of democracy has a more emphatic role because it is seen as legitimate and not self-serving. Where it did appear self-serving to critics, as in the case of Iraq, it failed.

These claims may all contain elements of the truth. I believe, however, that something more complex, and indeed important, is occurring that may explain this puzzle as well as more general trends in global politics, beyond formulations that link theory to policy, either through an overt reliance on traditional formulations such as unilateralism, multilateralism, or imperialism, or through a predominant focus on state or non-state actors.

One temptation is to focus on arguments suggesting that hard (material) power has less significance than soft (social) power in the dynamics of current global politics. Such a position would imply that the globalization of trade and arms, along with the resulting diffusion of technology, has made the use of hard power – as traditionally employed by states – of lesser strategic significance. In this formulation, international institutions – and, within them, both weaker states and transnational actors – act as a brake on the ambitions of more powerful states and can thus explain American policy failures. Such a position, however, cannot explain American policy successes. An obverse position, focusing on the utility of hard power, suffers from the same problem – it cannot explain varied outcomes.

So, rather than contemplating a choice between hard (material) and soft (social) power, I argue that the policy choices facing the US have altered. The foreign policy posture is no longer a conventional choice framed in terms of the traditional options of "isms:" unilateralism, bilateralism, multilateralism, or even imperialism. The shift towards transnational problems – ecological, economic or military – has eviscerated the distinction between domestic and foreign policy. State power has been tempered by the legitimacy (and therefore the preferences) of non-state constituents. Coupled with that, the shift in the content of the primary foreign policy challenges has made the linkage between hard and soft power both more complex and more important. This shift is explained, in theoretical and policy terms, through the evolution of global norms. Given the combination of new challenges, new actors and reduced legitimacy, the variant I present in this book focuses on the exercise of influence through the concept of "sponsorship" rather than "leadership" – entailing the selective use of hard power in the context of the more subtle application of soft power by societal actors. Global norms capture the essence of this formulation.

As discussed at greater length below, the construction of a global norm entails the marriage of institutions and power while avoiding the impression of stridency given by a superpower in asserting itself as a "first among equals." Global norms entail the linkage of soft and hard power. They require the initiative of civil society actors, and are built on achieving consensus, yet may necessitate the use of coercion by the US (in its current capacity as hegemon). In sum, the construction of a global norm may both explain part of the dynamics of global politics and simultaneously, in practical terms, serve American interests by addressing problems that the US is incapable of addressing alone. Global norms may reflect US preferences, but not US preferences alone. Indeed, they must – a priori – reflect support among a broad base of civil society actors.

The fact that the construction of a global norm is not simply a restatement of a multilateralist argument, nor a matter of getting other states to support the US position through persuasion or leadership, is key. Indeed, for a global norm to effectively influence the behavior of other states, a hegemonic power has to play a critical role in supporting and enforcing a global norm, but must *not* be seen as its major proponent. This would be counterproductive, because it would be construed as an expression of narrow self-interest. It is not the expression of social or material power that is required; it is the capacity to refrain from doing so that is key.

The successful construction of a global norm requires advocacy from societal actors who are seen as independent and representative of a broad swath of public opinion. Furthermore, such a process requires state support and codification through international institutions in order to gain legitimacy. It does, however, require US support (as a hegemon) and its willingness to use tangible resources for implementation and enforcement. As a policy choice, global norms therefore differ in character from the "isms" – bilateralism, imperialism, multilateralism or even isolationism – in subtle but nonetheless important ways, as reflected in Table 1.1.

Table 1.1   Foreign policy: separating global norms from the "isms"

		Hegemon generally leads foreign policy initiative	
		Yes	No
Hegemon seeks consensus	Yes	Multilateralism	Global norm
	No	Imperialism	Isolationism Bilateralism Unilateralism

There are common features to the negotiation of a multilateral agreement and the construction of a global norm. As Table 1.1 indicates, a global norm is comparable to a multilateralist accord in that, in both cases, the actors seek to generate a consensus among participants, although both entail the possible use of force.

As policy options, however, multilateralism and global norms are generally distinguished from each other in key ways. First, multilateralist policy in practice seeks a narrower consensus from among purely "strong states" or "great powers." A global norm as a policy option seeks a broader consensus, involving both state and non-state actors. It may not, and indeed probably will not, achieve universal consensus. Yet the goal is to create an effectively uncontested position for a norm in the international community, whereby defiance of the norm is regarded as illegitimate and the limited and largely sanctioned use of coercion is acceptable.

Second, US proponents of multilateralism often talk of engagement, consensus and burden-sharing, but do so in the context of explicit American leadership: the commonly used term (at least in Washington) being *primus inter pares* – "a first among equals." In this context, multilateralism involves a process of negotiation and bargaining built around explicit, articulated values promoted by the dominant power. In practice, for example, the exercise of "soft power" is more likely to be a product of USAID programs than any civil society initiative. NGOs here are regarded largely as partners who implement state initiatives rather than setting the agenda.

Alternatively, the consolidation and enforcement of global norms involve significant American participation, but they are not the product of American initiatives even if they are consistent (as we will see, by necessity) with American values. Rather, part of their appeal and credibility lies in the fact that the actual initiative behind the creation of a global norm resides elsewhere – among the broad-based representatives of civil society. The multilateralist position is thus reversed in the case of a global norm; *civil society actors initiate and the hegemon largely enforces or underwrites a norm.*[20]

As forms of foreign policy, both multilateralism and the construction of global norms contrast with unilateralist, bilateralist, imperialist, or even isolationist forms of policy, in which autonomy is privileged over consensus, and none requires a process of engagement that seeks to generate consensus. Imperialism is distinct from unilateralism, bilateralism, and isolationism in that it does entail leadership – if only for the purpose of compliance and seeking to sustain the appearance of the legitimacy of imperialist rule against the background of coercion. Try as they may, however, none of these four options "below the line" generate legitimacy for hegemonic action; and usually none is suitable for dealing with the preponderant transnational challenges America currently faces.

Yet, in theory, a global norm is, perhaps surprisingly, consistent with isolationist, unilateralist, and bilateralist forms of foreign policy in at least one dimension. Both entail the state refraining from embarking on an explicit foreign policy leadership, albeit with the intent of achieving strategically different goals. Clearly, however, the two forms of policy differ in motive and the process by which they occur, as well as the intended outcome. Isolationism, unilateralism, and even bilateralism prioritize autonomy, while the pursuit of a global norm is intended to engender cooperation; the former involves detachment, and the latter engagement. What they share is the absence of a proactive element of foreign policy leadership. In the case of unilateralism and bilateralism, the hegemon does not "lead", it acts – with the possibility of inviting others to do so as well, depending on the circumstances. This, however, does not constitute leadership, but rather an independent action.

As a form of foreign policy, the option of promulgating global norms is currently available only to the US because, despite its current relative decline from power (at least according to some measures), it is still the only state whose resources approximate the capacities of a hegemon.

---

[20] In that sense, global norms are reminiscent of Steven Luke's conception of power, whereby force and social control are obscured behind a broader notion of interest, getting others to pursue your preferred option because they generally consider it in their interest. See Steven Lukes (1974), *Power: a Radical View*, (London: Macmillan Press).

Critics might reasonably argue that the recent recession has buffeted the US economy, with its burgeoning debt and dwindling manufacturing base.[21] Clearly, there are no uncontested indicators of hegemony, and the US capacity to underwrite the rules has declined. But the same is true of America's primary competitors, with the European and Japanese economies experiencing the same or greater relative shrinkage in the size of the economy and burgeoning public debt that they can ill afford (reflected, most emphatically, by the Greek debt crisis). Furthermore, the US military capacity still dwarfs those of its realistic competitors, as does the size of its economy. This situation is dynamic; hegemons rise and decline, and the PRC (whose economy doubled in size in the first decade of the century) may plausibly be only decades away from assuming the role. In the short term, however, there are no other prospective states willing and able to enforce global norms.

The US is privileged in this situation because constructing global norms involves a specific configuration of soft (social) and hard (material) power. Only the US (when it is willing) is able to bear the associated enforcement costs. While the scope and domain of the capacity of the US to achieve its goals unilaterally is increasingly limited, and imperialist forms of policy are both expensive and ineffective, the US is nonetheless the only country that can effectively (in the current context) sponsor the promulgation of a global norm; it is the only country with the material resources to do so.[22]

In the long term European states, collectively through the EU, might be a viable alternative source for the generation and enforcement of global norms, but not in the short term. This is because, as critics point out, Europe is beset with its own domestic problems and a preference for "soft" power instruments – due to cost, ideological proclivity or a combination of the two. Furthermore, Europe's share of global output continues to shrink. As Jim Manzi points out, "America's share of global output has been constant at about 21%. Europe's share, meanwhile, has been collapsing in the face of global competition – going from a little less than 40% of

---

[21] For an informed and insightful perspective on this issue, see Herman Schwartz (2009), *Subprime Nation: American Power, Global Capital, and the Housing Bubble* (Ithaca, NY: Cornell University Press).

[22] For a recent comparable argument in support of the importance of US sanctions for compliance, see Ivan Krastev (2004), *Shifting Obsessions: Three Essays on the Politics of Anticorruption* (Budapest, HU: Central European University Press). For a relatively notable book on the price of American imperialism, see Niall Ferguson (2004) *Colossus: the Price of America's Empire* (New York: Penguin Press).

global production in the 1970s to about 25% today."[23] As a result, while it may effectively veto the spread of a global norm (through non-cooperation), it lacks both the resources to sponsor global norms and the coercive instruments needed to enforce them. The enforcement costs are often simply too great. Europe remains in the throes of an identity crisis and, collectively, it has an inefficient economy, a burgeoning welfare state, the demographic problem of an aging population, and is beset by the problem of increased racism, largely as a product of a growing, alienated Islamic (first and second-generation) presence. Indeed, European states prefer to reject the pragmatic response to offset their aging population, allowing more immigrants from many of these Muslim states.

Notably during periods of American decline, proponents of the view of Europe as the emergent power compare national measures of productivity, social welfare, and life expectancy and extrapolate on that basis about Europe's collective capacity to achieve foreign policy goals. Certainly, these factors are relevant to a nation's (or region's) capacity to pursue an effective foreign policy. But such an approach fails to note the continued importance of force projection, Europe's relatively more limited technology base (and thus its inability to innovate more sophisticated military technologies) and its relatively weak coercive capacity to support its diplomatic initiatives (as a product of its smaller military budget and the slower development of a fully integrated and united defense force). Even those initiatives supported or sponsored by the European Union that have not been reliant on military capabilities have failed the acid test of becoming globally accepted and implemented. Soft power may be a requisite for the construction of a global norm, but it is insufficient to successfully generate one. As a result, while it can maneuver diplomatically, the EU is not able to effectively promote global norms in the absence of US support.[24]

---

[23] Jim Manzi (2010), "Keeping America's Edge", *National Affairs*, 2, http://nationalaffairs.com/publications/detail/keeping-americas-edge

[24] My position on the significance of the US relative to the EU therefore clearly differs from that adopted in work by scholars such as Daniel Drezner, who argues, in an important 2007 book based on a game-theoretic formulation, that international regulation is based on great power collaboration. Great powers are defined in terms of market size and relative vulnerability to external disruptions, and Drezner adjudges the US and EU to constitute comparable powers, with a reciprocal veto bloc, on that basis. Yet, ultimately, Drezner *assumes* them to have a reciprocal veto capacity, just as he *assumes* it legitimate to treat the EU as a unitary actor. He does not focus on their capacity to compel behavior, or their capabilities beyond the realm of international economic regulation. While these are perfectly legitimate positions for the purposes of his argument,

In fact, successive global initiatives that have been supported by European countries (individually or collectively) over the last three decades, but have lacked American support, have arguably proved of limited consequence. The refusal or withdrawal of American commitment has left a series of conventions, protocols, and initiatives more formidable on paper than in reality.[25] From the failure to ratify the Convention on Children's Rights in 1987 to the banning of landmines in 1997; from the dilution of the Anti-Ballistic Missile Treaty to the US refusal to sign the Kyoto Protocol, the results have been comparable. Lack of American commitment has given these initiatives few teeth and few resources to support their efforts. The use of child labor is a growing problem; landmines still kill and maim thousands each year; and the refusal of the US to sign the Kyoto Protocol has reduced the political pressures on countries such as the PRC to do so. As the US is still the predominant power (and the only current superpower), American willingness to materially support a global norm is intrinsic – a necessary condition – to its successful implementation.

There are two main criticisms of this perspective. The first is that other major states can veto any attempt to create a global norm, especially if a coalition of states opposes its implementation. This claim certainly has credence. Like a multilateral approach, global norms are reliant on cooperation where bilateral coercion fails. My point is that many actors may veto an attempt to generate one, but only a hegemon who is willing and able to pay enforcement costs can create one – both points being reinforced in the case studies that follow.

A second criticism is the claim that global norms (in essence, if not by that name) have been created without American support. Advocates of the success of the International Criminal Court (ICC), for example, argue that it has proven successful in universalizing a legal system of human rights despite America's refusal to support the Court. But in doing so they ignore the fact that those prosecuted by the court have generally

---

he does not attempt to defend either position theoretically or empirically. See Daniel W. Drezner (2007), *All Politics is Global: Explaining International Regulatory Regimes* (Princeton, NJ: Princeton University Press), especially pp. 33–9. For a statement of this type of argument, largely focusing on soft power, see Zaiki Laidi (2005), *La Norme sans la Force: L'énigme de la Puissance Européenne* (Paris: Presses de Sciences Po).

[25] For a major book on the destructive effects of UK and US behavior, see Philippe Sands (2005), *Lawless World: America and the Making and Breaking of Global Rules from FDR's Atlantic Charter to George W. Bush's Illegal War* (New York: Penguin Press).

been leaders detained from failed and fragile countries wracked by civil war, whose capacity to resist external intervention was severely limited. This hardly constitutes a "strong test" of the court's global authority. War criminals from the former Yugoslavia prosecuted by the ad hoc International Criminal Tribunal for the Former Yugoslavia (ICTY) were tried only after extensive military action by an American-led NATO force. Without such military support, the ability of the ICC to prosecute cases remains strictly limited.

America may have a bloated military budget and may have too readily resorted to coercive measures in the last decade, but European over-reliance on soft power diplomacy, coupled with its ever-present nationalist tensions and slow collective military build-up, limits its effort to export norms even to cases such as the EU accession candidates.[26] Europe, collectively, needs to balance soft and hard power if it is successfully to support and enforce global norms.

This is not to suggest that the situation is static. Different configurations of power, along with different states, could – in principle – sponsor global norms that are effectively implemented. It does not take too much creativity to imagine a more stable, less inwardly focused and mercantilist PRC supporting and enforcing global norms. It does not, in principle, even require a *hyperpower* to generate, consolidate, and enforce global norms. As Duncan Snidal argued in the context of the maintenance of international regimes, a preponderance of material power – whether held by a hyperpower or collectively achieved by a collaborative group of states – is sufficient (in principle) to generate a global norm.[27]

Nonetheless, while the development of a global norm in the context of a multipolar distribution of power is theoretically possible, the need for greater collaboration as a product of mutual interest makes it harder to attain and sustain one – a classic collective action problem. In theory, therefore, global norms can be generated under varied conditions and are not confined to the current context (as discussed in greater detail below). A hegemonic distribution of power, however, is the most *likely* condition for the effective formulation and implementation of such a norm because it requires the commitment of resources by fewer actors.

---

[26] Even in these cases, the EU's efforts have often failed, as discussed by Carolyn M. Warner (2007), *The Best System Money Can Buy: Corruption in the European Union* (Ithaca, New York: Cornell University Press).

[27] Duncan Snidal (1985), "The Limits of Hegemonic Stability Theory", *International Organization*, 39:4, 579–614.

The current distribution of power therefore makes the prospect of success more likely, even if that factor alone will not ensure it.

What makes a norm "global"?

An extensive array of literature posits a series of formal definitions of norms dating back to the work of Talcott Parsons in the 1950s.[28] Some focus on domestic norms, others on international ones. More recently, the conventional definition of a norm in international relations is that of a standard of appropriate behavior for actors with a given identity.[29] Generally considered a benchmark in the application of the concept of norms by constructivists in linking the domestic context to the dynamics of the international system, however, is the work of Martha Finnemore and Kathryn Sikkink. They effectively describe the "life cycle" of the ideal type of an international norm – invoking the stages of norm emergence, a tipping point, its acceptance, a cascade of support and a bandwagon effect towards internalization that essentially catapults a widely shared value from the domestic to the international level and then towards domestic acceptance again in an interactive process.[30] Norms are therefore promoted by activists, gather momentum and then become a force for change.

One example of this process might be the growth of the anti-slavery movement from its origins in British legislation to a global proscription. Another, studied by Audie Klotz, is the successful effort of the

---

[28] See, for example, Talcott Parsons (1951), *The Social System* (London: Routledge & Kegan Paul). Parsons defined norms as "generalized formulations – more or less explicit – of expectations of proper action by differentiated units in relatively specific situations." Parsons is quoted in Charles W. Kegley and Gregory A. Raymond (1990), *When Trust Breaks Down: Alliance Norms and World Politics* (Columbia: University of South Carolina Press), p. 14. Furthermore, Jepperson, Wendt and Katzenstein suggest that "Norms are collective expectations about proper behavior for a given identity" in Peter J. Katzenstein (ed.) (1996), *The Culture of National Security: Norms and Identity in World Politics* (New York: Columbia University Press), p. 54. In the same book Martha Finnemore maintains that norms "create permissive conditions for action" if not determinative of behavior, providing a standard against which policies are measured and behavior adjudged. See her chapter entitled "Constructing Norms of Human Intervention", ibid., p. 158.

[29] Ibid., p. 5.

[30] Finnemore and Sikkink (1998), op. cit., p. 893.

anti-apartheid movement to create a *global* norm.[31] Interestingly, she characterizes global norms as being "constitutive" of international politics, but does not further explore the issue of what makes them *global* in character, nor does she link material to social power.[32] Ethan Nadelmann's work also uses the term "global norm" when examining the importance of global prohibition regimes dedicated to the enforcement of laws relating to criminal behavior such as drugs and prostitution.[33] These are embedded in global regimes, he suggests, that generally prohibit or proscribe action; they are formed to prevent "regime leakage"; they provide legitimacy and assist in the codification of international law and therefore in the development of "an international society of human beings sharing common moral bonds."[34] Interestingly, he does suggest that norms emerge because they reflect moral and emotional interests, as well as security and economic considerations, of the most powerful states.[35] He then adds that those norms that evolve into prohibition regimes generally reflect the criminal laws of the most powerful societies. Finally, he does point out that the transnational character of the problem forms a significant incentive for states to act.[36]

Nonetheless, Nadelmann's insightful analysis is problematic for four reasons. First, like Klotz, he does not really focus on a definition of what makes a norm "global" in character. Second, he does not address the question of whether, and how, norms influence the behavior of actors, linking the process, from motive to outcome, in a comprehensive manner. Third, in common with much of the work on norms – according to Ian Hurd – there is a propensity to overstate the consensus that exists

---

[31] Audie Klotz (1995), "Norms Reconstituting Interests: Global Racial Equality and U.S. Sanctions Against South Africa", *International Organization*, 49:3, 451–78. Note, therefore, that Klotz describes and locates anti-slavery in the context of anti-racism as a global norm, thus discussing global norms more as a context than an explanatory instrument.

[32] Ibid., p. 461.

[33] Ethan A. Nadelmann (1990), "Global Prohibition Regimes: The Evolution of Norms in International Society", *International Organization*, 44:4, 479–526.

[34] Ibid., p. 484. Interestingly, and importantly for my argument, Nadelmann does note the central importance of America in the twentieth century in the promulgation of these norms.

[35] Ibid., p. 484.

[36] Ibid., p. 524.

over norms.[37] Finally, his work emphasizes the initiation of a norm at the expense of its consolidation. In that sense, it elaborates on the issue of social power rather than material power. How these two dimensions are fused remains largely unaddressed.

So what are the attributes of global norms? Five elements distinguish a global norm. First, it has broad geographic application across space on a worldwide basis. Second, beyond a simple moral imperative, its legitimacy is based on a recognized body of knowledge that includes explicit philosophical and normative elements at its foundations. Third, global norms include explanatory, descriptive, and prescriptive elements – thus incorporating a notion of praxis. Fourth, global norms have a functional utility as a device designed to generate consent, cooperation, and burden-sharing through the generation of their own supportive institutional structures embodied in constitutions, conventions, and protocols expressed in international organizations. Finally, global norms have mechanisms for an unprecedented coercive capacity for domestic enforcement through the actions of great powers, because this formulation explicitly links material and social power. *These components – scope, legitimacy based on a theory of justice (rather than simply an ethical proposition), praxis, their embedded nature and capacity for enforcement – collectively define a global norm, as opposed to other forms of norms discussed in the literature of international relations.*

Let us examine these attributes in greater detail. First, global norms are distinct in scale from *universal* and *international* norms. *Global norms represent the relative predominance of an expressed value.* Global norms are therefore *probably* likely (not *universally* likely) to be observed in terms of the behavior of actors across cultures, contexts, and potentially even time, subject to local adaptation. Finnemore and Sikkink suggest that domestic norms become internationalized as a result of the actions of norm entrepreneurs – if they can convince enough state leaders to accept the norm.[38] The authors also argue that they may be regional or international but cannot be global – although subsequent work by others has specifically focused on both their regional and their local inter-

---

[37] Ian Hurd (2005), "The Strategic Use of Liberal Internationalism: Libya and the UN Sanctions, 1992–2003", *International Organization*, 59:3, 495–526.

[38] Finnemore and Sikkink (1998), op. cit., p. 895.

pretation and application.[39] Finnemore and Sikkink do not say why that is the case.[40]

In practice, however, the terms "global norm" and "international norm" are often conflated. Nadelmann provides one such example in his discussion of global regimes, while Ramesh Thakur provides another with his analysis of the growth of humanitarian law.[41] Neither author, however, defines the meaning of a global norm. Finnemore and Sikkink are reasonable in denying that "global norm" is a meaningful term in an absolute sense if, by that, they mean that a norm cannot be universal in its meaning or acceptance because the term "universal" implies an unchallenged consensus. A global norm, as I employ the term, is not a universal norm in a practical sense, because any sort of shared value meets with dissent – especially any sort of expressed value that seeks to transcend space, culture, and (possibly) time. No norm is universally accepted in that absolute sense.

But this kind of distinction potentially ignores the political dimension of norms. Conflict over the importance, appropriateness, interpretation, and enforcement of norms is inevitable and should be anticipated. Exceptional behavior regarding a norm therefore does not dilute the notion that it is "global." It is not fruitful to dismiss the idea of a global norm because it might not be universally embraced. The key questions thus become: is it considered legitimate according to the international community, even if it is disliked by some actors? And is it enforced with reasonable consistency, based on that shared understanding as being legitimate? If the answer to those two questions is yes – that it is understood as legitimate and enforced on that basis on a global scale – then it meets one precondition of a global norm. Of course, this definition narrows the breadth of norms that can be defined as global. Arguably, it also leads to a focus on some of the most important ones.

---

[39] See, as examples, Amitav Acharya (2004), "How Ideas Spread: Whose Norms Matter? Norm Localization and Institutional Change in Asian Regionalism", *International Organization*, 58:2, 239–75; Peter Katzenstein (2005), *A World of Regions: Asia and Europe in the American Imperium* (Ithaca, New York: Cornell University Press).

[40] Finnemore and Sikkink (1998), op. cit., p. 892.

[41] In addition to the earlier discussion of the works of Klotz and of Nadelmann, an important example of this tendency focused on the policy world is evident in the work of Ramesh Thakur. See, as an example, Ramesh Thakur (2001), "Global norms and international humanitarian law: an Asian perspective", *International Review of the Red Cross*, 841, 19–44.

Second, global norms are predicated on the foundation of a theory of justice, not simply a moral imperative. All norms, for sure, as Finnemore and Sikkink point out, are considered "good and appropriate" by their proponents, however questionable to others.[42] Furthermore, much of the work on norms generally offers recourse to an ethical absolute that is biblical in character, such as "thou shalt not kill" or "all people are created equal" (and therefore, in the latter case, slavery is abhorrent). Even the advocates of what might be regarded by many as morally more questionable norms make absolutist claims – such as the innate superiority of one race over another. Regardless of the content, those propagating such claims consider abrogation of these propositions repugnant. Yet these claims often make a simple appeal and offer little in the way of foundational substance or depth.

Global norms generally go further, attempting to legitimate their appeal with reference to a body of knowledge that claims an authoritative principled position based on rights and obligations. As discussed in the case studies that follow, even when ultimately unsuccessful, proponents of potential global norms make reference to long established, deeply debated principles. These have often (although not exclusively) emerged from – and are embedded in – the values of enlightenment, justified by democratic theories of state and society, social justice, or economic prosperity.

Candidates for global norms need not, however, offer recourse to such liberal principles. The presence of a moral imperative should not be equated with either "the good" or with the processes of modernity, post-industrialism or technological innovation, as some have claimed.[43] Indeed, such a claim of innate justice was evident in the principle of the "Divine Right of Kings," an early candidate for a global norm, widespread in Europe and its borders in the sixteenth and seventeenth centuries.[44] The idea was prominent in a parallel form in China and East

---

[42] Finnemore and Sikkink (1998), op. cit., p. 899.

[43] Coral Bell (2002), "Normative shift", *The National Interest*, 70, 44–54.

[44] Among the most famous proponents of Divine Right was Jacques-Benigne Bossuet, who developed many of the ideas offered earlier by Jean Bodin in *Six Books of the Commonweal*, first published in 1576. In response to successive waves of rebellion in Europe, Bodin's exhaustive treatise argued for indivisible and unlimited sovereign power as a solution to instability and violence. As an archetypal progenitor of a norm entrepreneur, Bossuet developed Bodin's argument further in fomenting the notion that monarchical rule could not be challenged. As God's anointed representatives on earth, not surprisingly, many powerful monarchs of Europe promulgated this doctrine in response to a fear that Papal

Asia, where it was referred to as the "Mandate of Heaven." With Charles I's execution, the principle of Divine Right was repudiated in England and gradually faded out in Europe over the next century. Ultimately, it had no hegemon to enforce it, and was thus reliant on national power configurations to sustain it. Its capacity to flourish wilted as these configurations shifted. Its authoritative claim, however, sprang not simply from a biblical edict but rather from a professed ethical set of propositions about the relationship between man and God. From this emerged a fusion of legitimacy and power that solidified monarchical rule, its last vestiges disappearing with the Russian revolution. Ultimately, it failed because it could not establish its legitimacy beyond a narrow (albeit very powerful) group of stakeholders.

A third element of global norms builds upon this normative foundation, offering some broad body of "scientific" theory, in which principles about a theory of justice are linked to formulations about how societies operate and are applied to behavior. In other words, it generally claims descriptive, explanatory, and prescriptive elements – what is collectively termed "praxis." The phrase is often associated with Marxists, dating from the discussion of its usage by Antonio Labriola, although it is more commonly associated with the later work of Antonio Gramsci in his Prison Notebooks.[45] But we should not limit any association of the notion of praxis purely to Marxists. Montesquieu, Locke, and Tocqueville, for example, all generated a body of knowledge about liberalism that included a theory of justice, a set of principles about the division of authority, and a design for action that was the basis for a process of implementation for institutional reform and public

---

authority would venture into the political sphere of kings. Louis XIV was a famous proponent of divine right. Henry VIII used it as a tool to oppose the Pope's denial of his right to divorce and King James I wrote two books that defended the doctrine. The principle of Divine Right, therefore, rested on a theory of justice and a more general body of knowledge, despite its all too evident reliance on inequity. From the early seventeenth century onwards, Bossuet's formulation was preeminent across Europe and beyond – arguably approximating the status of a global norm. See Jean Bodin (1955), abridged and translated by M. J. Tooley, *Six Books of the Commonwealth* (Oxford: Basil Blackwell), http://www.constitution.org/bodin/bodin.txt; Richard Hooker (1996), *The European Enlightenment Glossary: the Divine Right of Kings*, http://www.wsu.edu/~dee/GLOSSARY/DIVRIGHT.HTM; King James I (1609), *Works (On the Divine Right of Kings)*, Chapter 20, http://www.wwnorton.com/college/history/ralph/workbook/ralprs20.htm

[45] Antonio Gramsci (1975), *Prison Notebooks* (New York: Columbia University Press), p. X.

policies. Indeed, Thomas Locke was supported by Dutch patrons intent on developing plans to cast off Spanish rule. Such theories were later seized upon and advocated by scholars such as Friedman, Hayek, and Strauss, who formed what Gramscian analysis would later conceive of as intellectuals who reinforced the hegemony of the dominant class controlling the state.[46]

Economic neoliberalism and political neoconservatism are two of the more recent expressions of approaches linking philosophical, political, and economic theory to public policy – from the privatization of national economies in Latin America to the democratic "liberation" of countries in the Middle East, even though the simultaneous transition to democracy and capitalism is notoriously difficult to accomplish.[47] One variant of the expression of this norm is illustrated by the claims made by proponents of the "liberal democratic peace" argument. Proponents trace the lineage of the argument that a democratic world is more stable and peaceful back to Immanuel Kant's Perpetual Peace. This claim forms the basis of an extensive literature that debates whether democratic forms of governance are beneficial because democratic states do not fight each other. It is further linked to neoconservative policy prescriptions advocating the democratization of Iraq on the strategic principle that it would serve as the lever for a democratic, and thus a peaceful, Middle East. Likewise, advocates of deregulation and privatization argue their case predicated on the supposition that the liberation of the individual from state control, through the mechanisms of the marketplace, will enhance both democracy and wealth. Both elements – the peaceful effects of democratization and the democratizing effects of market capitalism – have become part of this liberal intellectual construction in the course of the last two decades, thus legitimating public policies proposing to engineer liberal democratic states and capitalist economies.

Fourth, global norms are generally codified in international law. They are embodied in international constitutions, conventions, and protocols, and even, on occasion, international law. But such norms extend beyond simple declaratory statements. These often find comprehensive

---

[46] For an application of this term see Ting-Hong Wong (2002), *Hegemonies Compared: State Formation and Chinese School Politics in Postwar Singapore and Hong Kong* (New York: Routledge), p. 22; Stephen Gill (1990), *American Hegemony and the Trilateral Commission* (Cambridge: Cambridge University Press).

[47] On this point see Leslie Armijo, Thomas J. Biersteker and Abraham F. Lowenthal (1994), "The Problems of Simultaneous Transitions", *Journal of Democracy*, 5:4, 161–75.

expression in international regimes and, as a result, generate – when successfully implemented – their own supportive institutional structures that reinforce the validity of the norm and substantiate an enforcement mechanism. When successful, they, in effect, reproduce themselves.

The importance of this component is that it assists in legitimating a structure of power and process as authoritative.[48] It has a functional component, however, which can be invoked by the hegemon to garner cooperation and burden-sharing in policies intended to address collective action problems and generate consent. Beyond shared values, it justifies shared action. This allows global norms to have important functional attributes; when successful, they generate a degree of consistency and stability in terms of expectations, enhancing the prospect of shared costs as well as shared benefits.

Invoking a global norm, however, carries within it a risk. When claims for shared interests or values by a hegemon appear contrived, disingenuous, or inconsistent with such conventions, the effect is paralyzing, undermining collective action by isolating the hegemon. A hegemonic state may therefore invoke global norms to justify unilateral actions. It may invade another in the name of humanitarianism. But, in doing so, it runs a great danger of undermining its claims if these actions seem unjustified or unwarranted by the norm itself. Invoking established norms, or trying to construct new ones, to justify unilateral action is therefore a double-edged sword. When other states and transnational actors broadly reject the claim that the norm justifies a hegemon's action, then its credibility and capacity to garner material, political, or even moral support are severely damaged.

Finally, *and crucially*, norms are global if they have a coercive enforcement mechanism and are consistently enforced. Political opposition to all norms should be anticipated. That is why enforcement mechanisms are required. It is when abrogation of a norm becomes routine, and the effective capacity for consistent enforcement is stymied, that its *global* quality becomes questionable. A global norm *has legitimating utility as a political force* in conflict. Generating these institutional structures and enforcement mechanisms, however, requires not only substantiating ethics but also material resources from the dominant political force. Global norms do not simply "float" in an "apolitical" environment; they require sponsorship – and that requires material resources.

---

[48] This general principle is discussed by Ian Hurd in "Legitimacy and Authority in International Relations", op. cit., especially p. 404.

The way that norms are discussed in the current literature distinguishes between support for the norm and its implementation. Doing so reinforces the division between material and social power. Arguably, norms are only relevant if they can be judged in behavioral terms, and the respect for global norms requires a coercive regulatory component: putting the material power "back in" to the study of norms. It is not only the effect of norms on what individuals, NGOs, or states think that matters; it is the institutional structures that they generate, the policies that ensue, and ultimately how those measures change behavior, that are important. Global norms integrate material and social power because they incorporate the idea that dominant political forces must be willing to commit their resources to such values if they are to substantially influence the behavior of other actors.

Sponsoring global norms: why should the US care?

So, in more formal terms, how are global norms generated? Beyond hegemons, how do they influence the form of policy and the subsequent behavior of other states? And why should the US care about a strategy of sponsorship as a foreign policy option?

I argue that the answer to how they are created lies in systematically understanding the relationship between hard and soft power, and between the interaction of civil society representatives and the US in the context of global institutions. We should care about them as a form of foreign policy because global norms provide a means whereby the US can address both many of its own narrow strategic problems *and* a series of broader collective action problems – where a reliance on "isms" has failed. Doing so requires patience, a new strategic approach, and a sense of timing. Yet it provides an effective, productive, and often relatively low-cost way to address foreign policy problems.

In support of this argument, the remainder of this book is divided into three sections. In the next chapter, I briefly address the question of how scholars in international relations conceive of norms in terms of the relationship between hard and soft power, and then explain why global norms are becoming increasingly important as an avenue of foreign policy. I then lay out the conditions for the formulation, codification, and enforcement of global norms and the alternative forms that policy takes when other conditions prevail.

In the third to sixth chapters of the book, I offer four case studies that examine US foreign policy in order to illustrate my argument.

There I look at efforts to generate global norms in four policy areas: the trafficking of humans (global norm), preventive military interven- tion (unilateralism), cybersecurity (multilateralism), and anticorruption (imperialism). Each is reflective of a different approach to foreign pol- icy: three employing variants of "isms" generated by different configu- rations and the fourth configuring, in a way consistent with a global norm, widespread civil society support, codification through global institutions, and US sponsorship through enforcement. I do not offer these studies as strict "tests" of my argument in a causal sense. Rather, each is offered as a heuristic device, intended to illustrate how variations in the linkages between hard and soft power – and between broad-based civil society organizations, global institutions and US power – lead to very different kinds of foreign policy with very different policy patterns and outcomes.

In the concluding section of the book, I consider the implications of my argument for a variety of issue areas, including further brief examples, and the capacity of the US to mount global responses to transnational problems through the construction of global norms.

2
Sponsorship: Linking Resources, Legitimacy and Institutions

How the scope and substance of challenges have changed

It has become almost a truism to acknowledge that the primary foreign policy problems faced by governments have become overwhelmingly *transnational* in scope – from pandemics and climate change to proliferation, terrorism, and clandestine migratory flows. As a consequence, the breadth of policy problems, their complexity, and the character of suitable responses have all altered. Formerly, the size and scope of the US economy, its relative geographic isolation, and its disproportionate military capability meant that it was relatively insulated from global forces and it could often pass on the costs of adjustment to other states, whether through trade protection, an overvalued dollar, or the demand for "burden-sharing" in times of crisis.

Much of this has changed in the last two decades. Although the greatest advocate of globalization (defined largely as the free flow of trade and finance, the privatization of ownership, and the spread of civil and political rights), the US was sheltered more than most countries historically by both geography and its material capacity – and was ill prepared to deal with many of the unforeseen consequences of globalization. As a result of the coupling of these new challenges and the lack of adaptation to this new environment, the US clearly no longer enjoys the privileged ability to act unilaterally that it held at the height of its power. Power defined in terms of material resources is still important, but is now insufficient to achieve many prescribed policy goals. Furthermore, the transnational character of the problem that it confronts often blunts power used in conventional strategic ways.

Pointedly, as a part of the changing policy landscape, security threats are evidently no longer territorial in character, and increasingly emanate from a large number of failed and fragile states where there is little evidence of a centralized state or the rule of law. Despite historic cases of mass violence against civilian populations in war (most monstrously, the Holocaust), it was never a convention. Now violence is often primarily aimed at civilian populations rather than the state apparatus, with civilian fatalities and injuries no longer simply constituting "collateral damage." Addressing such threats requires shared information and often a willingness on the part of the other (often failed or fragile) states to consent to the violation of their sovereignty for the purpose of intelligence-gathering, covert operations, or troop deployment. Military action increasingly requires collaboration with the armed forces of other states to reduce cost or provide specialized skills or local knowledge that is generally lacking. These limitations apply to the US as they do to other states, despite its abundant resources. Although in a process of transition, the American security apparatus is still not built primarily to cope with the plethora of new transnational threats at this relatively early point in the new century. Neither military drones, a symbol of both America's technological capacity and its independence, nor large contingents of troops can address most security threats in an age characterized by asymmetric warfare, which is often fought through subnational conflict in diverse global contexts.

Due to their global nature, economic, environmental, and security problems impose themselves across continents, not simply local borders. Economic contagion in 1998, for example, began in Thailand and spread as far as Russia, before washing up at Wall Street's shore in the famous Long Term Credit Management bailout organized by the Clinton Administration.[1] The more recent financial crisis circled the globe and returned to American shores, generating unprecedented US public debt and unemployment levels not seen in nearly three decades. We are increasingly aware that the child soldiers of today are the suicide bombers of tomorrow; that an outbreak of swine flu, Ebola or Marburg virus, if not controlled, threatens large-scale populations continents away; and that the proliferation and illegal sales of fissile materials used

---

[1] Paul Blustein (2001), *The Chastening: Inside the Crisis that Rocked the Global Financial System and Humbled the IMF* (New York: Public Affairs); J. Bradford DeLong and Barry Eichengreen (2001), "Between Meltdown and Moral Hazard: The International Monetary and Financial Policies of the Clinton Administration", *National Bureau of Economic Research, Working paper 8443*, http://www.nber.org/papers/w8443

in the making of nuclear weapons (small and large) pose a threat to national security and require, in the words of then US Senate Foreign Relations Committee chairman Richard Lugar, "building extraordinary international relationships."[2]

In this respect, the events of 9/11 illustrated to the American public the oft-cited "darker side" of globalization. They merely made this evident to a broader American audience unaware that globalization entailed substantially more than economic interdependence. New technologies and porous borders allowed sinuous actors to incur enormous damage in an unanticipated manner. The inevitable postmortem of the "9/11 Commission" pointed an accusatory finger at a breakdown in US intelligence. It conveyed the comforting thought that the attack could have been avoided or its effects mitigated. But whether a corrective action could have averted the attack remains questionable. The alternative course is an admission that, in a transnational world, the US is inevitably vulnerable and that it may be only a matter of time until America endures another major attack. Such an admission, even if true, is politically unpalatable. Efforts to reinforce homeland security have therefore reduced the prospects of a major attack but do not guarantee safety.

The response of scholars to the changing environment

Some leading scholars who study international relations have clearly recognized these changes. Yet they offer little adaptation beyond an incremental adjustment to existing approaches, particularly to US foreign policy. Joseph Nye, for example, has long advocated recognizing the importance of "soft power" as an aspect of US foreign policy. He has been less clear, despite his wealth of foreign policy experience, in addressing the critical questions of when and how it is to be used.[3] In his most recent work – although recognizing the importance of integrating "soft" and "hard" power (what he collectively terms "smart power") – he remains analytically and tactically focused on leadership

---

[2] CNN News (2002), "'High risk' of WMD attack in decade: U.S. survey finds more nations will acquire nuclear weapons", 22 June, http://edition.cnn.com/2005/US/06/21/wmd.threat/index.html

[3] Nye had served as deputy undersecretary of state in the Carter Administration. Between 1977 and 1979, Nye served as Deputy to the Undersecretary of State for Security Assistance, Science and Technology, and chaired the National Security Council Group on Nonproliferation of Nuclear Weapons. In 1993 and 1994, he was chairman of the National Intelligence Council. In 1994 and 1995, he served as Assistant Secretary of Defense for International Security Affairs.

as a key ingredient.[4] Other scholars have been slow to integrate such recognizable changes effectively into their work. Traditional realists regard norms and ideas as largely ephemeral. Authority is a product of a hierarchical structure based on – and reflective of – the presiding distribution of power. Coercion therefore dominates as the mode of social control, in which, in the words of Ian Hurd, "fear produces acquiescence."[5]

This position is difficult to reconcile with the position of the neoconservatives in the Bush Administration who emphasized the significance of values as transformative – reflective of their quest to create democratic regimes in the Middle East.[6] Among realist scholars, Stephen Krasner is a notable exception, acknowledging that norms are of significance, if not in any way determinative of behavior. Krasner characterizes some norms as resilient yet institutionally weak in the sense that transgression by the powerful is commonplace. While suggesting that norms are not irrelevant, he acknowledges that power is not simply embedded in underlying institutional structures, and that norms have a limited impact on actual behavior.[7] Krasner's sophisticated formulation moves well beyond a basic force model in explaining outcomes by pointing to the strategic use of contradictory norms by policymakers as well as the potential employment of social power resources. This may, in part, explain his appointment as the Director of the Policy Planning Staff at the US Department of State between 2005 and 2007. Nonetheless, for him, material power is the key factor in explaining behavior (whether in the context of unilateral policy or within international regimes),

---

[4] Joseph Nye (2008), *The Powers to Lead* (Oxford: Oxford University Press). For a concise discussion of the linkage between hard and soft power, see Joseph Nye (2008), "Obama's Foreign Policies Must Combine Hard and Soft Power", *Huffington Post*, 3 December, http://www.huffingtonpost.com/joseph-nye/obamas-foreign-policies-m_b_147108.html

[5] For a helpful discussion of this point see Ian Hurd (1999), "Legitimacy and Authority in International Relations", *International Organization*, 53:2, 379–408, especially 383–9.

[6] See Peter Katzenstein's discussion regarding constructivism and rationalism in the introduction to Peter J. Katzenstein (1996), "Introduction: Alternative Perspectives on National Security", in Peter J. Katzenstein (ed.), *The Culture of National Security: Norms and Identity in World Politics* (New York: Columbia University Press). In this regard, Katzenstein notes the work of Stephen M. Walt (1991), "The Renaissance of Security Studies", *International Studies Quarterly*, 35:2, 211–39.

[7] Stephen D. Krasner (1999), *Sovereignty: Organized Hypocrisy* (Princeton: Princeton University Press), especially pp. 50, 51 and 57.

defined ultimately as military capability and a product of the pre-eminent power position of the US.[8]

The logic of this position, however, is that the US should be able to both make and break norms at will to achieve its policy goals. The Iraq case clearly demonstrates that this is not true. Power defined as force and will has only limited utility. It is effective only under very limited conditions – and policymakers, therefore, can neither condition nor ignore the potential influence of either norms or global institutions. In that sense, material power (like norms or institutions) may play a role, but the key issue is how and under what conditions.

Since the 1970s, liberal theorists in international relations have argued that military power has declined in importance as an explanation for the behavior of states. The growing importance of global organizations – such as the International Monetary Fund (IMF), the World Bank and the United Nations – coupled with the expansion of global trade, and the evolution and spread of technology, has created an interdependent world in which economic, political, and military affairs have become inextricably intertwined.[9] New protocols, laws and conventions, collectively often characterized as "international regimes," magnify the importance of these changes by providing emergent non-state actors with a conduit to exercise an unprecedented moral authority. Liberals contend that these institutions and their accompanying new legal structures therefore mediate power's effects, forming a prism through which military power (and thus force) is refracted or diluted rather than reflected. Furthermore, the coercive aspects of both military and economic power are diluted in a world in which "the enemy" is not always tangible and visible, even if the threat and corresponding vulnerability are clear. It is hard to destroy an enemy that one cannot find, as the examples of terrorists or computer hackers illustrate.

On the one hand, therefore, the US may dominate other potential state challengers such as Western Europe militarily, but the economies of the two are so integrated that dominance, let alone conquest, is unthinkable. American military capability, for example, may dwarf that

---

[8] Such views are epitomized in Stephen Krasner's noted analysis of regime theory in the *International Regimes* edited volume. See Stephen Krasner (1983), 'Regimes and the Limits of Realism: Regimes as Autonomous Variables', in Stephen Krasner (ed.), *International Regimes* (Ithaca, NY: Cornell University Press), especially pp. 355–8.

[9] This argument is most notably made by Robert Keohane and Joseph Nye in Robert Keohane and Joseph Nye (1977), *Power and Interdependence* (Boston, MA: Little Brown).

of the PRC, but America's economic vibrancy is, in large part, contingent on the sale of Treasury bonds bought by the Chinese government. Competitors are, correspondingly, also collaborators.

For over two decades, neoliberal institutionalists have argued that they provide an answer to the question of the conditioning effects of power in the context of new transnational forces by focusing on the role of material interest, defined as incentives in the context of intergovernmental institutions. Such global governance is often defined by them more broadly in terms of international regimes; it is part of a research agenda that attempts to demonstrate that cooperation in addressing collective action problems is possible, even in the context of an anarchical international system.[10] Institutions affect uncertainty through reduced transaction costs and increased information flows specifying the costliness of violation and severity of punishment.[11] Such scholars link the notion of international regimes to a discussion of the significance of global institutions.[12] Norms constitute a component of the definition, although proponents have still failed to address the central question of how and to what extent norms influence behavior. Neoliberals have, in the past, suggested that the US can generate norms and institutions through regime formation but that their capacity to break them is relinquished once they have been fashioned. This approach is subject to two forms of criticism: first, that regime theory is too often overly

---

[10] There is an extensive literature on this issue, for example Robert Keohane (1984), *After Hegemony: Cooperation and Discord in the World Political Economy* (Princeton, NJ: Princeton University Press); Lisa L. Martin and Beth A. Simmons (1998), "Theories and Empirical Studies of International Institutions", *International Organization* 52:4, 729–57; Kenneth A. Oye (ed.) (1986), *Cooperation under Anarchy* (Princeton, NJ: Princeton University Press).

[11] Robert Keohane, op. cit.; Douglass C. North (1990), *Institutions, Institutional Change, and Economic Performance* (New York: Cambridge University Press), p. 28. Constructivists challenge the notion that international organizations (defined as institutions) are efficient in the way conceptualized by neoliberals. Rather, IOs develop pathologies and contribute autonomously to social learning. As Michael Barnett and Martha Finnemore suggest, "Because the neorealist and neoliberal arguments we engage have focused on intergovernmental organizations rather than nongovernmental ones, and because Weberian arguments from which we draw deal primarily with public bureaucracy, we too focus on intergovernmental organizations in this article and use the term international organizations in that way." See Michael N. Barnett and Martha Finnemore (1993), "The Politics, Power and Pathologies of International Organizations", *International Organization*, 53:4, 699–732, esp. footnote 3, p. 700.

[12] Oran R. Young (1999), *Governance in World Affairs* (Ithaca, NY: Cornell University Press), p. 11.

generalized in its narrative, and has yet to successfully explain behavioral change by large states on a micro level of decision-making; second, that regime theory has not been effectively applied in the policy context because the operational utility of the concept is too limited. In terms of "praxis" the concept is therefore, incomplete.

Liberals do, however, make a powerful point. The challenges faced by nations – rich and poor, strong and weak – have fundamentally altered in large part as a result of these changes in global patterns. By this, I mean not simply the *substantive* content of the issue but the *scope* of the issues themselves. With the acceleration of globalization, little now stops at the border as it did in a world of nationally managed capitalism, and of respective American and Soviet spheres of influence, where the spillover effects of problems were constrained by institutions designed to buffer domestic populations from the effects of the outside world.

Rejecting a rationalist impulse, alternative "constructivist" or "postmaterialist" scholars have reemphasized the role of discourse, identity, norms and values and, therefore, social forms of power in explaining the new dynamics of global politics in a post-Cold War world.[13] Focusing on a *normative shift* in world politics, they lay particular stress on the renewed significance of civil society actors in the promotion of new norms as a form of *social power* – the power of persuasion and ideas through the process of framing a debate – in contrast to a more traditional emphasis on *material power*. They emphasize the role of (primarily single-issue) social groups and transnational organizations whose activists tend to represent the disenfranchised, who appear to have no conflict of interest, and thus steep themselves (often very effectively) in the language of moral authority. Using what Krasner (amongst others) terms "sociological theories", for constructivists "shared principles and norms are the critical determinants of actual outcomes. These norms, not directly observable, are the underlying structure that is manifest in actions and the reasons that are offered to justify them. Power is

---

[13] Finnemore notes this distinction, claiming that materialist explanations have limited utility, but does not theoretically extensively develop the relationship between these two forms of power in her subsequent analysis; Michael N. Barnett and Martha Finnemore, op. cit., pp. 6–8. See James Fearon and Alexander Wendt (2002), "Rationalism v. Constructivism: A Skeptical View", in Walter Carlsnaes, Thomas Risse and Beth A. Simmons (eds), *Handbook of International Relations* (London: Sage Publications). For an application of these types of principles to current great power issues, see Charles A. Kupchan, Emanuel Adler, Jon-Marc Coicaud and Yuen Foong Khong (eds) (2001), *Power in Transition: The Peaceful Change of International Order* (Tokyo: United Nations University Press).

not ignored but is comprehended as being embedded in an underlying institutional structure."[14]

Coral Bell ascribes this shift towards the power of norms and values to three sequential causes: the global institutionalization of diplomacy since 1945, the end of American and Soviet bipolarity in the 1980s, and the information and communication revolution of the 1990s.[15] The cumulative effect, she argues, has been to hasten the *pace* of change and to shift the *substance* of the prevalent norms away from nationalism towards cosmopolitanism. Although cosmopolitanism does not reify a particular set of values, it does stress the importance of the individual as a global, rather than national, citizen – and in that sense is "subversive of state authority."[16]

Understandably, the activism implied by this analysis generates liberal visions of human rights, and economic and social emancipation. Bell herself mentions the popularity of norms regarding environmental protection, nonproliferation and the responsibilities (and not just rights) of states to address such issues as genocide or the broad denial of human rights.[17] But equally as forceful, Bell notes, are the illiberal norms of pan-Islamism and the still powerful attractiveness of nationalism, the latter being the intellectual justification for genocidal behavior such as ethnic cleansing. All of these could be defined as cosmopolitan norms, including militant jihadism and neoliberalism, with their pernicious effects. All have activist proponents, but that does not render them progressive or humanitarian in a political sense. Norms are therefore ambivalent in character and should not be mistaken for progressive.[18]

---

[14] Stephen D. Krasner, *Sovereignty: Organized Hypocrisy*, op. cit., p. 50.

[15] Coral Bell (2002), "Normative Shift", *National Interest*, 70, 44–54.

[16] Ibid., p. 47.

[17] Ibid., p. 49.

[18] For an informative discussion of this mistaken distinction between "good" and "bad" norms in the context of norm diffusion, see Amitav Acharya (2004), "How Ideas Spread: Whose Norms Matter? Norm Localization and Institutional Change in Asian Regionalism", *International Organization*, 58:2, 239–75. Finnemore and Sikkink state, more broadly, that "One logical corollary to the prescriptive quality of norms is that, by definition, there are no bad norms from the vantage point of those who promote the norm. Norms most of us would consider 'bad'... were once powerful because some groups believed in the appropriateness of the norm, and others either accepted it as obvious or inevitable or had no choice but to accept it." Martha Finnemore and Kathryn Sikkink (1998), "International Norm Dynamics and Political Change", *International Organization*, 52:4, 887–917, esp. p. 892.

Norms, from this constructivist perspective, therefore shape the way actors see the world and thus define their interests. More formally, Martha Finnemore maintains that norms "create permissive conditions for action," even if they are not determinative of behavior, providing a standard against which policies are measured and behavior adjudged.[19] Other constructivists, however, see norms as increasingly causative, arguing that they shape not only the identity and interests of actors, but also their behavior.[20]

Where constructivism has devoted attention to global policy issues, the focus has predominantly been on the role of non-state actors in defining the agenda and interests of international organizations. In Martha Finnemore's solely authored work, she has focused on the idea of the endogenous sourcing of preferences.[21] In her co-authored work with Kathryn Sikkink, they suggest that the domestic or sociological roots of norms "are deeply entwined with the workings of international norms" as part of a two-level game.[22] In that sense, international institutions serve as organizational platforms through which norms are promoted, along with NGOs and larger transnational advocacy networks. As Finnemore and Sikkink state:

> Sometimes these platforms are constructed specifically for the purpose of promoting the norm, as are many nongovernmental organizations (NGOs) (such as Greenpeace, the Red Cross, and TransAfrica) and the larger transnational advocacy networks, of which these NGOs become a part (such as those promoting human rights,

---

[19] Martha Finnemore (1996), "Constructing Norms of Human Intervention", in Peter J. Katzenstein (ed.), *The Culture of National Security: Norms and Identity in World Politics* (New York: Columbia University Press), p. 158.

[20] For a discussion see Emanuel Adler (1991), "Arms Control, Disarmament, and National Security: A Thirty Year Retrospective and a New Set of Anticipations", *Daedalus*, 120, 1–20 and, more recently, Michael Barnett and Raymond Duvall (2005), "Power in International Politics", *International Organization*, 59:1, 39–75. For examples see Audie Klotz (1995), *Norms in International Relations: The Struggle Against Apartheid* (Ithaca, NY: Cornell University Press); and Nina Tannenwald (1999), "The Nuclear Taboo: The United States and the Normative Basis of Nuclear Non-Use", *International Organization*, 53:3, 433–68.

[21] Martha Finnemore's seminal work on this subject includes her book, Martha Finnemore (1996), *National Interests in International Society* (Ithaca, NY: Cornell University Press), pp. 9, 17.

[22] Martha Finnemore and Kathryn Sikkink (1998), "International Norm Dynamics and Political Change", op. cit.

environmental norms, and the ban on land mines or those that opposed apartheid in South Africa).[23]

International organizations as conduits play a crucial role in diffusing norms. For example, Finnemore and Sikkink suggest that:

> The structure of the World Bank has been amply documented to affect the kinds of development norms promulgated from that institution; its organizational structure, the professions from which it recruits, and its relationship with member states and private finance all filter the kinds of norms emerging from it. The UN, similarly, has distinctive structural features that influence the kinds of norms it promulgates about such matters as decolonization, sovereignty, and humanitarian relief.[24]

Professionals, with legitimacy born of their expertise and access to information, influence the behavior of other actors, including states. Those within international organizations such as the World Bank or the IMF have the benefit of the possibility of coercive leverage over states, while networks of NGOs and International Governmental Organizations (IGOs) generally do not. Still, they collectively comprise what constructivists regard as "global governance."[25]

IGOs are dynamic agents linking states and NGOs to international society, not simply to be treated as static. Their roles, according to Barnett and Finnemore, are not simply functional but can, in fact, be dysfunctional. Barnett and Finnemore therefore contend that:

> Neo-liberal-institutionalists actually disadvantage themselves in their argument with realists by looking at only one facet of IO power. Global organizations do more than just facilitate cooperation by helping states to overcome market failures, collective action dilemmas and problems associated with interdependent social choice. They also create actors, specify responsibilities and authority among them, and define the work these actors should do, giving it meaning

---

[23] Ibid., p. 899.

[24] Ibid., p. 899.

[25] For a representation of this perspective see Robert O'Brien, Anne Marie Goetz, Jan Aarte Scholte and Marc Williams (2000), *Contesting Global Governance: Multilateral Economic Institutions and Global Social Movements* (New York: Cambridge University Press).

and normative value. Even when they lack material resources, IOs exercise power as they constitute and construct the social world.[26]

These three approaches thus offer distinct perspectives in explaining the motives for behavior and limited guidance in terms of policy choices. They contrast in numerous ways: on their definitions and importance of norms as marginal or central to explanations of behavior; on the importance of social and material power as the primary catalysts for behavior, assuming in each case that one "explains" or "is embedded" in the other; on whether preferences are exogenously or endogenously determined; and of the relative importance of structure and agency in determining the behavior of state and non-state actors in a global context. What they have largely left unaddressed is how material and social power pragmatically relate to each other, in either the study or the conduct of foreign policy.

So what is the cost of dogmatism in the face of global change?

A harsh critic might ask: can all this effort actually explain, in more than a partial sense, the dynamics and greatest problems that we currently face? If "norms matter," then the key questions are "under what circumstances?" and "to what extent?" in the formation of foreign policy. The same is true for the use of power or the role of institutions. Comprehensive explanations have been frowned upon by many of those engaged in what has been proverbially termed "the paradigm wars" as merely "over-specification of the argument;" a coded language for criticizing the use of too many factors (on methodological grounds) to explain behavior. This rejection of such comprehensive approaches, however, has a major cost, evident in the inability of these approaches to link hard and soft power effectively – in other words, to explain the dynamics of global politics in its broadest sense, and to explain US foreign policy in a narrower sense.

Liberals and constructivists have focused on aspects of soft power, suggesting that the role of hard power has either been overstated historically or become diluted over time. They have largely ignored the question of how the two are related and applied to foreign policy. They seem not to address questions of under what conditions one predominates,

---

[26]Michael N. Barnett and Martha Finnemore (1993), "The Politics, Power and Pathologies of International Organizations", op. cit., p. 700.

or how they might be related rather than "embedded" or "fused," so that variations in their linkages account for different patterns of policy outcomes. There has been a cost to this dogmatism. The cost of focusing on theoretical consistency and the search for parsimony has been an inability to explain events, analyze variations in the forms of foreign policy, or, ultimately, prescribe solutions.[27]

Proponents of the importance of institutions and of norms support their arguments, critics suggest, by focusing on anecdotal evidence while maintaining a relatively abstract level of analysis. The principles of soft power have proved hard to implement in terms of policy, as the Obama Administration has discovered in a variety of policy contexts; mass popularity does not translate into favorable foreign policy, whether in Iran or Europe. By the end of his first year in office, from the climate summit in Copenhagen to cooperation over global economic policy, President Obama failed to garner the cooperation he might have anticipated given his global popularity. Likewise, the Bush administration could neither thwart the growth of militant Islam, nor push back the tide of anti-Americanism after the invasion of Iraq, despite democracy's global attractiveness.

Clearly, despite the rhetoric, the commitment of American governments to the importance of soft power as an instrument of foreign policy has been historically limited in recent decades. Concerns about reputation or legitimacy, for example, were soon cast aside after Colin Powell's UN speech on Iraq failed to garner sufficient Security Council support in favor of what might most generously be described as a qualified unilateralist policy – the US supported by a small group of states, each with its own motives for joining the coalition. For US officials, worries about America's international standing were dismissed as trivial when thoughts of revenge for 9/11, coupled with future national security concerns, predominated. The Obama Administration may have emphasized its differences with its predecessor, but what are more remarkable are the continuities in security policy between the two despite the changes in the tone and lexicon.

It would, therefore, be simplistic to unquestioningly accept that the new environmental or economic challenges have changed the central determinants of policy to a point where material power – whether

---

[27] Krasner, for example, makes this point more eloquently in regards to constructivism when stating that its "emphasis on inter-subjectively shared understandings provides only limited guidance." Stephen D. Krasner (1999), *Sovereignty: Organized Hypocrisy*, op. cit., p. 54.

military or economic – is irrelevant. To suggest that power has been diffused to the point where institutions, reputation, or legitimacy have become more central in explaining either the form that foreign policy takes, or the outcome it generates, seems to miss a key point: *it is the conditions under which hard power can be used successfully to achieve prescribed goals, the way that it engages with both soft power and global institutions, that has changed. Soft power matters; what is key is how it matters and when it matters and how it relates to military power and economic resources, in the context of global institutions.* Hard power, norms and global organizations now integrate in different ways because of the shifting dynamics of global politics and economics. States, particularly the United States, must understand these changing dynamics if they want to implement policies successfully. *The major foreign policy problems we face have changed; as a result, so have the relevant policy prescriptions.*

Immigration provides a telling example. American mythology is replete with stories of the arrival of people at Ellis Island to be accepted or refused entry. Historically, immigration was a less complicated issue: to be dealt with by passport control and US Embassies, relatively easy to address despite America's extended borders. The American state's ability to control immigration meant that even desperate refugees, sometimes fleeing Europe for their lives, could be turned back from its borders and ports.

Yet, immigration as an issue has grown steadily in importance and complexity as the consequences of immigration policies spread into new areas of American life. Critics of the wave of immigration in the 1980s focused on the social and economic dimensions of the arrival of illegal boat people in the Southeast of the United States, and of both drugs and human smuggling in the Southwest. These dimensions expanded after 9/11 into matters of national security, civil liberties, the future of the American higher educational system, and the vibrancy of its economy. The consequences of US immigration policy have an impact not only on potential migrants but also on the health of firms in Silicon Valley, student applications to American universities, the rules under which people can be detained without trial, and issues regarding surveillance and privacy – in a historically unprecedented and complicated policy "mix."

The same tendency is true of terrorism, an issue predominantly national in character until the 1970s. The Irish Republican Army (IRA) or Euskadi Ta Askatasuna (ETA) focused on local targets, just as the Islamic Salvation Front (FIS) in Algeria and the Irgun in Israel had done decades earlier in their wars of liberation. The Palestinian hijacking of European planes and killing of Israeli Olympians in Germany represented an expansion of terrorist targets, but nonetheless, their geographic scope remained limited.

The 1990s, now infamously, witnessed the dramatic expansion of these operations to a global scale. Combating terrorism was no longer national in scope. Islamic militant groups were not geographically concentrated as earlier groups had been. They both operated and trained globally, using new technologies that allowed them to remain isolated in small cells of operatives and hard to detect across continents. Yet terrorism clearly has a large and important domestic dimension; large ethnic populations from outside "the West," whose radical fringe (often born within these countries) act as suicide bombers, pose an unprecedented and complex threat. Enhanced border security offers little more than a band-aid as the relationship between security, immigration, and integration has altered.

These are just two examples of problems that have now become global in scale and can no longer be addressed in an insular fashion within the context of America's foreign policy establishment. To this list could be added the smuggling of the biological, chemical, and fissile materials that are the foundation of weapons of mass destruction; drug contravention; or multiple aspects of environmental degradation. In all these cases, the military, political, and economic aspects of these problems have become increasingly complex, and the threats to the health and welfare of civilian populations ever more intertwined, leading to the increasing popularity of terms such as environmental, economic, and human security. As a result, collaboration has become functional, even for a supposed waning "hyper-power," with state and non-state actors alike.

How the American response has not changed – and how it might

What is the response of the US in this new environment? The major foreign policy options have remained relatively static: the menu of "isms" outlined in the first chapter. While all but a handful of people reject isolation, elements of it persist – such as in the demands of both right-wing republicans and Lou Dobbs populists that America should build a fence along its southern borders. This central element of the immigration debate was supposed to assure us of border control, regardless of the fact that thousands of miles of the southern border, and the entire northern border, would remain unfenced.

More common in foreign policy has been a debate between three groups: first, Wilsonian Internationalists who emphasize the importance of American leadership in the context of multilateralism; second, neoconservative imperialists with triumphal grand designs about the reconstruction of the world around politically conservative and economically neoliberal principles; and third, an assortment of unilateralists intent on the use of force to strike at what they consider to be security threats with little regard for questions of foreign sovereignty. All are willing to intervene abroad, albeit for very different reasons; all are subject to the usual oscillating US cycle between triumphalism and fatalism; and all assume the primacy of American leadership.

Nonetheless, European critics are often, surprisingly, relatively unsophisticated in not recognizing the variations in the position of proponents of US policy, although the tone of the criticism may change according to US administrations. They maintain that the US is unwaveringly one-dimensional with a reliance on force, and that military power is increasingly irrelevant in this context.[28] The implications of such arguments suggest that America is naturally ill equipped to achieve its foreign policy goals in the new century. Diplomatic skills count for rather more than coercive powers – war-making needs a strong coercive capacity, while peacekeeping and nation-building do not.

Such hostility, however, understates the possibility that there is a continued, essential role for hard power that may complement diplomacy or the value of ideas. This is not to imply that a rehash of a now-defunct debate about the ethical virtues of consensus-building is required. Nor does it suggest a reconstruction of arguments about the virtues of collective security among states.[29] America's global role

---

[28] See Tony Judt (2005), 'Europe vs. America', *New York Review of Books*, 52:2, 10 February; Zaiki Laidi (2005), *La Norme sans la Force: L'énigme de la Puissance Européenne* (Paris: Presses de Sciences Po); Philippe Sands (2005), *Lawless World: America and the Making and Breaking of Global Rules from FDR's Atlantic Charter to George W. Bush's Illegal War* (New York: Allen Lane); and Jeremy Rifkin (2004), *The European Dream: How Europe's Vision of the Future is Quietly Eclipsing the American Dream* (New York: Tarcher/Penguin). A more optimistic approach is offered by Timothy Garton Ash, taken from his work in Timothy Garton Ash (2004), *Free World: America, Europe, and the Surprising Future of the West* (New York: Random House).

[29] The doyen of American policy-oriented experts who are proponents of collective security is John D. Steinbruner, former head of the Foreign Policy Studies program at the Brookings Institution. A relatively brief, albeit foundational, formulation of this approach is articulated in the paper: Ashton B. Carter, William J. Perry, and John D. Steinbruner (1992), *A New Concept of Cooperative Security*

is neither unconditional nor inflexible; it is built upon some enduring values. But these values are subject to the vagaries of shifting environments, emerging challenges, and the new positioning of novel actors who must be engaged in order to enhance the possibilities for effective policymaking.

Yet, it would be easy to dismiss the views of European commentators who focus on the dimensions of persuasion and negotiation as, ironically, inadvertently corroborative of Robert Kagan's contention that a weakened Europe relies on diplomacy rather than force. Perhaps the more significant, less dismissive, question that it generates is that sometimes the key issue is how to link strategy with military force and diplomacy (aspects of material *and* social power respectively) together to achieve a prescribed goal through the conduit of global institutions.

The evident, steadfast refusal by scholars to generate any theoretical linkage between hard (tangible resources) and soft power (and the legitimacy that it provides) has therefore undoubtedly had its costs.[30] In the search for a holy grail, little attention is paid to the issue of how contrasting intellectual approaches can be reconciled to construct a novel foreign policy approach that assails conventional assumptions.[31]

(Washington, DC: Brookings Institute). For a more comprehensive example of Steinbruner's work advocating a cooperative approach, see John D. Steinbruner (2000), *Principles of Global Security* (Washington, DC: Brookings Institution Press).

[30] Yet realist and liberal scholars have had an impact on US foreign policy, and not to acknowledge an element of praxis in their work is reasonable in principle but often problematic in practice. This list could be long. But, among notable recent and contemporary scholars, its distinguished members include the work of Zbigniew Brzezinski, Alexander George, Samuel Huntington, Bruce Jentleson, John Mearsheimer, Joseph Nye, and Henry Nau. Even Condoleezza Rice, former US Secretary of State, was at one time an academic. As Ido Oren has comprehensively demonstrated, American political scientists, arguably to a greater extent than academics elsewhere, have – through their individual or collective work – played a vital role in establishing the priorities and strategies of US foreign policy. For a historical account of this process see Ido Oren (2003), *Our Enemies and Us: America's Rivalries and the Making of Political Science* (Ithaca, NY: Cornell University Press).

[31] They have been content with the claim that research programs differ. In each program, proponents attempt to show either the greater utility of material power or how social power "ideationally constructs" material power. Left with this situation, it is unclear whether and how material and social sources of power can be reconciled within the context of one form of analysis. This formulation of the argument as rival explanations is described in Judith Goldstein and Robert Keohane (1993), "Ideas and Foreign Policy: An Analytical Framework",

Nonetheless, an important dialogue recognizing this problem has begun over the last decade in attempting to reconcile these approaches in the scholarly community,[32] although little research has been conducted in that vein. As Richard Ned Lebow suggested, for example, power and persuasion are intimately related.[33] Legitimacy (which the US often lacks), like material resources (of which it has plenty), is fundamental to sustaining power – requiring a more "operational" understanding of norms in order to develop a novel approach to foreign policy.

Translating scholarly debates into the policy context is rarely easy. Recognizing and reconciling the use of hard and soft power, however, is the key to developing a novel response to new foreign policy challenges – as an explicit part of a broader effort to link theory to policy. Such efforts have been frustrated by their evident explanatory and prescriptive shortcomings. I begin with the supposition that, for the purpose of explanation, it might be more useful to explore an alternative avenue. So, how do we link hard and soft power in a way

---

in Judith Goldstein and Robert Keohane (eds), *Ideas and Foreign Policy: Beliefs, Institutions, and Political Change* (NY, Ithaca: Cornell University Press), p. 4.

[32] There is indeed a limited but nonetheless important dialogue that attempts to reconcile approaches emphasizing material and social conceptions of power. See James Fearon and Alexander Wendt (2002), "Rationalism v. Constructivism: A Skeptical View", op. cit. Thomas Risse similarly argues in favor of a complementary synthesis between constructivism on the one hand, and realism and neoliberalism on the other. Thomas Risse (2002), "Constructivism and International Institutions: Toward Conversations Across Paradigms", in Ira Katznelson and Helen Milner (eds), *Political Science: The State of the Discipline* (New York: Norton & Co.), pp. 597–623. Martha Finnemore also argues that rationalism and constructivism are complementary, because of constructivism's focus on the shaping of interests. See Martha Finnemore (1996), *National Interests in International Society*, op. cit., p. 27. Neither, however, offers a practical means by which they can be reconciled. Others have clearly discussed the linkage without generating operational criteria. See also Michael Cox (2005), "Beyond the West: Terrors in Transatlantia", *European Journal of International Relations*, 11:2, 203–33, esp. pp. 203, 227. For an application of these types of principles to great power issues see Charles A. Kupchan, Emanuel Adler, Jon-Marc Coicaud and Yuen Foong Khong (eds) (2001), *Power in Transition: The Peaceful Change of International Order*, op. cit. One possible counterexample to this claim may be found in the work of Alistair Iain Johnston. See Alistair I. Johnston (2001), "Treating International Institutions as Social Environments", *International Studies Quarterly*, 45:4, 487–515. A realist initiative that explicitly attempts to link power to identity is found in Henry Nau (2002), *At Home Abroad: Identity and Power in American Foreign Policy* (Ithaca, NY: Cornell University Press).

[33] See Richard Ned Lebow (2005), "Power, Persuasion and Justice", *Millennium – Journal of International Studies*, 33:3, 551–81.

that offers a novel, practical, and effective way of conceiving of US foreign policy? It is to this question that I now turn.

So what to study? Linking civil society, power, and institutions in US foreign policy

US foreign policy suffers from a credibility crisis. In effect, while Americans often support the goals of international organizations, and conceive of many of their policies as well intended, they remain focused on assertive leadership and even America's closest allies remain skeptical of the motives behind what Christian Reus-Smit has called "America's material preponderance" despite the varying popularity of its presidents.[34] This skepticism may explain what he identifies as the US' "frustrated political influence." Traditional idealist and realist formulations of US foreign policy (unilateralism, multilateralism, and imperialism) are all overly reliant on assertive approaches coupled with the use of those material capacities, albeit for varying purposes – notably insulation, deterrence, and compellence.

I argue that there are three components to the effective exercise of power: generating legitimacy for a norm, having appropriate institutions to broaden and codify protocols consistent with that norm, and sufficient material capability to enforce that norm. While tangible resources and global institutions matter for both the form and substance of foreign policy, so does the legitimacy provided by norms. The key questions are: how do all three components work interactively? And do they do so in a systematic way that can explain variance in policies and foreign policy outcomes?

To answer these specific questions, I begin with a central proposition: the relative success of a global norm in terms of its emergence, widespread acceptance, and enforcement is generally contingent upon three necessary and sufficient factors. The first is the presence of aggressive moral entrepreneurs, seen as representative of broad public opinion, in advocating norms and garnering broad-based support for them. They provide the credibility needed to generate legitimacy for a norm. The second is the existence of formal global organizations that act as conduits for the codification and monitoring of policies based on those norms. The third is American commitment to provide resources and implement policy based on specified norms in order to generate their

---

[34] Christian Reus-Smit (2004), *American Power and World Order (Themes for the 21st Century Series)* (Malden, MA: Polity Press), p. 1.

enforcement. *If all three of these factors are present, they will produce a global norm. If two of these three factors are present, they will prospectively produce different kinds of US foreign policy, depending on the combination of factors present: unilateralism, multilateralism, and imperialism.*

I outline the defining features and functions of moral entrepreneurship, global institutions, and American power before delineating how variations in their presence generally result in corresponding variations in the form of US foreign policy.

Moral entrepreneurs and the issue of legitimacy

American policymakers often assume a degree of legitimacy of their policy positions which is clearly not in evidence. As Reus-Smit notes, "one can assert one's legitimacy as loudly as one likes, but it is meaningless if others do not agree."[35] Indeed, proclaiming the rectitude of one's own policy position is often counterproductive, leading to a credibility gap. Americans, blinded by both their own sense of moral rectitude and the preference of foreigners for many American cultural icons, are often oblivious to the fact that foreigners are suspicious of the intent that lies behind many US foreign policies. Claiming that the invasion of Iraq was motivated by a fear of an arsenal of weapons of mass destruction (WMDs) and (belatedly) the promotion of democracy, for example, did nothing to allay suspicions abroad that the invasion was part of an imperial design to control oil.

Joseph Nye's analysis of soft power implies that the American state has the ability to export values, political as well as cultural. But Tony Judt's caricature of European anti-Americanism may be more reflective of popular views, casting doubt on Nye's views:

> The US is a selfish, individualistic society devoted to commerce, profit, and the despoliation of the planet... The US rides roughshod over laws and treaties and threatens the moral, environmental and physical future of humanity. It is inconsistent and hypocritical in its foreign dealings, and it wields unparalleled military clout. It is, in short, a bull in the global china shop.[36]

Public opinion surveys echo such hostility towards America, even within NATO countries, generally regarded as among the closest of America's allies. A major 2005 report on popular attitudes in Europe

---

[35] Ibid., p. 5.

[36] Tony Judt, "Anti-Americans Abroad", *New York Review of Books*, 50:7, 1 May 2003, http://www.nybooks.com/articles/16219

towards the US, for example, noted that antipathy towards the second Bush Administration remained high, despite the survey coming on the heels of a series of initiatives designed to improve relations with its European partners. Seventy-two percent disapproved of Bush's foreign policies while – distinguishing Bush from America's role in general – over 59 percent of those polled thought US global leadership undesirable. National variations abounded and were predictable. The French topped the poll in their disapproval of Bush (85 percent) and were among the leaders in their questioning of US leadership (69 percent). Yet even the more receptive publics among the ten countries polled were relatively hostile. Only in Poland did a majority not disapprove of Bush's policies; and only four of the ten, a slim plurality, disagreed with the assessment that US leadership was undesirable.[37]

The findings of this poll were echoed elsewhere – largely with greater disapproval of the US and its policies as one moved further away from Europe. The Pew Global Survey carried out the same year, for example, reported an almost universal downward slope in favorable opinion towards the US dating from 1999, although even the more dramatic declines (such as in Indonesia, where favorable attitudes towards the US had fallen from 75 percent to 38 percent) seemed to have bottomed out by then. Nonetheless, the authors of the survey reported that "Indeed, opinion of the US continues to be mostly unfavorable among the publics of America's traditional allies, except Britain and Canada. Even in those two countries, however, favorable views of the US have slipped over the past two years."[38] Predictably, the view of the US in Arab and Muslim nations in surveys was repeatedly and overwhelmingly negative and unstinting.[39] More surprising (and referring back to the issue of US promotion of democracy), the Pew Survey suggested that many favor democracy in their country and think the US does too.[40] Even more damning, however, were the results of a question polled by Pew about

---

[37] See *Transatlantic Trends 2005*, Chart 2, p. 6.

[38] Pew Research Center Project (2005), "American Character Gets Mixed Reviews: US Image Up Slightly, But Still Negative", *The Pew Global Attitudes Project*, 23 June, p. 2, http://pewglobal.org/reports/pdf/247.pdf

[39] For the results of this poll see Shibley Telhami (2006), "University of Maryland/Zogby International 2006 Annual Arab Public Opinion Survey: A Six Country Study", *Brooking Institution*, http://brookings.edu/views/speeches/telhami20070208.pdf. A summary of the results is available at http://abuaardvark.typepad.com/abuaardvark/2007/02/new_telhamizogb.html

[40] Pew Research Center Project (2005), "American Character Gets Mixed Reviews", op. cit., p. 3.

whose interests US foreign policy serves. In no European country did a majority come close to suggesting that America is concerned with their country's interests. The survey results supported the proposition that the war in Iraq and reelection of George Bush only seemed to enhance skepticism towards the United States.[41]

It would be tempting to assume that this skepticism is a reflection of global attitudes towards the Bush Administration rather than the United States *per se*. After all, there could not be a greater contrast in global popularity than that between George Bush and Nobel Peace Prize winner Barack Obama. Global public opinion about the US image at the end of the Bush Administration had universally suffered (with the notable but curious exception of sub-Saharan Africa).[42] So it would be reasonable to assume that the personal popularity of a president is key to the credibility of US foreign policy. Although there has clearly been a benefit to America's legitimacy as a result of both "Obamamania" and the president's policies, the evidence that American policies or the president's personality is a determinative factor is hardly compelling.

At around the same time that Barack Obama was, according to one opinion poll, the most popular leader in the world,[43] public opinion about US foreign policy remained skeptical in key countries despite the President's strenuous efforts to generate support for his initiatives.[44] Even in countries where general skepticism towards the US had declined due to Obama's popularity, such as Germany, the general public still

---

[41] Ibid., pp. 4, 5.

[42] Pew Research Center Project (2008), "Global Public Opinion in the Bush Years (2001–2008) America's Image, Muslims and Westerners, Global Economy, Rise of China", *Pew Global Attitudes Project*, 18 December, http://pewglobal.org/reports/display.php?ReportID=263

[43] See World Public Opinion (2009), "Obama Rockets to Top of Poll on Global Leaders", 29 June, http://www.worldpublicopinion.org/pipa/articles/views_on_countriesregions_bt/618.php?nid=&id=&pnt=618&lb

[44] World Public Opinion Poll (2009), "Egyptian Public to Greet Obama With Suspicion", 3 June, http://www.worldpublicopinion.org/pipa/articles/brmiddleeastnafricara/613.php?nid=&id=&pnt=613&lb=brme; World Public Opinion (2009), "Pakistani Public Turns Against Taliban, But Still Negative on US", 1 July, http://www.worldpublicopinion.org/pipa/articles/brasiapacificra/619.php?nid=&id=&pnt=619&lb. For a relevant commentary on this issue see Andrew Kohut (2009), "Obama Unlikely to Find a Quick Fix for U.S. Global Image", *Pew Research Center Publications*, 31 March, http://pewresearch.org/pubs/1175/obama-europe-trip-bush-legacy

questioned American policy in key areas. As one World Public Opinion report on Germany characterized the situation:

> .... The German public's more benign view of the US does not extend to every global issue. A clear majority (56%) disapproves of how the US is dealing with climate change; only 25 percent approve. A full two-thirds think "the US uses the threat of military force to gain advantages." Fifty-four percent disapprove of the recent increase of US troops in Afghanistan.... And on the world financial crisis, a big majority (68%) thinks US economic policies have "contributed a lot" to the downturn in the German economy.[45]

This German ambivalence can be generalized to other countries. Six months into Obama's presidency, one global survey suggested that:

> Around the world US foreign policy continues to receive heavy criticism on a variety of fronts, even though in 13 of 19 nations most people say they have confidence in President Obama to do the right thing in international affairs... The US is criticized for coercing other nations with its superior power (15 of 19 nations), failing to abide by international law (17 of 19 nations), and for how it is dealing with climate change (11 of 18 nations).... asked how the US treats their government, few–on average just one in four–say it "treats us fairly," while two-thirds say that it "abuses its greater power to make us do what the US wants." Overall, these views are no better than they were in 2008.... In all nations polled, majorities say that the US "use(s) the threat of military force to gain advantages." Majorities range from 61 percent in India and Poland to 92 percent in South Korea and include America's close ally Great Britain (83%). On average, across all nations polled, 77 percent perceive the US as threatening.[46]

Perhaps what is most interesting about these findings is that the higher negative scores were recorded in countries traditionally regarded

---

[45] See World Public Opinion (2009), "Obama Changing the Way Germans See US, But Many Oppose Continuing Afghan Mission", 3 June, http://www.worldpublicopinion.org/pipa/articles/breuropera/614.php?nid=&id=&pnt=614&lb
[46] See World Public Opinion (2009), "Though Obama Viewed Positively, Still Much Criticism of US Foreign Policy: Global Poll", 7 July, http://www.worldpublicopinion.org/pipa/articles/views_on_countriesregions_bt/623.php?nid=&id=&pnt=623&lb

as being among the closest allies of the US, where one might anticipate its credibility would be greatest.

How do these findings relate, in the poll, to the question of US leadership? On average, only one in four agreed that the US is "an important leader in promoting international laws and sets a good example by following them," while two-thirds said that "the US tries to promote international laws for other countries, but is hypocritical because it does not follow these rules itself." Here too, overall, there has been no significant change from 2008.[47]

Subsequent polling indicates an improvement in America's image, although the figures themselves still present a daunting picture in terms of US global legitimacy. Conducted by the Program on International Policy Attitudes (PIPA), their 2010 survey of nearly 30,000 adults in 28 countries indicated that negative ratings of US influence had declined by nine points. Indeed, 46 percent of respondents supported the view that the US had a "mostly positive" influence, the highest figure recorded for the US in this polling series since the second Iraq war. Clearly, Obama and the administration's policies have had some positive effect on global attitudes towards the US.

These figures, however, have to be put in a comparative perspective. First, the percentage of respondents holding positive attitudes towards the United States significantly trailed those of other countries such as Germany (59 percent), Japan (53 percent), Canada (51 percent), the United Kingdom (52 percent), and France (49 percent). Even the European Union, widely berated as both intrusive and ineffectual, received a higher score – of 51 percent. Second, despite an overall global improvement, negative views of the US actually increased in some countries of key strategic importance to the US, notably India and Turkey. Fifty-two percent of Pakistani respondents retained a negative view of the US.

Second, although the overall increase in positive responses might be encouraging to American policymakers, the fact remains that the majority of those polled still do *not* have a positive view of the United States. Rather, unlike many of their European counterparts, only a plurality does. The majority are either neutral or critical. Indeed, no country in the survey generated as many negative responses as the US

---

[47] See World Public Opinion (2009), "Though Obama Viewed Positively, Still Much Criticism of US Foreign Policy: Global Poll", 7 July, http://www.worldpublicopinion.org/pipa/articles/views_on_countriesregions_bt/623.php?nid=&id=&pnt=623&lb

(34 percent) in terms of global influence among advanced industrial states, with Germany (at 14 percent) being regarded as the most benign among that group. Even the charismatic and multilateralist presidency of Obama appears to have its limits when it seeks to address the issue of American legitimacy on the global stage.[48] The presiding point is therefore as powerful as it is simple; regardless of the personal popularity of the President, the US retains a credibility problem. Even as popular an American president as Obama has a limited capacity to enhance American legitimacy. Policies advocated by the US are regarded with great skepticism, if not outright hostility, elsewhere – predicated on the assumption that the US is (whether transparently or covertly) pursuing a narrow self-interested agenda.

So how can the United States address this seemingly abiding credibility gap to achieve foreign support for its initiatives? One option is to act in a way that publics elsewhere deem acceptable, one consistent with international law and not skewed towards US self-interest – thus assuming a leadership role within the context of broad global support. Given the levels of skepticism, faith in such an approach seems optimistic. Another option is to let other actors set the agenda, supporting those initiatives with which they agree. Yet appearing to defer to the leadership of other state actors is, realistically, too politically unpalatable domestically to be a pragmatic strategy for most American presidents.

The same is not true for moral entrepreneurs, given the burgeoning support for leadership drawn from civil society and global organizations over the last two decades. Indeed, their growth in popularity and legitimacy has added another ingredient to the complex mix involved in global governance – causing the introduction of the term "stakeholders" into the lexicon of global politics and policy. Whether termed moral entrepreneurs or norm entrepreneurs, these actors are of key importance in providing legitimacy for any foreign policy initiative that the US supports. In this context, moral entrepreneurs armed with (at least the appearance of) moral authority, who are considered reflective of broad swathes of the global public, play an invaluable role in establishing the legitimacy of global norms.

---

[48] For data and analysis on the US and other countries see "Global Views of United States Improve While Other Countries Decline", WorldPublicOpinionPoll. Org, 18 April 2010, http://www.worldpublicopinion.org/pipa/articles/views_on_ countriesregions_bt/660.php

Margaret Keck and Kathryn Sikkink are among the most notable of those who focus on the strategic role such entrepreneurs play in promoting norms.[49] As Finnemore and Sikkink contend:

> Norms do not appear out of thin air; they are actively built by agents having strong notions about appropriate or desirable behavior in their community. ... consistent with the description Ethan Nadelmann gives of 'transnational moral entrepreneurs' who engage in 'moral proselytism'... Norm entrepreneurs are critical for norm emergence because they call attention to issues or even 'create' issues by using language that names, interprets, and dramatizes them. Social movement theorists refer to this reinterpretation or renaming process as 'framing'. The construction of cognitive frames is an essential component of norm entrepreneurs' political strategies, since when they are successful the new frames resonate with broader public understandings and are adopted as new ways of talking about and understanding issues.[50]

Finnemore and Sikkink explain what motivates behavior. "Ideational commitment is the main motivation when entrepreneurs promote norms because they believe in the ideas and values embodied in the norms, even though the pursuit of the norms may have no effect on their well-being."[51] Rock stars such as Bono or Bob Geldof personify such entrepreneurs when they actually engage in the political process, although they are hardly characteristic of the majority who work on single-issue policies relating to some aspect of social or economic justice. More often, they establish legitimacy through either the principled nature of the issues they represent on a nonpartisan basis (e.g. human rights organizations such as Amnesty International or Human Rights

---

[49] Margaret E. Keck and Kathryn Sikkink (1998), *Activists Beyond Borders: Advocacy Networks in International Politics* (Ithaca, NY: Cornell University Press), p. 17. See also Finnemore and Kathryn Sikkink (1998), "International Norm Dynamics and Political Change", op. cit, p. 893.

[50] Finnemore and Kathryn Sikkink (1998), "International Norm Dynamics and Political Change", op. cit., pp. 896–7.

[51] Ibid., p. 898. Note that there are alternative explanations for the same behavior. Dennis Chong offers a more skeptical view, suggesting that such altruistic behavior is explained either by the need to get along in the context of an iterative game or because of the selective incentives offered by the enhancement of one's social reputation. Dennis Chong (1991), *Collective Action and the Civil Rights Movement* (Chicago, University of Chicago Press), pp. 44, 48–55.

Watch) or because they represent the fight against injustice, whether the target of their accusation is an individual, a group, or, commonly, a state. O'Brien *et al.* suggest that the complainants are generally associated with social movements as:

> A subset of the numerous actors operating in the realm of civil society. They are groups of people with a common interest who band together to pursue a far-reaching transformation of society. Their power lies in popular mobilization to influence the holders of political and economic power... They can be distinguished from interest groups in that their vision is broader and they seek large-scale social change.[52]

Such moral entrepreneurs are to be found working for NGOs or their international equivalents, Global Social Movements (GSMs). O'Brien *et al.* suggest that such actors play a key role as the representatives of civil society in influencing the agenda of global organizations, if not the policies, in a new form of multilateral engagement.[53] The authors do suggest that:

> International public institutions are modifying in response to pressure from social movements, NGOs and business actors, but this varies across institutions, depending upon institutional culture, structure, role of the executive head and vulnerability to civil society pressure.[54]

Ultimately, the most that the authors can claim from the evidence of their cases is that GSMs may influence the agendas, *but not the policies*, of global institutions. If true, this example thus has a broader implication: that GSMs, NGOs, or (more generally) "moral entrepreneurs" (who are individuals who may represent such organizations) may play a role in influencing what gets on the agenda. Yet, as states learn avoidance techniques, these entrepreneurs find that they cannot participate in the key elements of negotiations – and certainly cannot get policies enacted without the advocacy of states, particularly the largest of states.[55] Nonetheless,

---

[52] Robert O'Brien, Anne Marie Goetz, Jan Aarte Scholte and Marc Williams (2000), *Contesting Global Governance: Multilateral Economic Institutions and Global Social Movements*, op. cit., p. 12.

[53] Ibid., p. 3.

[54] Ibid., p. 6.

[55] For a discussion of this point see Ann Marie Clark, Elizabeth Friedman and Kathryn Hochstetler (1998), "The Sovereign Limits of Global Society", *World Politics*, 51:1, 1–35.

their involvement is key, because through their advocacy they provide legitimacy for global norms that is distinct from the perception of self-interest generally associated with the claims made by states, particularly – more acutely – predominant powers like the United States.

Critical to their credibility is the absence of the appearance of any conflicts of interest, and that their representative position is not viewed as unjustly skewed to narrow interests, economically motivated, or broadly at odds with broader humanitarian interests. Above all, echoing my earlier comments, moral entrepreneurs must be seen as independent of the interests of powerful states or corporations if they are to establish their credibility and be reflective of a broad conception of global opinion. Scientists sponsored by industrial organizations, for example, who argue that there is no such phenomenon as global climate change are as likely to be dismissed and discredited as economists who work for neo-conservative think tanks and who argue in favor of neoliberal financial policies. In both cases, only the converted are listening. In contrast, advocates working on behalf of poverty alleviation, nuclear disarmament, or climate reduction are more likely to be considered independent in their perspective, however passionate their claims.

So how do we capture the essence of legitimacy? Defining legitimacy, in operational terms, is inevitably a challenging problem. Ian Hurd, for example, draws a distinction between the "objectivist approach" offered by Mark Suchman and the "subjectivist approach" employed in his own work when suggesting that:

> Legitimacy... refers to the normative belief by an actor that a rule or institution ought to be obeyed. It is a subjective quality, relational between actor and institution, and defined by the actor's *perception* [sic] of the institution. The actor's perception may come from the substance of the rule or from the procedure or source by which it was constituted. Such perception affects behavior because it is internalized by the actor and helps to define how the actor sees its interests.[56]

Hurd is careful to distance himself from the claim that legitimacy automatically confers morality. Yet few claims of legitimacy, while not being absolutist, do lack a claim of authority based on some appeal to morality. Hurd does acknowledge, however, that a claim of legitimacy implies a moral obligation,[57] however perverse, as well as an

---

[56] Ian Hurd, "Legitimacy and Authority in International Relations", op. cit.
[57] Ibid., p. 387.

appropriateness of action consistent with such values. In that sense, his views are consistent with the definition of a global norm adopted in this book.

Representatives of civil society are key in the formation of global norms because, when effective, they advocate values seemingly distinct from the self-interest of states, transcending context and time. In contrast, being associated with the interests of states, particularly the dominant one, is a recipe for failure even among the most earnest of NGOs.

Global Organizations as conduits and consolidators of global norms

So what constitutes an institution? What is its purpose in this context? If moral entrepreneurs provide the legitimacy needed for the global exercise of power, global organizations play a key role in consolidating and codifying the principles laid out in such a norm. Such institutions thus both reproduce and reinforce the initial norm, and often (when effectively consolidated) act as forums for discussion, adjudicators of rules, and conduits for sanctions against whose who transgress.[58]

If realists see institutions as simply reflective of material power, neo-liberals regard institutions as structures for addressing collective action problems and constructivists closely align norms with institutions, viewing them as normative contexts themselves, which play a more autonomous role and thereby redefine power.[59] James March and Johan

---

[58] Realists generally tend to support the proposition that institutions are reflective of broader power structures. Even more sophisticated variants, such as those offered by Stephen Krasner, view global institutions (in the context of regimes) as intervening factors, refractive if not reflective of the preferences of the most powerful states. Alexander Cooley, however, questions the notion that the relationship between the distribution of power and policy outcome is relatively seamless. He effectively demonstrates the attenuated nature linkage of this relationship in a variety of hierarchies. See Stephen Krasner (1983), "Regimes and the Limits of Realism: Regimes as Autonomous Variables", op. cit., pp. 355–8. Krasner develops this formulation further in Stephen D. Krasner (1999), *Sovereignty: Organized Hypocrisy*, op. cit. See also Alexander Cooley (2005), *Logics of Hierarchy: The Organization of Empires, States, and Military Occupations* (Ithaca, NY: Cornell University Press).

[59] For the sociological origins of such arguments, see, for example, John W. Meyer and Brian Rowan (1977), "Institutional Organizations: Formal Structure as Myth and Ceremony", *American Journal of Sociology*, 83:2, 340–63; John W. Meyer and W. R. Scott (1983), *Organizational Environments: Ritual and Rationality* (Beverley Hills, CA: Sage Publications). See also Paul J. DiMaggio and Walter W.

Olsen were among the forerunners of the adaptation of this latter version of institutional analysis. They emphasize the significance of political structure, defining it as:

> A collection of institutions, rules of behavior, norms roles, physical arrangements, buildings, and archives that are relatively invariant in the face of turnover of individuals and relatively resilient to the idiosyncratic preferences and expectations of individuals.... theories of political structure assume action is the fulfillment of duties and obligations ... we assume that political actors consult personal preferences and subjective expectations, then select actions that are as consistent as possible with those preferences and expectations... that political actors associate certain actions with certain situations by rules of appropriateness. What is appropriate for a particular person in a particular situation is defined by the political and social system and transmitted through socialization.[60]

Symbols become important here "not as devices of the powerful for confusing the weak, but more in the sense of symbols as devices of interpretative order."[61] In describing the concept of "normative order," March and Olsen note that "action is often based more on discovering the normatively appropriate behavior than on calculating the return expected from alternative choices. As a result, political behavior, like other behavior, can be described in terms of duties, obligations, roles, and rules ... A broader theoretical examination of normative order would consider the relations among norms, the significance of ambiguity and inconsistency in norms, and the time path of the transformation of normative structures."[62]

Peter Katzenstein, following much of this logic, suggests that, in essence, institutions are more abstract in character in the sense that they are inherently cognitive.

Powell (eds) (1991), *The New Institutionalism in Organizational Analysis* (Chicago: University of Chicago Press).

[60] James G. March and Johan P. Olsen (1984), "The New Institutionalism: Organizational Factors in Political Life", *American Political Science Review*, 78:3, p. 741. For another example of important formative work on this subject, see Herbert A. Simon (1982), *Models of Bounded Rationality* (Cambridge, Mass: MIT Press).

[61] James G. March and Johan P. Olsen, "The New Institutionalism: Organizational Factors in Political Life", op. cit.

[62] Ibid., p. 744.

Bargaining theory typically overlooks a central aspect of all bargaining – the framework or context in which a particular issue should be seen. A richer conception thus emphasizes not only how institutions facilitate bargains among political actors. It also investigates how institutions affect the context of bargaining, primarily through the effects they have on the identity of the political actors who make political choices.[63]

Yet Barnett and Finnemore see international organizations as autonomous and authoritative bodies generating norms, not as embodying norms themselves – effectively using international organizations as a factor in explaining norms.[64] I do not concur. No doubt organizational culture and rules influence the behavior of actors to some degree, but the extent to which norms are molded in the political arena, rather than reinforced, remains an open question.

Working on the assumption that norms originate among moral entrepreneurs, I employ an approach more commonly associated with historical institutionalism – viewing institutions in a more conventional, perhaps narrower, manner as structures and processes which may impinge on policy outcomes, but which largely act as conduits for negotiation and consolidation. An organization is neither a rule nor a norm.[65] Institutions determine the identity and number of the legitimate actors, the ordering of action, the information that actors will have about each other's intentions and, cumulatively, a relevant agenda – what Theda

---

[63] Peter J. Katzenstein (ed.), *The Culture of National Security: Norms and Identity in World Politics*, op. cit., p. 14.

[64] Bo Rothstein offers one solution consistent with Barnett and Finnemore. He suggests that "political institutions in a narrower sense can be defined as 'formal arrangements for aggregating individuals and regulating their behavior through the use of explicit rules and decision processes enforced by an actor or set of actors formally recognized as possessing such power.'" Bo Rothstein (1996), "Political Institutions: An Overview", in Robert E. Goodin and Hans Dieter Klingemann (eds), *A New Handbook of Political Science* (New York, Oxford University Press), p. 145. Elsewhere Peter Hall and Rosemary Taylor concur, suggesting that "many sociological institutionalists put a new emphasis on what I might think of as the 'cognitive'", in Peter A. Hall and Rosemary C. R. Taylor (1996), "Political Science and the Three New Institutionalisms", *Political Studies*, 44:5, 936–57.

[65] Nicholas Onuf deliberates on the meaning of rules in Nicholas Onuf (1989), *World of Our Making: Rules and Rule in Social Theory and International Relations* (Columbia, SC: University of South Carolina Press), especially pp. 78–95, 127–54.

Skocpol labeled a "Tocquevillian" approach. Here "organizational configurations, along with overall patterns of activity, affect political culture, encourage some kind of group formation and collective political actions (but not others), and make possible the raising of certain political issues (but not others)."[66] Organizations thus cohere; they do not autonomously formulate or determine policies.

Nonetheless, I recognize that a global institution, such as the United Nations, the International Monetary Fund, or the World Bank, may potentially refine norms through the process of debate and (possibly) consensus. It certainly consolidates an understanding of norms through protocol, laws, and conventions. It may even reject norms advocated by some moral entrepreneurs. But it does not create them. When successfully advocated, global organizations attempt to formally specify such norms and formulate policies based upon them. Such an organization, ultimately, may even legislate behavior consistent with, or in transgression of, a norm. Generally, however, although it may sanction measures against those who routinely and/or blatantly transgress its more cherished norms, it lacks the material resources necessary to compel state (and, where appropriate non-state) actors to conform to such protocols. Policies based on a consensus enhance the legitimacy of both the organization and – thereby – the norm. Those that narrowly reflect the wishes of stronger states and, most pertinently, the United States are viewed as instruments of coercion and imperialism rather than promoting a global norm.

American material power and sponsorship through its enforcement capability

Gone is the brief period at the end of the Cold War when commentators proclaimed American power so great that it was a unipolar moment. Indeed, US power measured in terms of tangible resources may arguably be in decline relative to the rest of the world, set against the astounding growth of the PRC and India coupled with the enormous costs of the two wars in Iraq and Afghanistan over the course of the last decade.

---

[66] Theda Skocpol (1985), "Bringing the State Back In: Strategies of Analysis in Current Research", in Peter Evans, Dietrich Rueschemeyer, and Theda Skocpol (eds), *Bringing the State Back In* (New York: Cambridge University Press), p. 21. She employs such an approach in Theda Skocpol (1992), *Protecting Soldiers and Mothers: the Political Origins of Social Policy in the United States* (Cambridge, Mass.: Belknap Press of Harvard University Press).

The triumphalism of American supremacy has been truly punctured. Nonetheless, by most relevant economic and military measures, the US outdistances its potential rivals by such a great degree that it may still fittingly be regarded as the only superpower in a world where other states have enormous power in singular dimensions. Increased by the wars in Iraq and Afghanistan, the US still spent more on its military budget than the next fifteen largest countries combined by the middle of the first decade of the twenty-first century.[67] By 2008, according to the Stockholm International Peace Research Institute, the US accounted for 41.5 percent of the global expenditure on defense ($607 billion), the next largest expenditure being by the PRC at 5.8 percent ($84.9 billion).[68] Its navy is larger than the rest of the world's navies combined, and its real-time digitized warfare capacity is relatively absolute. While, as I have already made clear, this combined military capability cannot be relied upon to achieve all foreign policy goals, such overwhelming capacity does provide a firm foundation for the projection of force or the use of deterrence or compellence in many situations. While US economic power is not as disproportionate, especially in the aftermath of the global crisis, the US still hosts the world's largest stock and consumer markets; remains responsible for 21 percent of global output, as it has for the last three decades; still provides the currency of last resort in periods of crisis and the largest reserve currency globally; still outdistances all other competitors in terms of technological innovation; and is still responsible for 33 percent of global annual GNP. Furthermore, the fact that a US mortgage crisis was able to generate a global crisis unprecedented in the last 50 years speaks to its structural power.[69] In tandem, its military and economic capacity is immense, despite its inability to translate that capacity into policy outcomes.

Such frustration in terms of policy outcomes, therefore, should not mislead us into assuming that such material power is irrelevant. Despite the work of scholars and the claims of foreign policymakers that focus exclusively on the importance of civil society actors or international organizations, few norms get enforced on a widespread basis without

---

[67] International Institute for Strategic Studies (2005), "The Military Balance 2005–2006", cited in Jolyon Howorth, *Security and Defence Policy in the European Union* (London & New York: Palgrave, 2007).

[68] See Stockholm International Peace Research Institute, Appendix 5A. Military expenditure data, 1999–2008, *SIPRI Yearbook*, http://www.sipri.org/yearbook/2009/05/05A

[69] See Herman Schwartz, *Subprime Nation*, op. cit.

American support.[70] Daniel Drezner, for example, recognized as much in commenting on the prospects for a global environmental accord, when he suggested that "objections in the United States about the Kyoto Protocol's costs of implementation, the distribution of costs, and the lack of enforcement measures have made implementation unlikely."[71] The same is true in case after case – the banning of landmines, carbon reduction, and, as we shall see in one of the case studies that follow, the globalization of cybersecurity.

Indeed, I offer a counterproposition to those who suggest that either American decline or the changing dynamic of world politics has made American power less relevant; *that American support – through spon-sorship – may have become more, not less, central to the fortune of global norms*. I offer this proposition because, in a world increasingly beset by transnational problems, the US is the only country currently able and potentially willing to expend its material resources globally in sup-port of such norms. The spread of human rights, for example, might primarily be explained by the fact that the "export of democracy," sponsoring groups and programs, was the foreign policy cornerstone of the Clinton Administration for the duration of his presidency.[72] In effect, in this interpretation, the spread of democracy was largely the product of sponsorship by a hegemonic power, just as the success of the anti-slavery movement of the nineteenth century was largely the product of Britain's effort when it was the dominant world power.[73]

---

[70] See, as examples, Martha Finnemore and Kathryn Sikkink, op. cit.; Thomas Risse, Stephen C. Ropp and Kathyrn Sikkink (1999), *The Power of Human Rights: International Norms and Domestic Change* (New York: Cambridge University Press); Robert O'Brien, Anne Marie Goetz, Jan Aarte Scholte and Marc Williams (2000), *Contesting Global Governance: Multilateral Economic Institutions and Global Social Movements,* op. cit.; Michael N. Barnett and Martha Finnemore (1993), "The Politics, Power and Pathologies of International Organizations", op. cit.

[71] Daniel W. Drezner (2001), "Globalization and Policy Convergence", *International Studies Review,* 3:1, p. 74.

[72] See, for example, Douglas Brinkley (1997), "Democratic Enlargement: The Clinton Doctrine", *Foreign Policy,* 106, 110–28. For a broad version of this argu-ment see Tony Evans (2001), *The Politics of Human Rights* (London: Pluto Press), pp. 15–23, 33–4.

[73] Notably, the British anti-slavery policy was the product of a campaign headed by the members of Britain's Anti-Slavery Society, a group who would be described in contemporary parlance as moral entrepreneurs. For a view on this issue see Chaim D. Kaufmann and Robert A. Pape (1999), "Explaining Costly International Moral Action: Britain's Sixty-year Campaign against the Atlantic Slave Trade", *International Organization,* 53:4, 631–68. They note that "the mobil-ization of British abolitionists for their cause as well as their willingness to

In the same spirit, global norms, in the absence of American sponsorship, face an uphill struggle, lacking vitality, material sources, and enforcement capacity.

Focusing on American commitment, however, is clearly distinct from claiming that the US must initiate the development of a norm. Audie Klotz provides compelling evidence that the United States joined a "bandwagon effect" in supporting the anti-apartheid position in the case of South Africa (although she does point to the sociological sources of US support for the norm).[74] Yet my analysis does allow Americans, if not the American state, to act as moral entrepreneurs. Indeed, there are many examples where American moral entrepreneurs have played a critical role in creating a "bandwagon," whether it was the support of American veterans for the Landmine Ban or demonstrations across American campuses against apartheid. It would be misplaced to ignore the American sociological sources of the momentum in the process of generating possible global norms that the US may have ultimately supported (as in the case of the anti-apartheid movement).[75]

Vocal support – and persuasion – is clearly not enough. Nor are protocols, laws, and the formation of international regimes. Key is the commitment of hard resources. Even if they do not supply the troops on the ground, no really large-scale peacekeeping operation, for example, can take place without American logistical support. Arguably, other states can and do intervene in small-scale operations, but only the US has the logistical capability to support the movement of the thousands of troops generally required in

---

accept high costs were driven ... by a parochial religious and political imperative to reform their domestic society; suppression of the slave trade was one part of a wider program to root out corruption in all aspects of English society" (see page 632). There is a wealth of literature on the role of Britain in the abolitionist movement, but see, as recent examples, Christopher Leslie Brown (2006), *Moral Capital: Foundations of British Abolitionism* (Chapel Hill, NC: University of North Carolina Press); Adam Hochschild (2005), *Bury the Chains, The British Struggle to Abolish Slavery* (Basingstoke: Pan Macmillan); Hugh Thomas (2006), *The Slave Trade: The Story of the Atlantic Slave Trade: 1440 – 1870* (London: Phoenix Press); Steven Wise (2004), *Though the Heavens May Fall: The Landmark Trial That Led to the End of Human Slavery* (New York: Da Capo Press).

[74] Audie Klotz (1995), *Norms in International Relations: The Struggle Against Apartheid.*

[75] For an account of the American domestic involvement in the Landmine Treaty, see Fen Hampson, Jean Daudelin, John B. Hay, Holly Reid and Todd Marting (2001), *Madness in the Multitude: Human Security and World Disorder* (New York: Oxford University Press).

		Yes	No	Outcome
1	Entrepreneurial support	X		Articulation, consolida-
	Institutionalization	X		tion and implementation
	American support	X		of global norm
2	Entrepreneurial support		X	Articulation and
	Institutionalization	X		implementation of
	American support	X		imperialist policies
				lacking global legitimacy
3	Entrepreneurial support	X		Weak multilateralism
	Institutionalization		X	
	American support	X		
4	Entrepreneurial support	X		Norms articulated and
	Institutionalization	X		consolidated but weakly
	American support		X	implemented
5	Entrepreneurial support	X		Norms articulated but
	Institutionalization		X	not consolidated or
	American support		X	implemented
6	Entrepreneurial support		X	US unilateralism or
	Institutionalization		X	bilateralism
	American support	X		
7	Entrepreneurial support		X	Empty cell
	Institutionalization		X	
	American support		X	
8	Entrepreneurial support		X	International regime in
	Institutionalization	X		decline. Very weakly
	American support		X	implemented

Figure 2.1   Variations in Explanatory Variables and Outcomes

such situations, whether under NATO or UN auspices. Without such support, both UN officials and scholars note, extended operations cannot be carried out.[76] The proposed norm of humanitarian intervention, therefore, cannot be enforced in major cases without a US commitment.

---

[76] See, for example, Edward C. Luck (1995), "The Case for Engagement: American Interest in Peace Operation", in Donald C. Daniel and Bradd C. Hayes (eds), *Beyond Traditional Peacekeeping* (New York: St Martin's Press), p. 73. A current, comparable debate is taking place over the role of the US in the Darfur conflict. See UN Office for the Coordination of Humanitarian Affairs (2005), "Sudan: Give more support to AU forces in Darfur, US urged", 22 July, http://www.globalsecurity.org/military/library/news/2005/07/mil-050722-irin01.htm. For a discussion about the indispensable role to be played by the US in Darfur, for example, see Samantha Power and John Prendergast (2004), "Break Through

Three factors are therefore necessary for a global norm to take root: independent civil society advocacy representatives of broad global publics; global organizations where such norms are advocated; and the American commitment of material resources – largely in that sequential order. Where one of these factors is absent, and thus a different configuration ensues, the result is one of a number of different types of US foreign policy – one of the options outlined in the first chapter.

How does this variation look in practice? Figure 2.1 outlines these variations by systematically demonstrating the form that foreign policy takes under alternative configurations.

Although it might be argued that it represents only a mechanistic "first cut," Figure 2.1 attempts to delineate the variations in the degree of widespread entrepreneurial support, institutional consolidation, and American commitment. The outcomes, I argue, lead to variations in the form of policy. Several of the cells are of no relevance to the discussion, most obviously option 7 where none of the conditions apply. In terms of US foreign policy engagement, the most reflective are options 1, 2, 3, and 6. These respectively reflect the four major outcomes delineated in Chapter 1: unilateralism (6), imperialism (2), multilateralism (3), and the consolidation of a global norm (1). In all of these but the first outcome, the US attempts to assume a dominant role with predictable results.

From a methodological perspective, the most interesting cases are when all or at least two of the three conditions I have outlined are met. So the fourth case of interest from a methodological perspective is the fourth outcome, where American support is weak, one that I argue many proponents mistakenly seize upon to demonstrate the robust nature of global governance. The rest, where one or none of the conditions outlined are met, are largely irrelevant for the purposes of this argument except the key case of unilateralism. We therefore need to examine four options (outcomes 1, 2, 3 and 6) in assessing the utility of this argument. I do so in the ensuing set of case studies.

---

to Darfur: Combine leverage, internationalism and aid to stop the killing in Sudan", reprinted from *The Los Angeles Times*, 2 June, http://www.hks.harvard.edu/cchrp/pdf/Break%20Through%20to%20Darfur%20_LAT_.pdf

US State Department officials clearly concurred with this assessment that American logistical support is indispensible, according to the comments made by Andrew Natsios, cited in Fox News (2007), "U.S. Official Says Sudan Must Accept Non-African Peacekeeping Troops", 8 August, http://www.foxnews.com/story/0,2933,292526,00.html

While the following four chapters should be considered more heuristic in value than decisive in supporting the argument laid out in the opening two chapters, they serve to illustrate the application of this framework, and how the systematic variation in US policy can be explained in the current context. The study of the attempt to prioritize the anti-corruption norm at the World Bank illustrates the challenges facing American policymakers seeking to impose their values through an imperialist foreign policy, even under the most likely of circumstances. The fourth chapter, on the Bush Doctrine, demonstrates the problems of constructing and enforcing a unilateralist policy in the absence of the legitimacy provided by a global institution. The fifth chapter, on cybersecurity, examines a case common to the global governance chapter, of efforts to generate a norm through multilateral negotiation but without US enforcement. All entail US efforts at leadership. Finally, the sixth chapter outlines the successful case of the construction of the anti-trafficking global norm, where NGO support has been broad-based, the principles have been enshrined in a global institution, and the US has spent material resources sponsoring its enforcement.

3
"If I Ruled the World:" Imperialism, Anti-corruption and the World Bank

> The FY 2010 Budget puts the United States on a path to double U.S. foreign assistance. This funding will help the world's weakest states reduce poverty, combat global health threats, develop markets, govern peacefully, and expand democracy worldwide.[1]
>
> President Barack Obama

At the end of October 2006, Luiz Inacio Lula da Silva won a resounding victory and was reelected as Brazil's president in a run-off against his conservative challenger, Geraldo Alckmin, with over 61 percent of the popular vote.[2] Lula's first term in office had been marked by a concerted policy thrust designed to reduce Brazil's historic gross inequalities. Vowing to eradicate hunger, he had embarked on a series of social reforms that not only endeared him to millions of Brazil's poor, but also appeared effective. The billions of dollars spent on health, education, and welfare were matched by a real 22 percent rise in the minimum wage between 2003 and 2006.[3]

---

[1] See Department of State and other International Programs, "A new era of responsibility", *Department of State*, p. 87, http://www.whitehouse.gov/omb/assets/fy2010_new_era/Department_of_State_and_Other_International_Programs1.pdf

[2] See BBC News (2006), "Brazil re-elects President Lula", 30 October, http://news.bbc.co.uk/2/hi/americas/6095820.stm

[3] See Timothy Powers (2006), "The Brazilian Elections: The Morning After Round 2", 30 October, unpublished manuscript, p. 9.

Critics, however, also characterized Lula's presidency as being endemically corrupt – the highlights including his party's purported bribing of congressional politicians in exchange for votes. Lula was also accused in the latter stages of the election of employing a "dirty tricks" campaign against his opponent, as a result of which his reelection campaign chief, Ricardo Berzoini, was forced to resign. The evidence against Lula in both cases seemed compelling. Yet Brazil's poor, and the overwhelming proportion of the electorate, did not seem to care. In numerous interviews, Brazilians expressed their admiration for Lula's emphasis on poverty alleviation, either rejecting or trivializing claims regarding Lula's alleged corruption.[4] Newspapers hailed Lula's re-election, emphasizing his defense of the poor.[5] In the battle for hearts and minds of the Brazilian electorate between poverty alleviation and reforms intended to counteract corruption, the former had triumphed. Fighting poverty had proved more legitimate with the voters than fighting for "the rule of law."

Two months later when Hugo Chavez stood for reelection in Venezuela, the country ranked 138th out of 163 on the Transparency International (TI) Corruption Perceptions Index for that year.[6] Critics accused him of cultivating a "culture of corruption,"[7] suggesting that:

> The soaring price of oil has flooded government coffers with petrodollars and fanned the same endemic corruption that thoroughly discredited Venezuela's two major political parties in the 1990s. As part of his commitment to end poverty within 20 years, Chávez has lavished government *largesse* on a plethora of welfare programs mostly devoid of parliamentary oversight or any other supervision. Not surprisingly, vast sums of money have stuck to the wrong hands, and most polls show that corruption now ranks among the top three concerns of ordinary citizens.[8]

---

[4] See BBC News (2006), "Brazil poor feel benefits of Lula's policies", 18 September, http://news.bbc.co.uk/2/hi/americas/5301240.stm

[5] For a summary of their statements see BBC News (2006), "Brazil press looks to future", 30 October, http://news.bbc.co.uk/2/hi/americas/6098314.stm

[6] See Transparency International Corruption Perceptions Index (2006), http://www.transparency.org/policy_research/surveys_indices/cpi/2006

[7] See Dave Eberhart (2006), "Venezuela's Chavez Caught in Culture of Corruption", *NewsMax.com*, 31 March, http://www.newsmax.com/archives/articles/2006/3/31/114227.shtml

[8] See Phil Gunson (2006), "A Question of Graft: As gushing petrodollars stick to the wrong hands, corruption threatens the regime of Hugo Chávez", *Newsweek*, 31 July, http://www.newsweek.com/id/46219/page/1

While Chavez certainly devoted huge sums of money to poverty allevi-ation programs,[9] the electorate shrugged aside concerns about corruption. His policies were rewarded, the electorate swepting Chavez back into power, as he gained nearly 63 percent of the vote against his social democratic opponent – by an even greater margin of victory than in the prior elec-tions of 1998 and 2000.[10] Poverty alleviation once again, it seemed, carried greater weight with the electorate than concerns about corruption.

In Iran in 2005, Mahmoud Ahmadinejad, then the Mayor of Tehran, campaigned on a platform of poverty reduction.[11] Again, in 2009, he ran his campaign for reelection on a similar platform, targeting the support of both Iran's rural and urban poor. The Western media, which focused more on the protests and Ahmadinejad's flagrant anti-Semitism, largely missed this point. Once again, poverty alleviation was clearly shown to be more popular than competing values.

Developments in these three countries could not have been in starker contrast to those at the World Bank, where a major shift had taken place during the same time period. Dating from the arrival of Paul Wolfowitz as president, anti-poverty had been usurped by anti-corruption as the dominant institutional concern. This restatement of World Bank prior-ities signaled a conspicuous, indeed dramatic, shift from the halcyon days of 2000. Then the World Bank's *World Development Report* was published with the subtitle "Attacking Poverty," and its then-president James Wolfensohn's mantra was that "major reductions in human deprivation are indeed possible, and that the forces of global integration and technological advance can and must be harnessed to serve the

---

[9] As examples of the discussion regarding expenditures, see Steven Mather (2006), "Chavez Highlights Two of Venezuela's Social Programs", *Axis of Logic*, 13 August, http://www.axisoflogic.com/artman/publish/article_22746.shtml. Also see Kevin Sullivan (2004), "Embattled Chavez Taps Oil Cash In a Social, Political Experiment", *The Washington Post*, 18 June, p. A19, http://www.wash-ingtonpost.com/ac2/wp-dyn/A50593–2004Jun17?language=printer

[10] See Stephanie Hanson (2006), "Six More Years of Chavez", *Council on Foreign Relations*, 4 December, http://www.cfr.org/publication/12086/six_more_years_of_chavez.html; also see BBC News (2006), "Chavez named presidential vic-tor", 5 December, http://news.bbc.co.uk/2/hi/americas/6209258.stm. On the prior election see Medea Benjamin (2004), "Why Hugo Chavez Won a Landslide Victory", *www.commondreams.org*, 17 August, http://www.commondreams.org/views04/0817–01.htm. On the linkage between Chavez's social policy and his reelection, see BBC News (2006), "Chavez wins Venezuela re-election", 4 December, http://news.bbc.co.uk/2/hi/americas/6205128.stm

[11] See China Daily (2005), "New Iranian President Offers 'Moderation'", 28 June, http://www.chinadaily.com.cn/english/doc/2005–06/28/content_455077.htm

interest of poor people." In a sweeping statement, Wolfensohn's definition of poverty extended beyond income and consumption "to include
powerlessness and voicelessness, and vulnerability and fear."[12]

This chapter is about the unsuccessful, explicit attempt of the United
States, through the personal efforts of Paul Wolfowitz as successor
President to Wolfensohn, to use the World Bank as a conduit to create
anti-corruption as a global norm and utilize its capacity as a coercive
enforcement mechanism. In terms of the framework outlined in the
opening chapters, this case study chapter is about American attempts
to promote a norm on the basis of very limited societal support – thus
looking more like imperialism to America's critics. Fighting poverty
had received widespread support as the number one priority during the
Wolfensohn era among a broad array of constituents.

In contrast, fighting corruption was considered legitimate as the World
Bank's primary goal among only a select group of stakeholders drawn
from the US government and a few European countries, a few large
Northern NGOs, notably TI, and a handful of small Southern ones. In
the case of the norm of anti-corruption, the advocacy that comes from
civil society is from a narrow base and is financially supported by self-
interested stakeholders, and the norm appears more justified by technocratic principles (albeit augmented by the occasional rhetoric of a moral
imperative) rather than a theory of justice.[13] It was, nonetheless, selectively enforced through coercive measures. The result, however, was a
series of policies lacking popular support, and had limited effectiveness
during Paul Wolfowitz's reign. It is a norm whose proponents tried to
enforce it through a global institution; but is not a global norm.

For many of the World Bank's constituents, the importance of fighting corruption seemed to pale in comparison to the poverty and hunger
experienced in the Global South. Certainly, no one argued *in favor* of
corruption, as petty dictators amassed fortunes in offshore accounts.
According to many critics, however, making the fight against corruption
the primary goal as a means to address global poverty seemed a rather

---

[12]James D. Wolfensohn (2000), "Foreword", *World Development Report
2000–2001: Attacking Poverty* (New York: Oxford University Press), p. V, http://
siteresources.worldbank.org/INTPOVERTY/Resources/WDR/English-Full-Text-
Report/toc.pdf

[13] For a cogent, if non-technical, justification for the relationship between anti-
corruption, the rule of law and growth, see Ana Isabel Eiras and Brett D. Schaefer
(2005), "A Blueprint for Paul Wolfowitz at the World Bank", Backgrounder
#1856, *The Heritage Foundation*, 2 June, http://www.heritage.org/Research/
TradeandForeignAid/bg1856.cfm

indirect way of combating the problem – reminiscent of "trickle-down economics" rather than attacking the problem at the root. The primacy of anti-corruption has therefore been, as this chapter details, a policy without the widespread legitimacy of anti-poverty measures.

Some societal support for propagating the anti-corruption norm clearly exists. Yet the effort is spearheaded by TI, an organization that is staffed by a leadership that originated from the World Bank itself; has a narrow constituency of (primarily) Northern states and (secondarily) a few members of the (Northern) business community; and is overwhelmingly funded by Northern States and the European Union. Furthermore, the concerns expressed by TI's leadership about social justice may well be sincere (corruption is evil; it undermines the moral basis of society), but that seems a "thin reed" as a foundation upon which to generate widespread support in comparison with competing claims by groups whose primary concerns focus on issues such as indigenous rights, environmental degradation, and poverty alleviation (defined as redistribution through social service provisions) in the Global South. The fact that TI worked its way into a position of preeminence within the sinews of the World Bank, that it collaborates with relatively few other NGOs, and that the US government (symbolized in the form of controversial then World Bank president, Paul Wolfowitz) is the most avowed proponent of the same norm, only serves to further reduce the credibility of TI's goals in the eyes of many in a wary Global South.

The result was the World Bank's sponsorship of a norm that appeared to be the product of top-down pressure from stakeholders in the North with a vested interest rather than bottom-up advocacy from NGOs or stakeholders in the South. It is a norm that lacks the necessary endorsement from a broad selection of increasingly alienated (and even hostile) civil society actors needed to establish its legitimacy.[14] It is a norm whose enforcement meets with resistance, whether active or passive – and requires local acceptance in order to be implemented effectively. As a Heritage Foundation background report on the issue of anti-corruption at the time suggested, "Developing countries must make their own internal reforms for their own reasons; reforms imposed through

---

[14] For a general discussion of the importance of civil society organizations, at least from their and the World Bank's perspective, see (2003) "The World Bank and Civil Society", *Bretton Woods Project*, 17 November, http://www.brettonwoodsproject.org/art-27513

external pressure are likely to be short-lived or poorly implemented."[15] To advocates, its application looks like a formula for growth and development in the Third World; to opponents, it looks like imperialism.[16]

The context: global poverty and international financial institutions

Critics of neoliberalism and globalization often focus on American policy in explaining the reputed growth in the disparities between the rich and the poor nations dating from the 1960s.[17] Susan Strange focused on a series of unilateral US decisions in explaining the breakdown in the national regulation of markets and the onset of globalization.[18] In contrast, however, much of the literature addressing this issue has more generally pointed to the role of the International Monetary Fund and the World Bank as conduits of American power in advancing the neoliberal agenda, famously coined by economist John Williamson in 1990 as the "Washington Consensus."[19]

---

[15] Ana Isabel Eiras and Brett D. Schaefer (2005), "A Blueprint for Paul Wolfowitz at the World Bank", op. cit.

[16] Albeit it is a form of imperialism that looks more neocolonial than colonial (lacking the formal attributes of political control). For an elaboration of this distinction see John Gallagher and Ronald Robinson (1953), "The Imperialism of Free Trade", *The Economic History Review*, second series, 6:1, 1–15.

[17] For an admittedly dated review of these figures see Lant Pritchett (1996), "Forget Convergence: Divergence Past, Present and Future", *Finance and Development*, June, http://www.imf.org/external/pubs/ft/fandd/1996/06/pdf/pritchet.pdf. For an updated version see Branko Milanovic (2001), "Chapter III- Growth, Inequality and Poverty", *World Development Report 2001:Attacking Poverty*, http://siteresources.worldbank.org/INTPOVERTY/Resources/WDR/English-Full-Text-Report/ch3.pdf; John T. Passé Smith (2008), "Characteristics of the Income Gap Between Countries", in Mitchell A. Seligson and John T. Passé Smith (eds), *Development and Underdevelopment: the Political Economy of Global Inequality* (Boulder, CO: Lynne Rienner). Note that there is not a consensus on the growth in disparities. See, for example, Jeffrey G. Williamson (1996), "Globalization, Convergence and History", *Journal of Economic History*, 56:2, 277–306. The World Bank's own data presents a mixed picture but suggests that the situation of the poorest of the poor (in Heavily Indebted Poor Countries or HIPC), generally located in Africa, is not improving. See http://web.worldbank.org/WBSITE/EXTERNAL/NEWS/0,,contentMDK:20040961~pagePK:64257043~piPK:437376~theSitePK:4607,00.html

[18] See, for example, Susan Strange (1998), *Mad Money: When Markets Outgrow Governments* (Ann Arbor, MI: University of Michigan Press).

[19] John Williamson (1990), *Latin American Adjustment: How Much Has Happened* (Washington DC: Institute for International Economics). For a recent, succinct overview of the historical development of the neoliberal paradigm at the World

Critics may overstate this characterization of international financial institutions (IFIs) as simple conduits for the US economic agenda. However, the mass protests that have often accompanied the annual meetings held by the world's most notable IFIs clearly attest to the questionable legitimacy of these policies – even among a portion of the mass publics of the Global North whose countries are, they themselves argue, among the primary beneficiaries of such policies.[20]

Although the gap between IFI loan rates and those charged on capital markets have shrunk in the last few years, many of the poorest states that are borrowers from the IMF or the World Bank do not realistically have the option of exit, or even of much dissent, if they want access to the capital generally needed to finance financial crises or long-term, large-scale development projects. Their credit rating is too poor to qualify for market-based loans. They therefore tend to try and negotiate the formal terms of their compliance as best they can. Ultimately, however, acquiescence within the limited contours of asymmetric bargaining is essentially assured, especially in periods of crisis. Formal compliance does not, however, necessarily imply legitimacy. Often the story of the recipient countries' response to World Bank policy is a combination of formal rhetorical compliance coupled with non-implementation or outright informal resistance at the national or local level. It is a story of power without legitimacy. In the absence of legitimacy, as I have suggested earlier, policy initiatives therefore prove ineffective.

This chapter illustrates the dynamics of that relationship: where US power is exercised and policy is institutionalized at a global level through the promulgation and enforcement of the norm of anti-corruption. However, it is a norm that is considered as imposed from the top rather than adopted from the bottom, and therefore lacks widespread support

---

Bank, see Robin Broad (2006), "Research, knowledge, and the art of 'paradigm maintenance': The World Bank's Development Economics Vice-Presidency (DEC)", *Review of International Political Economy*, 13:3, 387–419.

[20] See Walden Bello (2006), "The Crisis of the Globalist Project & the New Economics of George W. Bush", *Transnational Institute*, 1 May, http://www.tni.org/article/crisis-globalist-project-new-economics-george-w-bush. These criticisms were given greater credibility by the attack launched on the relationship between the US and the World Bank by Joseph Stiglitz, the former Chair of the US Government's Council of Economic Advisors (1995–7) and the World Bank's former Chief Economist and Senior Vice-President between 1997 and 2000, in his famous book, *Globalization and Its Discontents*. See Joseph Stiglitz (2001), *Globalization and Its Discontents* (New York: W.W. Norton).

among key stakeholders.[21] Admittedly, as I document, one group of civil society organizations, led by TI, is supportive of the World Bank leadership's emphasis on anti-corruption as a global norm. However, TI was so much associated with the goals of the World Bank's leadership under Wolfowitz, identifiable as a coherent group of Northern states (mostly European), the US government and the business community – and so estranged from the primary concerns of most other major NGOs – that it added little credibility to the World Bank's mission among the vast majority of stakeholders, NGOs and Southern states alike.[22] Critically lacking the kind of widespread political support generated by what are perceived as the independent representatives of civil society, however, the policies generated a "blowback" of both active and passive resistance among many governments, and hostility among NGOs. The result is that policies are implemented, but their enforcement is narrow in scope, reliant on material power rather than social power, and widely regarded as illegitimate.

Lifelong World Bank officials might argue otherwise – that anti-corruption has not come to dominate as an operational norm, usurping other contenders because of US advocacy. They might point, understandably, to the institutional drag created by intra-organizational dynamics within the World Bank. They might tout their own efforts to pursue an agenda designed more to respond to the imperative of addressing scarcity in the Third or Fourth World rather than the exigencies of US policy, and on that basis might claim some tacit independence. They may have a point; within the contours of such a large organization they may have capacity for some maneuverability. However, what they are exhibiting is only flexibility within limited contours – which are largely defined by American leadership.

I illustrate those limits by charting both the continuities and the changes in the dominant organizational norm between the Clinton and Bush Administration appointees – and how a change in US presidents altered the World Bank leadership's policy thrust in two stages.

---

[21] For the list of 74 NGOs hostile to Wolfowitz and his efforts to promote the norm of anti-corruption, see Jubilee USA (2006), "World Bank Finances Corporate Corruption", 20 April, http://www.jubileeusa.org/fileadmin/user_upload/Resources/Policy_Archive/bankcorporatecorruption.pdf

[22] One of TI's closer relationships is with the Global Integrity Alliance, a group whose membership is composed of a curious mix of governments, foundations devoted to business ethics (many of whose web home pages could not be located), multinational corporations, TI chapters, and a scattering of academics. For a list of member organizations see http://www.ethics.org/gia/organizations.html

The first transition was between Wolfensohn's first term under Clinton and his second under Bush. The second was an accelerated policy shift between Wolfensohn and his successor, Bush appointee Paul Wolfowitz, who was eventually replaced by Robert Zoellick. In effect, this period marked the rise and decline of Paul Wolfowitz's leadership, and with it the corresponding failure of an attempt to institute a new norm of anti-corruption, one associated with American imperialism.

In the remainder of this chapter I first outline the basis for US power. I then describe the differences between the two Wolfensohn terms of office, before outlining the hard shift towards the anti-corruption norm under Wolfowitz and the new policies introduced as a result of that shift. It concludes with a discussion of the reactions to that policy shift and its implications for any attempt at the construction of a global norm in the context of US leadership.

The US government and the World Bank

The literature on the US dominant influence on the policies of the World Bank is far too extensive to recount in this context.[23] Of course, the United States was responsible for the creation of the World Bank, and authoritative in the writing (and rewriting) of its mandate and bylaws. The US government sanctions the choice of the Bank's President, and the appointment of senior advisers lies within the President's mandate – as Paul Wolfowitz demonstrated with his subsequent appointment of several controversial advisors who were described broadly as political appointees at odds with the staff and career leadership.[24] Yet, beyond the selection and reappointment of both

---

[23] See, for examples regarding the World Bank, Catherine Gwin (1994), *U.S. Relations with the World Bank, 1945–92* (Washington DC: The Brookings Institution); Robert H. Wade (2002), "US Hegemony and the World Bank", *Review of International Political Economy*, 9:2, 215–43; Robert H. Wade (2001), "The US Role in the Long Asian Crisis of 1990–2000", in Arvid Lukauskis and Francisco L. Batista-Rivera (eds), *The Political Economy of the East Asian Crisis and its Aftermath: Tigers in Distress* (Cheltenham: Edward Elgar), pp. 205–8. For a recent article regarding the purported politicization of the IMF, see Bessma Momami (2004), "American Politicization of the International Monetary Fund", *Review of International Political Economy*, 11:5, 880–904.

[24] See, for example, Florian Gimbelin (2006), "World Bank steps up anti-graft fight", *Financial Times*, 12 April, http:/news.ft.com/cms/s/c6aa8e5e-c9c4–11da-94ca-0000779e2340.html

its President and senior leadership,[25] formal American influence has three other major components.

First, the proportional formal vote exercised by the US (at 16.39 percent on the governing International Bank for Reconstruction and Development board responsible for "hard loans" and 20.86 percent on the newer International Development Agency (IDA) board responsible for "soft loans"), coupled with bylaws requiring a minimum 85 percent vote to approve loans, gives the US (as the largest donor) an effective veto power on both policy and loans.[26] Although other major donors can, in principle, coalesce to form a veto, only the US can do so unilaterally. The reported effect of this leverage, according to Ngaire Woods, is that policy proposals are routinely offered to the US Treasury Department (and them alone) for vetting prior to any formal vote on a loan in recognition of US formal power.[27]

Second, US law requires the relevant US Congressional appropriations committee to authorize its replenishment of the World Bank's IDA (the body responsible for lending concessions) on an annual basis, subject to broad US Congressional review and approval. This creates a complex, interactive negotiating process in which civil society groups lobby in Congress, and congressional representatives lobby the Treasury Department and World Bank officials, regarding World Bank policies.[28] As Woods states, "The Treasury formulates and implements virtually all policy towards the IMF, while the State Department has more input in policy towards the World Bank. However, other agencies, and most particularly the US Congress, bring significant pressure to bear on government positions, both through direct relations with the IMF and World Bank and through indirect pressure on the Treasury and State Department officials."[29] The threat is a realistic one. As Catherine

---

[25] For a discussion of the influence wielded by the US as a result of this capacity to select the leadership, see Robert H. Wade (2002), "US Hegemony and the World Bank", op. cit.

[26] Ngaire Woods (2003), "The United States and the International Financial Institutions: Power and Influence Within the World Bank and the IMF", in Rosemary Foot, Neil MacFarlane and Michael Mastanduno (eds), *US Hegemony and International Organizations* (NY: Oxford University Press), p. 8.

[27] Ibid., p.15.

[28] For a historical perspective on the role of Congress in the formulation of IDA policy, see Catherine Gwin (1994), *U.S. Relations with the World Bank, 1945–92* (Washington DC: The Brookings Institution), pp. 15–16, 26–32.

[29] Ngaire Woods (2003), "The United States and the International Financial Institutions: Power and Influence Within the World Bank and the IMF", op. cit., p. 6. It is no surprise, in view of these comments, that Robert Zoelleck,

Weaver points out, "congressional representatives have demanded specific organizational reforms at the World Bank prior to the authorization of funds."[30] Regardless of their disagreements, what apparently unites Congress and the Executive branch, according to Woods, is "the belief that the United States can and should set down terms and conditions for multilateral economic institutions."[31]

Third, given that primary donors pay to the IDA on a proportional basis, World Bank officials are cognizant that any drop in the US contribution would necessitate a proportionate drop in the contribution of other donors. This generates a multiplier effect to any American threat to cut its budget.[32] The US employs this threat on an occasional basis to ensure its policy and loan demands are met. During a 2005 IDA replenishment process, for example, the US demanded that new policies be instituted to strengthen a "results measurement" initiative such as the enhancement of the Country Policy and Institutional Assessment (CPIA) process. As a result of these demands, the final agreement also entailed a greater focus on private sector development.[33]

American institutional power is clearly unrivalled at the World Bank. Calls to democratize this power have consistently fallen on deaf ears.[34] In addition to these powers, US influence is enhanced by a variety of con-

---

Wolfowitz's successor, formerly held an appointment as a Deputy Secretary at the US Department of State.

[30] Catherine Weaver (2006), "The World's Bank and the Bank's World: Towards a Gross Anatomy of the World Bank", paper presented at the Annual Conference of the International Studies Association, 24 March, San Diego, CA, p. 9, http://www.allacademic.com//meta/p_mla_apa_research_citation/0/9/7/9/6/pages97968/p97968–1.php. BIC Toolkits for Activists (2003), "The Role of Congress in Multilateral Development Bank Reform", *Bank Information Center (BIC)*, November, http://www.bicusa.org/en/Article.304.aspx

[31] Ngaire Woods (2003), "The United States and the International Financial Institutions: Power and Influence within the World Bank and the IMF", op. cit., p. 7.

[32] Ngaire Woods (2003), "The United States and the International Financial Institutions: Power and Influence Within the World Bank and the IMF", op. cit., p. 9.

[33] See Jonathan E. Sanford (2005), "Multilateral Development Banks: Current Authorization Request", CRS Report for Congress, *Congressional Research Service*, 3 May, pp. 3–4, http://digital.library.unt.edu/govdocs/crs/permalink/meta-crs-7347:1

[34] For a discussion of this issue see, for example, Bruce Jenkins and Nancy Alexander (2005), "Who Rules the World (Bank)?", *Bank Information Center*, IFI Info Brief No. 1, http://www.bicusa.org/bicusa/issues/bic_ifi_info_brief_who_rules_the_world_bank.pdf

ventional norms. First, the US holds a near monopoly over the information key to the formulation of policy. Second, the World Bank is located within a close proximity to key economic departments in the US government. Weaver persuasively argues that the nearby locale of that bureaucracy "has facilitated a behind-the-scenes interaction that has permitted the US to proactively promote its foreign policy interests within the international organization."[35] Third, the huge and skilled US bureaucracy devoted to economic policy provides it with an unrivalled technocratic ability. The US employs numerous dedicated officials and Treasury Department officials who coordinate both at the IFIs in Washington and at the individual level of countries who receive World Bank loans.[36]

Furthermore, the use of English as the World Bank's dominant language, its overwhelming employment of economists, and the fact that an equally overwhelming proportion of those economists are trained at Anglo-American institutions, all lend to the formidable sway of neoliberal assumptions embedded in the policies adopted by the World Bank.[37] Indeed, Ngaire Woods cites data from a 1996 study suggesting that approximately 90 percent of employees with PhDs at that time received them from the United States or Canada, while another showed that 80 percent of the Bank's senior staff were trained in economics and finance at US and UK institutions.[38]

Overall, Woods concludes that the World Bank has become susceptible to more direct US influence as its activities and its resources have expanded.[39] The necessary replenishment of World Bank funds has provided the US with an opportunity to negotiate, or renegotiate, conditions for US contributions. According to Woods, "the overall result seems to have enhanced the capacity of the United States unilaterally to

---

[35] Catherine Weaver (2006), "The World's Bank and the Bank's World: Towards a Gross Anatomy of the World Bank", op. cit., p. 11.

[36] Ngaire Woods (2003), "The United States and the International Financial Institutions: Power and Influence Within the World Bank and the IMF", op. cit., p. 18.

[37] Catherine Weaver (2006), "The World's Bank and the Bank's World: Towards a Gross Anatomy of the World Bank", op. cit., pp. 11–12. See also Devesh Kapur, John P. Lewis and Richard Webb (1997), *The World Bank: Its First Half Century*, Volumes I and II (Washington DC: Brookings Institution).

[38] See Nicholas Stern with Francisco Ferreira (1997), "The World Bank as an 'Intellectual Actor'", in Devesh Kapur, John P. Lewis and Richard Webb (eds), *The World Bank: Its First Half Century*, Volume II. The figures are now dated, but nothing has occurred that challenges this basic insight.

[39] Woods provides a succinct but highly comprehensive table listing aspects of US influence in "The United States and the International Financial Institutions", Table 4.1, p. 96.

determine aspects of policy and structure within both the IMF and the World Bank."[40] She stridently states that: "The United States has used its dominant position in each of the Bretton Woods twins to radically reshape their finances since the 1980s, as well as to reinforce and elaborate the conditionality associated with their loans."[41] Robert Wade concurs, suggesting that: "where the USA sees its vital interests at stake it can virtually always prevail in lending situations."[42] Elsewhere he contends that "The World Bank has been an especially useful instrument for projecting American influence in developing countries, and one over which the US maintains discreet but firm institutional control."[43]

Wade argues that the US controls the World Bank's selection of leadership, its culture, and the dominant thinking. Its location, *lingua franca* and the structure of power within the World Bank reinforce these tendencies.[44] Opinions differ over the influence of NGOs: one view is that they are given a voice, only for their proposals to be either ignored at the policy stage or implemented in relatively trivial contexts.[45] The second, echoed by Ngaire Woods, is that the NGOs given primacy are largely those in agreement with the US agenda, because of their engagement in American politics through a Congressional membership likely to be sympathetic to their aims. Not all NGOs, therefore, are created equal.[46] Either way, the World Bank walks a fine line between the appearance of independence in order to sustain legitimacy and the exigencies created by American preferences. The mass protests and academic criticism suggest that, at least in some quarters, the patent exercise of American power comes at a loss of World Bank legitimacy.

---

[40] Ngaire Woods (2003), "The United States and the International Financial Institutions: Power and Influence Within the World Bank and the IMF", op. cit., p. 10.
[41] Ngaire Woods (2006), *The Globalizers: the IMF, the World Bank and Their Borrowers* (Ithaca, NY: Cornell University Press), p. 200.
[42] Robert H. Wade, "US Hegemony and the World Bank", op. cit., p. 208.
[43] Robert H. Wade (2001), "Showdown at the World Bank", *New Left Review*, 7, 127, http://newleftreview.org/?getpdf=NLR24109&pdflang=en
[44] Robert H. Wade, "US Hegemony and the World Bank", op. cit., p. 218.
[45] O'Brien *et al.*, for example, argue that NGOs have made inroads at the World Bank, only to demonstrate in their book that, while NGOs have attempted to influence the agenda, with some success, they have largely failed to influence policy. See Robert O'Brien, Anne Marie Goetz, Jan Aarte Scholte and Marc Williams (2000), *Contesting Global Governance: Multilateral Economic Institutions and Global Social Movements*, op. cit.
[46] Ngaire Woods (2006), *The Globalizers: the IMF, the World Bank and Their Borrowers*, op. cit., p. 112.

The guiding norms of the World Bank

Among the largest IFIs, the World Bank made a great effort, during James Wolfensohn's presidency, to enhance its legitimacy by presenting itself as being the "human face of capitalism."[47] A series of reforms initiated under the new presidency of Wolfensohn, commencing soon after his appointment by President Clinton in 1995, tried to integrate civil society organizations and NGOs into the World Bank's decision-making process in an attempt to address their concerns.[48]

A dialogue between World Bank staff and the representatives of some of these groups featured a discussion about concepts such as "empowerment of the poor," "poverty alleviation," and "sustainable development." The goal of NGOs was to get these concepts adopted by the organization as operational norms. The World Bank's goal was to co-opt the leadership of these NGOs, and thus enhance the World Bank's legitimacy.[49] The efforts of the NGOs bore fruit. The *World Development Report of 2000/2001* declared poverty to be:

> The result of economic, political and social processes that interact with each other and frequently reinforce each other in ways that exacerbate the deprivation in which poor people live. Meager assets, inaccessible markets, and scarce job opportunities lock people into material poverty. That is why promoting opportunity – by stimulating economic growth, making markets work better for

---

[47] In that sense, it represents a harder case to make of the appearance of "imperialism" outlined in my original schema, although examples of imperialism generally employ the rhetoric of a moral imperative, whether bringing the appropriate faith to the natives or economic freedom to the subjugated.

[48] For a description of the process leading to Wolfensohn's appointment, see Sebastian Mallaby (2004), *The World's Banker: A Story of Failed States, Financial Crises, and the Wealth and Poverty of Nations* (New York: Penguin Press), pp. 73–83.

[49] For an interesting perspective on the history of the efforts of civil society transnational advocacy groups to generate support broadly in the World Bank for the principles of sustainable development (in the context of large-scale dam projects), see Sanjeev Khagram (2004), *Dams and Development: Transnational Struggles for Water and Power* (Ithaca, New York: Cornell University Press), especially pp. 195–6 and 210–11. For an interesting perspective on the relative success of the environmental movement at the World Bank, see Jonathan A. Fox and L. David Brown (1998), "Assessing the Impact of NGO Advocacy Campaigns on World Bank Projects and Policies", in Jonathan A. Fox and L. David Brown (eds), *The Struggle for Accountability: The World Bank, NGOs, and Grassroots Movements* (Cambridge MA: MIT Press), pp. 485–39.

poor people, and building up their assets – is key to reducing poverty.[50]

The report, however, went on to point out a host of other problematic contributory factors: the customary norms, values, and practices within societies, and social exclusion by race, ethnicity, and gender often practiced within them – as well as addressing the underlying insecurities the poor faced as a result of "war, disease, economic crises, and natural disasters."[51] In sum, both proximate practices and underlying structural factors had to be tackled if the globe's widespread destitution and gross inequalities were to be addressed.

The report's prescriptive strategy was threefold. First, material opportunities targeted on the poor had to be promoted by a comprehensive package of:

Jobs, credits, roads, electricity, markets for their produce, and the schools, water, sanitation, and health services that underpin the health and skills essential for work... Mechanisms need to be in place to create new opportunities and compensate the potential losers in transitions. In societies with high inequality, greater equity is particularly important for rapid progress in reducing poverty.[52]

Second, poor people had to be empowered through the introduction of measures by state and social institutions designed to make them accountable and responsive to the poor: "access, responsibility, and accountability is intrinsically political,"[53] and reforms designed to strengthen the participation of poor people in the political process were needed. Finally, the report's authors intrinsically linked enhanced well-being and greater investment in the poor with a reduced vulnerability to both man-made and natural disasters. Effective national management of risk was key to bolstering the capacity of the poor to deal with shocks, and to build their assets.[54]

---

[50] See World Bank (2001), "Overview", *World Development Report 2000–2001: Attacking Poverty* (New York: Oxford University Press), p. 1.

[51] Ibid., p. 3.

[52] Ibid., pp. 6–7.

[53] Ibid., p. 7.

[54] See World Bank (2001), "Overview", *World Development Report 2000–2001: Attacking Poverty* (New York: Oxford University Press), p. 1.

The report stressed that three elements – opportunity, empowerment, and security – were complementary in building "a comprehensive approach to attacking poverty."[55] Effective implementation was contingent on local circumstances and the contribution of both the developed countries and multilateral organizations. However, the report did identify key measures that had to be implemented in each area – and by whom – if the fight to achieve poverty reduction was to be a successful one.[56]

While the goals of the World Bank were therefore explicitly stated, the evidence of mass protests suggests that the World Bank's strategy had mixed results.[57] Civil society organizations were frustrated by the lack of operational progress and questioned the World Bank's motives and ensuing policies, accusing the leadership of being disingenuous in their advocacy of poverty alleviation and supportive of private interests.[58] They protested and boycotted meetings, and many ultimately withdrew from discussions.

However, the World Bank was far more successful in establishing broader legitimacy as a result of its efforts to alleviate poverty, especially in the Global South, where the poorest of client states are less skeptical of the World Bank's contribution than either their Northern counterparts or the NGO community.[59] One public opinion survey of 32 countries completed in late 2005, based on 37,572 respondents (and thus before Wolfowitz's anti-corruption campaign got under way), revealed that the World Bank had a more positive rating than other IFIs or global companies. In 31 of the 32 countries, a majority or plurality claimed that the World Bank had a positive influence. "Countries that have been recipients of World Bank loans are particularly positive about its influence. Africans are especially enthusiastic – Kenya (81 percent

---

[55] Ibid., p. 7.

[56] Ibid., pp. 7–12.

[57] Indeed, Fox and Brown adjudge the impact of these efforts at reform to be "still quite limited." See Jonathan A. Fox and L. David Brown (1998), "Assessing the Impact of NGO Advocacy Campaigns on World Bank Projects and Policies", op. cit., p. 532.

[58] For a recent example of such dissent see ICFTU (2006), "Fighting for Alternatives: Cases of Successful Trade Union Resistance to the Policies of the IMF and World Bank", *The International Confederation of Free Trade Unions*, 20 April, http://www.icftu.org/www/PDF/IFI.pdf

[59] See World Public Opinion.Org (2006), "World Bank Receives Good Marks in World Poll", 24 January, http://www.worldpublicopinion.org/pipa/articles/btglobalizationtradera/162.php?nid=&id=&pnt=162&lb=btgl

rated it positively), Tanzania (79 percent) and Democratic Republic of the Congo (75 percent). Afghanistan was also quite positive (79 percent) as were Asians generally, especially Indonesia (80 percent)." Northern states were less enthused. "The British are among the most tepid with 45 percent positive and 37 percent negative, as are the Americans – 47 percent positive, 28 percent negative."[60] There is thus a high correlation between public support for the World Bank and the countries that have benefited most from Wolfensohn's poverty alleviation strategy. This is true even in countries where corruption is rampant; and the majority of respondents in these countries often reported in the same survey that they thought their own individual economic situation was getting worse (e.g. Congo 63 percent, Kenya 53 percent), or that the general economic situation in their country was worsening (e.g. Congo 79 percent, Kenya 57 percent).

Nonetheless, the respondents were by no means uncritical of the World Bank. Steven Kull, the director of PIPA who carried out the survey, notes that many saw the World Bank "as falling short of these goals and disproportionately serving the needs of the wealthy states – enough to drive many out on the street to demand that these institutions better fulfill their purpose and potential."[61] Still, there is a clear correlation between countries where the World Bank had committed funds and its degree of popularity: the policies resulting from Wolfensohn's Comprehensive Development Framework (discussed in greater detail below) won approval ratings among mass populations in the Global South.

In contrast, the general population in the major stakeholder countries polled were the least favorably disposed towards the World Bank.[62] Most were well below the global average of 55 percent positive. Notably, the World Bank was least popular among its major client states in Argentina (a remarkably low 26 percent positive) and Brazil (48 percent positive, just above the UK and US figures), two countries where the World Bank has provided loans, but where its policies are most closely associated with those of the IMF rather than the principles of poverty alleviation.[63] Finally, NGOs, the major proponents of poverty alleviation,

---

[60] World Public Opinion.Org (2006), "World Bank Receives Good Marks in World Poll", op. cit.

[61] Ibid.

[62] Unfortunately many stakeholder countries were omitted from the survey.

[63] For a full list of results in all 32 countries, see Globespan and PIPA, "BBC World Service Poll: Evaluation of Global Institutions and Economic Conditions

were overwhelmingly more popular globally than either IFIs or global companies. This (albeit limited and admittedly indirect) data suggests that policies designed to address poverty are popular and regarded as legitimate as a norm, at least among clients and stakeholders.

The origins of the shift

Nonetheless, some things seem clear. First, NGO criticism that Wolfensohn did retreat from his reformist strategy in his second term seems justified. The halcyon days of the *World Development Report*'s publication soon receded under pressure from the new George Bush White House administration. Second, a small cohort of civil society groups associated with the American focus on anti-corruption (led by TI) stayed in discussions with the World Bank's leadership and – with some vocal support from the US Congress – came to dominate other NGOs' concerns (such as poverty alleviation and sustainable develop-ment) in Wolfensohn's second term. Third, anti-corruption became the dominant focus of the World Bank under Wolfowitz's leadership, a shift consistent with American policy under the Bush administration.

The United States government has always been vocal about enforc-ing anti-corruption policies, dating from the passage of The US Foreign Corrupt Practices Act in 1977 (some of whose compliance provisions were updated in the USA Patriot Act) and was even more aggressive about it under George W. Bush.[64] In Wolfowitz, the administration chose a strident advocate in the crusade against corruption, someone ready to co-opt sympathetic states and NGOs in the North and to punish offenders in the South. As one commentator suggested, "Although his predecessor, James Wolfensohn, also highlighted corruption as a serious obstacle to development, Wolfowitz has significantly elevated the issue as a World Bank priority."[65] A leaked internal World Bank document

---

Questionnaire and Methodology", http://www.worldpublicopinion.org/pipa/pdf/jan06/GlobalPlayers_Jan06_quaire.pdf

[64] For a summary of the provisions see US Department of Justice and US Department of Commerce, "Foreign Corruption Practices Act: Anti-bribery Provisions', http://www.justice.gov/criminal/fraud/fcpa/docs/lay-persons-guide.pdf

[65] See Gail Hurley (2006), "Wolfowitz Needs to Look at Corruption of Yesterday, Not Just Today and Follow the Positive Example of Norway", European Network on Debt and Development (EURODAD), 1 June, http://www.eurodad.org/aid/article.aspx?id=3280&item=338

on the strategy for combating anti-corruption soon after Wolfowitz's arrival made this position crystal clear:[66]

The apparent replacement of poverty alleviation as a prime concern in favor of a greater focus on anti-corruption in the early period of Paul Wolfowitz's tenure served to undermine the legitimacy of the World Bank's claim that its primary interest lay in assisting the world's poor. In the words of Walden Bello, it was seen by many critics as part of an institutional structure "blatantly manipulated to serve the interests of the imperial center."[67]

Regardless of the veracity of this hostile view, I argue that the root of this widely critical perspective lies in three components: the power structure of the World Bank; the norms that guided its mandate; and the relatively nominal shifts in those norms over time. For, despite Wolfensohn's progressive rhetoric of inclusiveness, and allowing for his genuine efforts to institute reforms, the World Bank has consistently remained focused on those neoliberal, technocratic norms embedded in the "Washington Consensus." These norms are at odds with broader global conceptions based on a theory of economic justice most coherently initially articulated by the New International Economic Order and expressed by advocates of the UN's Millennium Goals (endorsed by 189 governments including the major donor governments, the World Bank, and the UN) or the International Covenant on Economic, Social and Cultural Rights (ICESCR).[68]

In his first term of office, Wolfensohn, with Clinton's approval, adopted an approach in which considerations of anti-corruption and economic justice were balanced in the context of Wolfensohn's broad

---

[66]The rationale for this reprioritization is laid out in the executive summary of a leaked confidential internal World Bank report entitled "Strengthening Bank Group Work in Governance and Anti-corruption" and dated 17 August 2006, available at http://www-wds.worldbank.org/external/default/ WDSContentServer/WDSP/IB/2006/08/18/000090341_20060818150004/ Rendered/PDF/37005.pdf

[67]Walden Bello (2006), "The Crisis of the Globalist Project & the New Economics of George W. Bush", op. cit.

[68]For a statement of these goals see http://www.undp.org/mdg/basics.shtml

For the official statement of the state of the UN's Millennium Goals in 2005, see http://unstats.un.org/unsd/mi/pdf/MDG%20Book.pdf. For a discussion of the background and components of both the MDGs and the ICESCR, see Paul J. Nelson (2007), "Human Rights, the Millennium Development Goals, and the Future of Development Cooperation", *World Development*, 35:12, 2041–55.

Comprehensive Development Framework.[69] While enjoining his staff to talk to NGOs about policies predicated on addressing poverty concerns, Wolfensohn, for example, initiated the focus on anti-corruption at the World Bank's Annual Meeting in 1996, the same year that the *United Nations Convention Against Corruption* was drafted (entering into force with US ratification in 2005).[70]

Wolfensohn's second term, however, coincided with the election of George W. Bush, whose agenda differed from his predecessor's. As Sebastian Mallaby states, "there was no getting around the fact that the new American President did not know the World Bank President and did not particularly want to know him."[71] According to Mallaby, Paul O'Neill, the new Treasury Secretary, was more hostile to Wolfensohn and the World Bank's policies under Wolfensohn than was Bush himself. Over the course of O'Neill's tenure, his deep skepticism about the purpose of the World Bank and its lack of efficiency, coupled with the Bush administration's new focus on the War on Terror, drove Wolfensohn "to promote cleaner governance around the world," justified by Bush administration officials on the grounds that this was part of a broad anti-terrorism strategy aimed at strategically important countries.[72]

O'Neill's aim was to get rid of Wolfensohn and reform the World Bank.[73] The Republicans generally had a dim view of Wolfensohn,[74] and the Republican Congress, led by Senate Foreign Relations Committee Chair Richard Lugar, focused on corruption involving World Bank projects.[75] Even O'Neill's successor, John Snow, found no

---

[69] The two men's personal affinity, notes Sebastian Mallaby in his biography of Wolfensohn's tenure at the World Bank, was powerful. See Sebastian Mallaby, op. cit., p. 287. In the context of the latter, Mallaby's account of Wolfensohn's reaction to his visit to Indonesia in 1996 – and meeting with Suharto – is instructive. With Suharto having actually boasted of his corruption, Wolfensohn, hitherto exclusively focused on poverty reduction, became more attendant to the "cancer of corruption". See Sebastian Mallaby, *World's Banker: A Story of Failed States, Financial Crises, and the Wealth and Poverty of Nations*, op. cit., p. 179.

[70] Corruption being broadly defined in this context as "the misuse of entrusted power for private benefit", in "Transparency International Sourcebook 2000", *Transparency International*, Notes to Chapter 1.

[71] Sebastian Mallaby, *World's Banker: A Story of Failed States, Financial Crises, and the Wealth and Poverty of Nations*, op. cit.

[72] Ibid., p. 304.

[73] This claim is made repeatedly by Sebastian Mallaby; ibid., pp. 291, 306.

[74] Ibid., p. 293.

[75] See, for example, Richard G. Lugar (2004), "$100 billion may have been lost to World Bank corruption", 13 May, http://www.thedailystar.net/2006/05/09/

common ground with Wolfensohn because of the latter's refusal to use World Bank funds to pay for the reconstruction of Iraq after the invasion in 2003.[76]

Nonetheless, Wolfensohn sought to retain a focus on poverty, employing a different tactic with the Republicans. He claimed that poverty created the foundation for terrorism in failed and fragile states such as Afghanistan and Sudan.[77] But, as Mallaby suggests, "The vision of a development agenda led by developing countries was hard to sustain," and Wolfensohn made a series of promises to the White House that the World Bank could not deliver. This did little to address either the White House's hostility toward the World Bank or the Treasury's preference for a change of leadership and sweeping reform.[78]

As a result of these combined pressures, Wolfensohn's authority dwindled, and so did his capacity to pursue a balanced agenda. Under US government pressure, he increasingly focused on American concerns – terrorism and anti-corruption. Those NGO groups pursuing other agendas became disillusioned and sometimes hostile. Only one, TI, became enamored and was embraced. Consistent with Ngaire Woods' expectations, TI and the World Bank both became closely identified with US goals and priorities – creating a major credibility problem for both, beyond their immediate stakeholders in the Global North.

Under Wolfensohn, the World Bank largely confined its work on corruption to analysis,[79] although it began to embark on building a few prototype domestic institutions in client countries designed to work against corruption.[80] Yet according to Jeffrey Winters, there was a basic paradox between the World Bank's concerns about corruption on the one hand, and their lending activities on the other, because

---

d605091504125.htm. Lugar was the subsequent architect of US legislation aimed at attacking corruption at multilateral development banks. See S. 1129, the Development Bank Reform and Authorization Act, eventually enacted into law in November 2005.

[76] Sebastian Mallaby, *World's Banker: A Story of Failed States, Financial Crises, and the Wealth and Poverty of Nations*, op. cit., p. 363.

[77] Ibid., p. 304.

[78] Ibid., p. 312.

[79] Ben W. Heineman, Jr and Fritz Heimann (2006), "The Long War Against Corruption", *Foreign Affairs*, 85:3, 75–86.

[80] See, for example, the auditing procedures designed to ensure no abuse of funds in the case of loans to Chad, as described by Sebastian Mallaby, *World's Banker: A Story of Failed States, Financial Crises, and the Wealth and Poverty of Nations*, op. cit., p. 352.

many Bank officials felt that the Bank's first priority was to lend money. Focusing on corruption entailed the prospect of reducing loans – and thus was at odds with the widely understood logic of the Bank's mission.[81]

As Sebastian Mallaby succinctly stated:

In the end, Wolfensohn would have to face a trade-off between two versions of the Bank. The first version cast the Bank as a partner of northern NGOs and Northern governments, who steer the machinery of the international system. The Bank's role, in this conception, was to act as a sort of secretariat for the North's global ambitions. The second vision cast the Bank as a partner of poor countries, not of NGOs and shareholders. Its role, in this conception, was to fend off the demands of Northern constituents as much as possible.

Wolfensohn's inability to walk a fine line between the two resulted in him retreating towards (the Bank's original mandate of) infrastructure development projects but nonetheless deeper into the American, Republican mandate of anti-corruption. The forced resignation of chief economist Joseph Stiglitz, Wolfensohn's subsequent reputed capitulation over the content of the 2000 World Development Report, and George W. Bush's election proved the unraveling of Wolfensohn's strategy. These events left him cautious about challenging the thrust of preferred US policy, if not neutered altogether in his second term, dooming both his broader agenda and the chances of being retained for a third term.[82]

As he sought to placate the Bush administration, increasing strains with advocates of the civil society agenda marked the final 24 months of Wolfensohn's presidency. By the end of 2004, NGO groups were boycotting meetings with World Bank officials in Berlin, London, Tokyo, and Washington, angry because "they say the meetings are merely a 'public relations exercise' and that the Washington-based bank is not serious about giving a greater say to indigenous and local

---

[81] Jeffrey A. Winters (2002), "Criminal Debt", in Jonathan R. Pincus and Jeffrey A. Winters (eds), *Reinventing the World Bank* (Ithaca, NY: Cornell University Press), p. 122.

[82] Paul Blustein (2005), "Wolfensohn Confirms Plan to Leave World Bank", *The Washington Post*, 4 January, p. E01, http://www.washingtonpost.com/wp-dyn/articles/A45819–2005Jan3.html

people affected by bank-financed projects carried out by international companies."[83] The Environmental Defense Fund even published accusatory pamphlets against Wolfensohn, quoting his claims that development was impossible within a corrupt environment.[84]

One of Wolfensohn's last major acts as World Bank President was to promote, and successfully complete, the construction of an oil pipeline between Chad and Cameroon. Chad is among the poorest countries in the world, with a per capita income of $238 per year, and the pipeline was intended to bring jobs and revenues to this landlocked country. The Bank had pioneered this high-risk project to prove that "petrodollars can benefit the poor."[85] One of Wolfensohn's successor's acts, within months of assuming office, was to suspend World Bank loans to Chad and freeze profits derived from the pipeline and held in an escrow account in London, which included royalties from the pipeline's operator, Exxon Mobil.[86] Thus Wolfowitz symbolically, and very publicly, snubbed his predecessor.

Changing US leadership, changing World Bank agendas

Paul Wolfowitz's tenure as president represented a significant contrast. Anti-corruption was emphasized as *the* central issue on the organization's agenda, defined as critical to the stimulation of growth. The focus therefore moved to a full-fledged emphasis on mainstreaming policies designed to address the issue in the World Bank's operational program on a results-oriented basis – in effect a more coercive implementation of policy.

Of course, Wolfowitz arrived with a powerful reputation for stridency and, despite pointing to the continuities in themes between himself and his predecessor at his first press conference at the World Bank, he did not take long to distance himself from his predecessor's agenda.[87] First, ousting many of the career senior officials at the World Bank, and his appointment

---

[83] Emad Mekay (2004), "World Bank Delays NGO Consultations", *Global Policy Forum*, 5 November, http://www.globalpolicy.org/ngos/int/bwi/2004/1105consultations.htm

[84] Cited in Sebastian Mallaby, *World's Banker: A Story of Failed States, Financial Crises, and the Wealth and Poverty of Nations*, op. cit., p. 356.

[85] See Bretton Woods Project (2006), "Bank freezes pipeline funds to Chad", 20 January, http://www.brettonwoodsproject.org/art.shtml?x=507557

[86] Ibid.

[87] For illustrations of continuities, according to Wolfowitz, including Africa, good governance and ownership, see Bretton Woods Project (2005), "Which

of a new set of senior staff drawn from his own former political advisors in the Republican Party as their replacements, did much to foment anxiety within the organization and clear the way for the enforcement of his new ideas.[88] Then he turned away from the issue of poverty alleviation, and immediately began to focus his attention on anti-corruption, claiming it was a key component of growth. The issue had first emerged at the World Bank in the aftermath of the Asian economic crisis of 1997–8 and the drafting of the OECD *Anti-Bribery Convention* in the same period, but interest clearly accelerated after Wolfowitz's arrival.[89]

Wolfowitz argued that: "corruption is often at the very root of why governments don't work. It weakens the systems and distorts the markets. In the end, governments and citizens will pay a price, in lower incomes, lower investment and more volatile economic swings. But when governments do work – when they tackle corruption and improve their rule of law – they can raise their national incomes by as much as four times."[90] Elsewhere he referred to corruption as a "weed."[91] The logic was simple; anti-corruption policies improve growth and growth enlarges the economy, thereby attacking poverty (employing the now-traditional trickle-down theory of economics).

There was certainly support for Wolfowitz's claim among American members of the business and policy community. Ben W. Heineman, Jr (formerly of General Electric) and Fritz Heimann (a cofounder of TI and its Chair from 1993 to 2005) offered a more comprehensive – if no less dramatic – statement about the logical relationship between anti-

---

way the World Bank?",13 June, http://www.brettonwoodsproject.org/art.shtml?x=235788

[88] For details see Brad DeLong (2006), "Bitter Conflict at the World Bank", *The Economist's View*, 23 January, http://economistsview.typepad.com/economistsview/2006/01/bitter_conflict.html. Also see Andrew Balls and Edward Alden (2006), "Wolfowitz triggers graft storm at World Bank", *Financial Times*, 23 January, http://www.ft.com/cms/s/0/e125344e-8b8c-11da-91a1-0000779e2340.html

[89] See Florian Gimbelin (2006), "World Bank steps up anti-graft fight", *Financial Times*, 12 April, http://www.ft.com/cms/s/0/fd8bfcec-c97d-11da-94ca-0000779e2340.html

[90] Wolfowitz, cited in World Bank (2006), "World Bank Announces Strategy to Combat Corruption", *The World Bank Press Release No: 2006/358/EXC*, 11 April, http://web.worldbank.org/WBSITE/EXTERNAL/NEWS/0,,contentMDK:20884956~pagePK:34370~piPK:34424~theSitePK:4607,00.html

[91] See Bretton Woods Project (2005), "World Bank anti-corruption: discourse versus practice", 21 November, http://www.brettonwoodsproject.org/art.shtml?x=438379

corruption and growth with their claim that: "The true impact of corruption is now widely acknowledged: corruption distorts markets and competition, breeds cynicism among citizens, undermines the rule of law, damages government legitimacy, and corrodes the integrity of the private sector. It is also a major barrier to international development – systemic misappropriation by kleptocratic governments harms the poor."[92] Heineman and Heimann also suggested that the goal of eradicating corruption entails a "multifaceted" strategy involving enforcement, prevention, state-building, and the building of cultural mores to undergird the other three components – and the significance of embedding anti-corruption practices in the activities of the World Bank and other IFIs in this regard.[93] One Heritage Foundation (a Conservative think tank) report suggested that: "Providing assistance to governments of countries that have a weak rule of law and that lack transparency and accountability invites corrupt use of assistance." Assistance should therefore only be awarded to countries that have demonstrably implemented necessary reforms, otherwise "providing assistance in bad policy environments is at best ineffective. At worst, it is counterproductive because it gives corrupt governments economic resources to maintain bad policies that retard development."[94]

The scope and goals of Wolfowitz's ambitions were stated in a leaked World Bank document early in his tenure, worth quoting at length:

> The World Bank Group has been a key player in the broader effort to improve governance, and the way the Bank and donors do business in some highly corrupt and poorly governed countries has begun to change. However, while some countries have made progress, the growing attention to these issues has yet to result in improved outcomes across the globe. The governance agenda needs to be translated more effectively into concrete results…. This paper proposes a comprehensive strategy for the World Bank Group to enhance and integrate governance and anti-corruption measures across the entire range of its activities and operations….The paper builds on the strong vision and strategic thrust President Wolfowitz outlined in his Jakarta speech on governance, and reflects lessons from

---

[92] Ben W. Heineman, Jr and Fritz Heimann (2006), "The Long War Against Corruption", op. cit., p. 76.

[93] Ibid., pp. 77–8.

[94] Ana Isabel Eiras and Brett D. Schaefer (2005), "A Blueprint for Paul Wolfowitz at the World Bank", op. cit.

the past decade of experience of the Bank and other partners in this area.[95]

The coercive aspect fairly boldly stated:

> For the group of countries in which governance is relatively strong and corruption is not a major hindrance to development, Bank efforts on governance will be largely responsive to the interests and direction of the government (and Bank strategies for well-performing middle-income borrowers will remain flexible and customized.) For the large middle group of countries where governance and corruption pose a challenge, governance will be treated more consistently and with greater depth in CASs. For some of these countries, the Bank's strategy will feature governance as the central theme and make use of tools such as anti-corruption action plans in projects, field-based governance advisors, and anti-corruption teams. For the small group of exceptional-risk countries where corruption and weak governance are blocking progress and the government and the Bank cannot agree on priorities, a more restricted interim strategy will be prepared, which will include the possibility of curtailed financing with specific triggers and may focus mostly or entirely on nonlending forms of engagement.[96]

Wolfowitz's approach conveniently ignored the World Bank's historical collusion in corrupt practices by lending to corrupt dictators around the globe and then forgiving their unpaid debts. He continued to advocate such loans.[97] Nonetheless, it would be naïve to assume that Wolfowitz's advocacy of anti-corruption was purely based on neoliberal economic postulates. He imbued anti-corruption with the kind of crusading language he had formerly used to justify the American invasion of Iraq, stating that: "corruption is the biggest threat to democracy since communism."[98] Echoing these

---

[95] See the first page of the World Bank (2006), "Executive Summary: Strengthening Bank Group Work in Governance and Anti-corruption", op. cit.

[96] Ibid., p. vii.

[97] His refusal to incorporate this aspect implies that anti-corruption is linked to growth policies but has only an indirect effect on poverty For a discussion of this point see Gail Hurley (2006), "Wolfowitz Needs to Look at Corruption of Yesterday, Not Just Today and Follow the Positive Example of Norway", op. cit.

[98] This quote is widely cited, but see, for example, The Monitor's View (2006), "World Bank's war on corruption", *The Christian Science Monitor*, 7 March, http://

sentiments, a World Bank report suggested that: "Unchecked corruption can destroy economies by undermining the legitimacy of state institutions, strangling the private sector, and damaging civil society ... Reforms that rationalize the role of the state, reduce red tape, and promote competition can help improve governance and reduce corruption."[99]

This rhetoric was linked to the World Bank's focus on press freedom as an informal measure of the capacity to expose and address domestic corruption.[100] Media independence has always been a key component of what the US has characterized as civil and political rights (as opposed to economic rights) in its campaigns at the United Nations. An emerging difference was that the World Bank's purported non-intervention in domestic political matters was therefore clearly reconsidered with a focus on the civil liberties most consistently favored by the US.

In sum, in the battle for supremacy between anti-corruption and poverty alleviation, there were elements of both continuity and change. The World Bank retained its interest in growth, but tilted towards anti-corruption designed to promote growth and very specific elements of rights (civil not economic) under Wolfowitz, while what critics such as Robert Wade term "paradigm maintenance"[101] continued. With the Bush Administration's selection of Wolfowitz, few concessions were made to the interests of the Global South. In the words of Robert Wade, the World Bank's "Finance Ministry Agenda" won out over its "Civil Society Agenda."[102]

Moral entrepreneurs and shifting norms

Wolfowitz, like his predecessor, stressed the importance of working with civil society actors. In a speech made after assuming the presi-

---

www.csmonitor.com/2006/0307/p08s02-comv.html

[99] World Bank (2006), "Executive summary: Strengthening Bank Group Work in Governance and Anti-corruption", op. cit.

[100] David Hoffman (2006), "World Bank should link loans to press freedom", *International Herald Tribune*, 5 April, http://www.iht.com/articles/2006/04/04/opinion/edhoffman.php

[101] Wade applies this term to the World Bank in many contexts. But see, for example, Robert H. Wade (2001), "Showdown at the World Bank", op. cit.

[102] For a characterization of the components and proponents of these agendas, see Robert H. Wade (2002), "US Hegemony and the World Bank: The Fight over People and Ideas", *Review of International Political Economy*, 9:2, 215–43.

dency he stated that: "civil society everywhere is one of our most important partners...because they [civil society groups] are key to holding governments accountable."[103] Wolfowitz's appointment, however, signaled an end to an ecumenical approach in dealing with civil society groups. Convention holds that civil society groups were empowered during the period of Wolfensohn's presidency, engaged in discussion about the Bank's policy agenda as stakeholders.[104] Certainly, the World Bank was initially relatively open in its discussions with NGOs in Wolfensohn's first term, engaging representatives of both the "Finance Ministry Agenda" and the "Civil Society Agenda."[105]

TI's founder and chairman, Peter Eigen, had himself left the World Bank in 1993 to pursue its anti-corruption agenda because the Bank's officials refused to endorse his prescription that battling corruption should be prioritized. TI's mission statement formally aims "to curb corruption by mobilizing a global coalition to promote and strengthen international and national integrity systems."[106] Bank officials opposed this shift on the grounds that this would contravene the national sovereignty of its clients (and thus would transgress the World Bank's founding principles).[107]

Eigen developed into a powerful entrepreneur, albeit one whose imperative reflected the agenda of the private sector and governmental constituencies primarily located in the Global North rather than the Global

---

[103] See (2006) "International watchdogs work to improve World Bank accountability", *CEE Bankwatch Network*, 21 April, http://www.bankwatch.org/project.shtml?qpc+147587--1&x=1801702&d=r

[104] See O'Brien *et al.* (2000), *Contesting Global Governance*, op. cit.

[105] This list included those working, for example, on the rights of indigenous peoples, environmental degradation (such as Friends of the Earth and the World Wildlife Fund), and poverty issues (War on Want, World Development Movement, Bretton Woods Project). For a succinct but informative statement about the relationship between NGOs and the World Bank under Wolfensohn, see James A. Paul (1996), "The World Bank & NGOs", *Global Policy Forum*, http://www.globalpolicy.org/component/content/article/177-un/31512-the-world-bank-a-ngos.pdf

[106] Cited in Fredrik Galtung and Jeremy Pope (1999), "The Global Coalition Against Corruption: Evaluating Transparency International", in Andreas Schedler, Larry Diamond and Marc F. Plattner (eds), *The Self-Restraining State: Power and Accountability in New Democracies* (Boulder, Co: Lynne Rienner), p. 260.

[107] See Peter Eigen, "The Magic Triangle", *The Focus*, 9:2, 46. For figures and a list of major contributors see http://www.transparency.org/about_us/annual/financial_reports

South. Not surprisingly, although the source of TI's contributions is diffuse, an overwhelming proportion of TI's financial support historically comes from the US and European governments, along with the European Union.[108] Some of the quasi-NGOs that align themselves with TI, such as the U4 Utstein Group and its Anti-corruption Resource Center, are composed of a number of Northern Development Ministries.[109] Others, such as the Chr. Michelsen Institute (CMI), declare their independence but their major "clients" are many of the same governments that support the U4 Utstein Group.[110] Support for this anti-corruption norm was therefore limited rather than representing broad swathes of global civil society.

Eigen certainly made significant headway in pursuit of this cause during Wolfensohn's incumbency, partially as a result of the greater priority given to corruption reform by the Clinton administration.[111] Despite Wolfensohn's limited support of TI's agenda, it was TI that grew increasingly influential at the World Bank, as it formed a partnership with the World Bank's Economic Development Institute (EDI) from 1993 onwards[112] and subsequently played a central role in the Corruption Action Plan Working Group in 1996. The working group eventually drafted a landmark publication the following year, one that guided the World Bank's anti-corruption strategy, entitled *Helping Countries Combat Corruption: The Role of the World Bank*.[113] Officially, this strategy included four components: preventing corruption in the World Bank's financial activity; helping recipient countries combat corruption; the mainstreaming of corruption considerations in the Bank's analysis and decision-making; and a broader contribution to international anti-corruption efforts.[114]

While strident, at least rhetorically, about maintaining its independence, TI worked assiduously to become both indispensable and vocal within the World Bank, integral as a partner rather than

---

[108] For details see, for example, Transparency International (2004), "Financial Information", 31 December, p. 7.

[109] For more details see http://www.u4.no/about/main.cfm

[110] For details see http://www.cmi.no/about/funding.cfm

[111] For the Clinton administration's effort to push this issue at the OECD, see Fredrik Galtung and Jeremy Pope (1999), "The Global Coalition Against Corruption: Evaluating Transparency International", op. cit., p. 265.

[112] Ibid., p. 266.

[113] Heather Marquette (2001), "Corruption, Democracy and the World Bank", *Crime, Law and Social Change*, 36:4, 395–407.

[114] Suzanne Akiyama (2004), "Perspective on Corruption", *Center for the Study of International Development Strategies (CSIDS)*, p. 2, http://www.grips.ac.jp/csids/perspectives/perspective02.pdf

remaining a critic. By the end of the decade, Galtung and Pope could comment that: "Several TI national chapters now work actively with the World Bank in the Bank's member countries, and there is a relatively free flow of information between the international financial institutions and TI."[115] The EDI also worked to forge partnerships with TI's local national chapters as monitors of national anti-corruption strategies.[116]

Nonetheless, TI remained somewhat critical of the World Bank even after that date, suggesting that the organization did not devote enough time or resources to implement its anti-corruption initiative.[117] Wolfensohn nonetheless proved conciliatory to TI until the end of his second term, praising their efforts even as they criticized the Bank's.[118]

From balance to focus

Not surprisingly, therefore, TI seems to have attained a privileged position, and was one of the most vocal proponents of Wolfowitz's agenda among civil society groups. Certainly, in Wolfowitz, Eigen has found a likeminded spirit. Like Wolfowitz, Eigen's focus has always been unambiguous, entitling one piece "Corruption is the Enemy of Development."[119] TI now enjoyed a growing access and influence, while those organizations working on poverty alleviation appeared to have little. Even prior to Wolfowitz's incumbency, Eigen attempted to distance himself from groups that focused on poverty alleviation, and to strengthen his credibility as a respected spokesperson among stake-

---

[115] See Fredrik Galtung and Jeremy Pope (1999), "The Global Coalition Against Corruption: Evaluating Transparency International", op. cit., p. 267.

[116] Ibid., pp. 270–1.

[117] See Press Release (2000), "World Bank needs to strengthen its anti-corruption work, says Transparency International", *Transparency International*, 30 August, http://www.transparency.org/news_room/latest_news/press_releases/2000/2000_08_31_worldbank. See also Transparency International (2000), "World Bank Urged to Strengthen its Anti-corruption Work", 31 August, http://www.afrol.com/Categories/Economy_Develop/eco002_wb_anticorruption.htm

[118] See World Bank (2005), "World Bank Hails Transparency International's Annual Report", *World Bank Press Release No:2005/385/S*, 16 March, http://web.worldbank.org/WBSITE/EXTERNAL/NEWS/0,,contentMDK:20395101~menuP :34463~pagePK:64003015~piPK:64003012~theSitePK:4607,00.html

[119] Peter Eigen, "Corruption is the Enemy of Development", *Corporate Responsibility*, http://www.responsiblepractice.com/english/issues/transparency/

holders favoring the anti-corruption agenda, by decrying what he has characterized as the "ugly face" of civil society – specifically, those who demonstrate against World Bank policies in the streets.[120] Now, whether more the product of the leadership's efforts or simply a fortuitous swing of the political pendulum, TI consolidated its position as the key civil society organization with influence both within the Bank's new senior leadership and on Bank policymaking. Eigen and TI mastered the ability to act authoritatively within the organization while sustaining the appearance of being outsiders to key constituents with vested interests in the Finance Ministry agenda of the World Bank.

Other than TI, the alternative and arguably more popular response to Wolfowitz's appointment among leading civil society activists, especially those associated with the poverty alleviation agenda, can probably be best summed up as lying between skeptical and hostile. Bob Geldof, former rock star and current moral entrepreneur *par excellence* in his role as organizer of Band Aid, as well as being a five-times Nobel Peace Prize nominee, offered a populist view. He was quick to attack the very underpinnings of Wolfowitz's claim about the relationship between corruption and growth. In articulating a view widely held in the Global South, Geldof inverted the causal logic offered by Wolfowitz. While recognizing the endemic nature of corruption in Africa, he suggested that "corruption is a byproduct of poverty" rather than its cause.[121]

Geldof is only one of the more famous among many who criticize the World Bank's new policy thrust. One extreme, but not unique, position is offered by the leadership of the Global Justice Ecology Project, who commented that: "The approval of Paul Wolfowitz, architect of the Iraq War, to head the World Bank advances the Bank's role as an extension of U.S. imperial power."[122] Jim Vallette of the Institute for Policy Studies offered the opinion that: "choosing Wolfowitz for this job makes perfect sense if the Bush administration intends to completely alienate the world community."[123] Other commentators were even more strident, if

---

[120] Peter Eigen, "Gala Dinner Keynote Speech", http://www.fese.be/efmc/2003/report/efmc_eigen.htm. This link is no longer available.

[121] See (2006) "Irish rocker-activist Geldof takes aim at corruption in Africa", *Mail & Guardian Online*, 25 April, http://www.mg.co.za/article/2006–04-25-geldof-takes-aim-at-corruption-in-africa

[122] See "Paul Wolfowitz: Symbol of A Global Crisis Behind and Beyond Iraq", Global Justice Ecology Project, http://archive2.globaljusticeecology.org/index.php?name=about_us&ID=313

[123] Jim Vallette (2005), "Why Wolfowitz?', 17 March, http://www.tompaine.com/articles/why_wolfowitz.php

possible, suggesting that Wolfowitz's appointment is part of a global US conspiracy for control.[124]

On Wolfowitz's first day at his new job he received a letter signed by over 300 civil society organizations, based in 60 countries, specifying benchmarks by which they would evaluate his performance.[125] The criticism is not confined to either populists or those that might be considered civil society groups in Washington. Joseph Stiglitz, former World Bank Chief Economist and respected academic, savagely attacked Wolfowitz's appointment, arguing that: "The World Bank will once again become a hate figure. This could bring street protests and violence across the developing world" and that Bush's appointment of Wolfowitz was "either an act of provocation or an act so insensitive as to look like provocation."[126]

Specifically, many critics suggested that the new President was missing the point that the focus on government corruption in recipient countries was errant. Northern governments facilitated corruption through legislation allowing bribes to be taken as tax deductions. Even where that had been discontinued, enforcement was often weak or nonexistent. Multinational corporations endorsed corruption by handing out bribes.[127] Indeed, the World Bank spurred the very process of privatization that in large part explained the dynamic growth of corruption. Furthermore, the World Bank's own "pressure to lend" and lack of due diligence over the administration of loans created a climate in which corruption could flourish. It had knowingly lent money to corrupt dictators who had stolen large portions of these loans, but continued to demand repayment nonetheless, creating a huge debt burden in many countries that continued to be serviced.

Respected Indonesian NGO, the International Forum for Indonesian Development (INFID), argues that "it is widely known that approximately

---

[124] See, for example, Shalmali Guttal (2005), "A Suitable Boy: Paul Wolfowitz and the World Bank", *Global Policy Forum*, 25 September, http://www.globalpolicy.org/socecon/bwi-wto/wbank/2005/0925suit.htm

[125] See Bretton Woods Project (2005), "Which way the World Bank?", 13 June, http://www.brettonwoodsproject.org/art.shtml?x=235788

[126] Stiglitz's comments were reported by Robert Preston (2005), "Stiglitz warns of violence if Wolfowitz goes to World Bank", *The Daily Telegraph*, 20 March, http://www.telegraph.co.uk/money/main.jhtml?xml=/money/2005/03/20/cnwbank20.xml&menuId=242&sSheet=/portal/2005/03/20/ixportal.html

[127] For a comprehensive statement of this position see Susan Hawley (2000), "Exporting Corruption: Privatisation, Multinationals and Bribery", *The Corner House Briefing*, 19 June, http://www.thecornerhouse.org.uk/item.shtml?x=51975

30% of the World Bank loans during the reign of Suharto were cor-
rupted." Moreover, the debts were accumulated by an authoritarian
regime and no public consultation took place. For years, the World
Bank continued making transactions with Indonesia. The Bank supported and strengthened the authoritarian regime, says INFID....
A leaked 1997 World Bank report supports these allegations. The
report found that as much as 20 to 30% of the budgets linked to
development funds were embezzled, and World Bank loans were
clearly involved. Other internal reports attest to staff knowledge of
the regime in place and the fraud taking place. Despite this clear
awareness, loans increased. There was also an increase in World
Bank loans to the Indonesian Government during the occupation
of East Timor.... Indonesia's total external debt stands at US$134
billion. Of this sum, public and publicly guaranteed debt amounts
to US$ 80 billion. To pay this debt, the government put aside 26% of
the 2006 state budget. In contrast, education was allocated only 5%
and health 2%. Poverty levels are high and increasing in Indonesia:
50% of the population lives in poverty and earns less than US$ 2 per
day. The World Bank is one of the country's largest creditors with
approximately US$12 billion in claims.[128]

Instead of focusing on guilty but powerful Northern constituents
or the World Bank's own past practices, these critics contended that
Wolfowitz has chosen to use this issue as an opportunity to control or
constrict loans to the Global South.[129] The following passage, especially
the interaction between Wolfowitz and Gail Hurley, the representative
of Eurodad, a European NGO focusing on the issue of debt and development, illustrates many of these points.

> Gail Hurley from Eurodad strongly challenged both Bank senior
> management and Mr Wolfowitz directly on their approach to cor-
> ruption. She asked whether they acknowledged that "any compre-
> hensive approach to corruption as claimed by the Bank necessarily
> involves a frank and open evaluation of World Bank lending in the
> past which leads inevitably to the question of how to deal with **odious**

---

[128] Gail Hurley (2006), "Wolfowitz Needs to Look at Corruption of Yesterday,
Not Just Today and Follow the Positive Example of Norway", op. cit.
[129] See Bretton Woods Project (2005), "World Bank anti-corruption: discourse
versus practice", op. cit. See also Anup Shah (2008), "Corruption", *Global Issues*,
27 December, http://www.globalissues.org/article/590/corruption

and illegitimate [sic] claims." Put simply: within the World Bank's so-called crusade against corruption, what is it going to do about odious and illegitimate debt? Wolfowitz, who was visibly taken aback by the question, was not quite sure how to respond, except to say that this was not really what he had in mind. He was also doubtful as to how shareholders would respond. Eurodad nevertheless urged Wolfowitz to raise the issue with the Bank's shareholders as part of his drive against corruption. Bank senior management responded by saying that they felt that the issue had been dealt with within the framework of the HIPC Initiative, even though this clearly covers only a small number of countries and leaves many others with very serious allegations of odious and illegitimate debt left to service their debt burdens.[130]

As Hurley herself notes elsewhere:

Remarkably absent from the anti-corruption strategy presented by officials so far is any critical examination of the Bank's lending practices to poor countries in the past. The World Bank has over the years been involved with and lent to some of the world's most notorious and despised regimes such as Mobutu Seke Seso of Democratic Republic of Congo and Ferdinand Marcos of the Philippines. Bank documentation at the time of these transactions, or published shortly afterwards, confirms that many Bank officials – at both country-level and in Washington DC – were perfectly aware of the nature of the regimes in place and that many loans were simply transferred into the bank accounts of the dictators and their generals. It was plain therefore that they did not reach the poor or foster economic development. Despite their odious and illegitimate nature most of these debts continue to be serviced today, at the expense of essential investments in poverty reduction and economic development.[131]

These claims vexed Wolfowitz's campaign, finding expression at the 2006 April Annual meeting of the World Bank when protestors interrupted

---

[130] See "Low-Down on World Bank/IMF Spring Meetings 2006", European Network on Debt and Development (EURODAD), 27 April, http://www.eurodad.org/whatsnew/articles.aspx?id=416&item=406&ArticleShowall=true

[131] Gail Hurley (2006), "Wolfowitz Needs to Look at Corruption of Yesterday, Not Just Today and Follow the Positive Example of Norway", op. cit.

his speech making these explicit claims.[132] Clearly, beyond the constituency backing of TI, Wolfowitz's appointment lacked support from major elements in civil society. He nonetheless pushed on with enforcement.

The new priority at the World Bank: institutional reforms and external resistance

Wolfowitz was determined to prioritize anti-corruption by building a coercive enforcement capacity hitherto lacking at the World Bank. At the beginning of his incumbency, he commissioned an external review of systems of transparency, accountability, ethics, and integrity led by Harvard University economics professor Robert Pozen. Little was publicly disclosed about the review in its immediate aftermath, but it was widely assumed that it informed many of Wolfowitz's subsequent actions.[133] He then increased both the size of the staff and budget to be spent on investigations and sanctions of the World Bank's Department of Institutional Integrity (DII) to over $10 million a year, creating a greater capacity to investigate the backlog of 387 cases of suspected corruption. Governance and anti-corruption measures were addressed in the Country Assistance Strategies (CAS), being mainstreamed into country programs where corruption was characterized as an "epidemic."[134] Staffs were instructed that, henceforth, these strategies had to address governance issues, and their field office staffs were also increased to ensure implementation, including a resident governance advisor and a fiduciary team that includes investigators and project advisors, as well as an anti-corruption committee in the field offices. In an attempt to enhance these initiatives' credibility, Wolfowitz employed the work of World Bank analyst Daniel Kaufmann to highlight the importance of anti-corruption in the first Global Competitiveness Report of his tenure, published by the World Economic Forum.[135]

---

[132] See (2006) "World Bank Finances Corruption – Activists Disrupt World Bank President Paul Wolfowitz's Press Conference", 21 April, http://www.nadir.org/nadir/initiativ/agp/free/imf/washington2006/0421wolfowitz.html

[133] Bretton Woods Project (2005), "The World Bank weeds out corruption: Will it touch the roots?", *Update 50*, 8 April, http://www.brettonwoodsproject.org/article.shtml?cmd[126]=x-126-531789

[134] See "Governance and Anti-Corruption", *The World Bank: News and Broadcast*, http://web.worldbank.org/WBSITE/EXTERNAL/NEWS/0,,contentMDK:200409 22%7emenuPK:34480%7epagePK:34370%7etheSitePK:4607,00.html

[135] See Daniel Kaufmann (2005), "Myths and Realities of Governance and Corruption", *Global Competitiveness Report 2005–2006*, World Economic Forum.

Consistent with Ngaire Woods' expectations, the NGOs engaged in the discussion over anti-corruption were dominated by Transparency International and the Global Integrity Alliance, two organizations whose concerns coincided with Wolfowitz's agenda and that were well versed in congressional lobbying.[136] Neither, given their limited agenda and close prior association with Wolfowitz's agenda, added significant credibility to an audience more concerned with economic justice and rights.

Wolfowitz was not content to confine institutionalizing the fight against corruption to the World Bank alone. In an effort to institutionalize the norm on a truly global basis, and thus expand both its monitoring and enforcement capabilities, he sought to engage the leadership of other global and regional institutions. By February 2006, the World Bank had therefore concluded discussions with the African Development Bank, Asian Development Bank, European Bank for Reconstruction and Development, European Investment Bank, Inter-American Development Bank, and the International Monetary Fund (IMF). As a result, they reached agreement to form a task force designated to create a "framework for preventing and combating fraud and corruption." According to the US State Department, "The task force plans to identify opportunities for collaboration among the institutions on helping countries strengthen their own capacity to fight corruption and on improving cooperation with other groups, including civil society group [sic] to enhance transparency and accountability" in an attempt to "increase information sharing, standardize definitions of corruption, improve the consistency of investigative procedures and ensure mutual support for compliance and enforcement."[137] Interestingly, although the mandate of the World Bank is economic, and explicitly not political, a USAID official was quoted in the same State Department announcement of the agreement suggesting that the attack upon corruption was critical to the spread of democracy.

In parallel, a comparable process was being pursued within the US Congress. As previously mentioned, Senator Richard G. Lugar used his influential position as Chair of the Senate Foreign Relations Committee from 2003 onwards to hold hearings berating the World Bank (albeit

---

[136] See "Governance and Anti-Corruption", op. cit.
[137] See US Department of State (2006), "International Banks to Collaborate on Corruption Problem', *US Department of State*, 23 February, http://www.america. gov/st/washfile-english/2006/February/20060222171157AEneerG0.6717035. html

one among a group of targeted multilateral banks) for its purported ineffectiveness in employing anti-corruption strategies.[138] Lugar articulated what became Wolfowitz's mantra, that corruption thwarts growth and thus threatens the welfare of the poor. By May 2004, he was promoting the idea that over $100 billion might have been lost to World Bank projects through corruption.[139] By 2005, Lugar led the introduction of the Development Bank Reform and Authorization Bill, co-signed by 11 senators out of the Senate Foreign Relations Committee. S. 1129 focused squarely on multilateral development banks and became law in November 2005. Lest there was any doubt that the Republican Congress and Wolfowitz were speaking with a coordinated voice, the law stated in its preamble that: "Officials of the World Bank have identified corruption as the single greatest obstacle to economic and social development" and that "the multilateral development banks are taking action to address fraud and corruption but additional measures remain to be carried out."[140] The law, among other things, authorized the Treasury Secretary to seek the creation of a pilot program designed to create an Anti-corruption Trust at the World Bank. The purpose of the Trust was (1) to assist poor countries in investigations and prosecutions of fraud and corruption related to a loan, grant, or credit of the World Bank; and (2) to determine whether such a program should be carried out at other multilateral development banks.[141] Furthermore, the legislation introduced monitoring and implementation provisions, new strengthened requirements for internal auditing at the World Bank, and established new requirements for recipients of US-funded loans. After passage, its advocates at the Department of State subsequently suggested that the law "promotes financial disclosure by staff member [sic], protection for whistleblowers, and establishment of ethics and audit offices in the banks. It also promotes transparency in the budgets of countries receiving aid,

---

[138] See (2005) "Lugar Commends Discussion to Advance MDB Anti-Corruption Plans", 20 October, http://lugar.senate.gov/pressapp/record.cfm?id=247532

[139] Richard G. Lugar (2004), "$100 billion may have been lost to World Bank corruption", op. cit.

[140] See The Orator (2005), "The Development Bank Reform and Authorization Act of 2005", *109th Congress, 1st Session, S. 1129*, 26 May, http://www.theorator.com/bills109/s1129.html, Section 2(4) and Section 2(6B).

[141] The Development Bank Reform and Authorization Act of 2005, Section 4(b).

with special requirements for natural resource extraction projects."[142] Clearly, Wolfowitz, the Bush administration and the Republican US Congress spoke with one voice.

Within the World Bank itself, Wolfowitz sought more than internal reforms and external agreements. He wanted enforcement, encouraging the staff to scrutinize borrowers' behavior. Indeed, World Bank publications proclaimed that: "The Bank has progressed rapidly from taking an ad hoc, low-visibility approach to instances of fraud and corruption in member countries, Bank-financed projects, and among staff, to a leadership role among the multilateral development banks in all three areas."[143]

Reputedly, a confidential internal report was leaked to Eurodad entitled "Raising the bar on anti-corruption."[144] In tandem, the World Bank's Board of Executive Directors voted to introduce a Voluntary Disclosure Program (VDP) to strengthen its ability to prevent corruption in its operations; it was, in effect, an amnesty program described as "an anti-corruption investigative tool designed to uncover corrupt and fraudulent schemes and patterns in bank-supported projects through the voluntary cooperation of participating firms and individuals." Managed by the DII, it was intended "to allow those involved in past fraud and corruption to avoid administrative sanctions if they disclose all prior wrongdoing and satisfy standardized, non-negotiable terms and conditions."[145] The message was clear; the focus would be on widespread action against client states and private sector actors.

The four-pronged approach of the implementation of the anti-corruption norm consisted of supporting good governance at the country level; preventing corruption in Bank-financed projects; addressing the private sector's role in public sector governance and anti-corruption

---

[142] Bruce Odessey (2006), "Development Banks Must Step Up Corruption Fight, Official Says", US Department of State, http://usinfo.org/wf-archive/2006/060328/epf210.htm

[143] "Governance and Anti-Corruption", op. cit.

[144] See Gail Hurley (2006), "Wolfowitz Needs to Look at Corruption of Yesterday, Not Just Today and Follow the Positive Example of Norway", op. cit.

[145] See World Bank (2006), "World Bank Launches Voluntary Disclosure Program: New Anti-corruption Tool Increases Risk to Firms Engaging in Fraud and Corruption", *World Bank Press Release No:2007/35/INT*, 1 August, http://web.worldbank.org/WBSITE/EXTERNAL/NEWS/0,,contentMDK:21011609~pagePK:34370~piPK:34424~theSitePK:4607,00.html

efforts; and supporting broader global initiatives (presumably as part of a US-inspired norm towards transparency).

Tangibly, in 2005, the first year of Wolfowitz's presidency, the number of World Bank projects including components addressing those issues jumped to almost 50 percent, with a growth to over 10 percent of the Bank's portfolio dedicated to the building of more "efficient and accountable public sector institutions."[146] The DII began to participate in Detailed Implementation Reviews of high-risk projects, developing plans for a formal voluntary disclosure program designed to encourage whistle-blowing by compromised firms involved in theft, bid-rigging, bribes, kickbacks, collusion, coercion, fraud, or the general misuse of World Bank funds in exchange for reduced sanctions.[147]

The results were almost immediate, with $35 million in loans to Bangladesh being cancelled after the department's examination revealed corruption in the bidding process on road-building contracts.[148] Similarly, health, nutrition, and municipal services projects were also cancelled for the same reason. Plans were made to ban the private firms involved from future World Bank contracts, and two officials were fired.[149] A local World Bank official termed the country's anti-corruption commission "a joke"[150] – forceful and undiplomatic language for a senior official visiting a client. Underlining the central components of the CAS for Bangladesh for the next three years, it was stated that: "The WB will also support the strengthening of key institutions of accountability, including the comptroller and auditor general, public accounts committee, Bangladesh Bank, the public service commission, securities and exchange commission, as well as the 'core' governance processes of public financial and budgetary management, public procurement, the National Board of Revenue, and legal and

---

[146] See Gail Hurley (2006), "Wolfowitz Needs to Look at Corruption of Yesterday, Not Just Today and Follow the Positive Example of Norway", op. cit.

[147] Ibid.

[148] See Celia W. Dugger (2006), "World Bank Chief Outlines a War on Fraud", *The New York Times*, 12 April, www.nytimes.com/2006/04/12/world/12wolfowitz. html?ex=1145505600&en=c62a0b65b7bde499&ei=5070&emc=eta1

[149] See Bretton Woods Project (2005), "The World Bank weeds out corruption: Will it touch the roots?", op. cit.

[150] See (2006) "World Bank Terms Anti-Corruption Commission in Bangladesh a joke", *Asian Tribune*, 18 May, http://www.asiantribune.com/index. php?q=node/143

judicial reform, in collaboration with other development partners."[151] Bangladesh ranked last in the TI Corruption Perception Index.

World Bank actions soon followed. Three hundred and thirty companies and individuals were sanctioned from doing business with the World Bank. Other loans were either suspended or delayed. As previously mentioned, loans to Chad were suspended and accounts frozen in January 2006 because of the Chadian government's purported abrogation of an agreement in which it sought to divert funds from previously agreed to general government accounts.[152]

The IDA funding committed for projects active in January 2006 in Chad totaled US$297 million. Of that sum, approximately US$124 million remained undisbursed and subject to the suspension.[153] The Chadian government did not give up easily, trying various "maneuvers to get out of an anti-corruption agreement signed with the Bank."[154] The resolution of the case took over six months, with an agreement being signed between the World Bank and Chadian government on 13 July 2006. The new agreement included provisions for explicit rules regarding the preparation of budgets, closer consultation with stakeholders on poverty reduction strategies, and increased spending on improved governance measures as part of the budget set aside for poverty reduction. Furthermore, it was noted that:

> During the 2007 period of budget implementation, the Government of Chad will develop a new Poverty Reduction Strategy Paper by 2008, in close collaboration with national stakeholders and international partners, which will form a solid basis for determining future expenditure priorities and enacting a revised law, in accordance with these development priorities. The Government will strengthen the *Collège* to ensure effective oversight, public confidence and transparent implementation of projects financed with oil revenues. The Government of Chad agreed with donors

---

[151] See (2006) "World Bank Terms Anti-Corruption Commission in Bangladesh a joke", *Asian Tribune*, 18 May, http://www.asiantribune.com/index. php?q=node/143

[152] For a list of loans suspended to Chad, see http://siteresources.worldbank. org/INTCHADCAMPIPE/Resources/SuspendedChadActivities.pdf

[153] See World Bank (2006), "Chad-Cameroon Pipeline Project", *World Bank Press Release No:2006/383/AFR*, 26 April, http://web.worldbank.org/WBSITE/ EXTERNAL/NEWS/0,,contentMDK:20903775~pagePK:34370~piPK:34424~theSi tePK:4607,00.html

[154] See "World Bank anti-corruption: discourse versus practice", op. cit.

short- and medium-term steps to be undertaken to strengthen budget management within a comprehensive plan for the modernization of public finances. These steps include quarterly publication of budget execution data and regular audits of procurement contracts.[155]

In the words of the World Bank, "The basic principles underlying the approach taken in Chad – greater transparency and accountability in the use of oil revenues – remain central in the Bank's dialogue with a range of oil-producing countries."[156] As one press report succinctly stated, "The World Bank said Chad would aim to enhance transparency and accountability through a new pledge of support for the role of the College of Control and Surveillance of Petroleum Revenues – Chad's independent oil revenue oversight authority. It will be strengthened to ensure it has the resources to more effectively perform its duties."[157] Chad ranked last of all countries in the TI Corruption perception index – tied with Bangladesh.

The Chadian agreement with the World Bank included provisions established under the Extractive Industries Transparency Initiative (EITI), established by the World Bank and run under its rules in collaboration with a now familiar cast of Northern governments (Germany, Netherlands, Norway and the UK) focused on addressing corruption in resource-rich countries.[158] The US government, through USAID, provided an unspecified amount in financial support of the EITI.[159] Twenty countries, out of 191, had signed up to the initiative, with – despite the organization's touting of its stakeholder base across states, firms, and civil society – a small support base.[160] Chad signed up to the EITI as part of its agreement with the World Bank. As Jai Singh,

[155] See "The Chad-Cameroon Petroleum Development and Pipeline Project: Questions and Answers", *The World Bank*, http://web.worldbank.org/WBSITE/EXTERNAL/COUNTRIES/AFRICAEXT/EXTREGINI/EXTCHADCAMPIPELINE/0,,menuPK: 843277~pagePK:64168427~piPK:64168435~theSitePK:843238,00.html

[156] Ibid.

[157] See "Chad: Agreement With World Bank Over Oil Revenues", *All Africa*, 17 July http://allafrica.com/stories/200607171197.html

[158] For details on the Extractive Industries Transparency Initiative, see http://www.eitransparency.org/eiti

[159] For the size of the British, Dutch, German and Norwegian contributions see http://www.eitransparency.org/supporters/countries

[160] For a list of "supporters" see http://www.eitransparency.org/

commenting on the case, stated in his dealings over Chad, Wolfowitz "has made a strong statement about the Bank's values–and placed other countries on notice that the Bank's emphasis on governance and corruption is real."[161]

At the end of January, the World Bank announced it would not clear delayed loans to Kenya amounting to $265 million due to the government's lack of conviction in tackling corruption, despite the Bank's own description of the government's steps in dealing with corruption as "courageous" as recently as 2003.[162] Indeed, the Kenyan government introduced a comprehensive anti-corruption action plan and, according to the World Bank, acted on many of these measures.[163] If domestic, "bottom up" support is therefore a key ingredient for the implementation of effective anti-corruption initiatives, then Kenya seemed to have acted consistently in accordance with historic World Bank demands.

Yet the World Bank focused on the Kenya Urban Transport Infrastructure Project in response to accusations of massive government fraud.[164] Timing may have played an important role, as one NGO report did state that this suspension "came after widespread criticism earlier in the month for its approval of two loans worth $145m, only days after a dossier produced by former anti-corruption official John Githongo chronicled corruption at the highest levels within the Kibaki government. Three ministers have been forced to resign as a result of the revelations."[165] Nonetheless, World Bank criticism seemed to focus not so much on the issue of whether corruption was being addressed as on the subsequent punishments not being punitive enough.[166] Notably, Kenya ranked 144th on TI's corruption perception index out of the 159 ranked in 2005.

---

[161] Jai Singh (2006), "Why Liberals Should be Applauding Wolfowitz", *The New Republic Online*, 24 January.

[162] See the World Bank's Country Brief for Kenya at http://web.worldbank.org/WBSITE/EXTERNAL/COUNTRIES/AFRICAEXT/KENYAEXTN/0,,menuPK:3565 20~pagePK:141132~piPK:141107~theSitePK:356509,00.html

[163] Ibid.

[164] David Hoffman (2006), "World Bank should link loans to press freedom", op. cit.

[165] See Bretton Woods Project (2005), "The World Bank weeds out corruption: Will it touch the roots?", op. cit.

[166] Jeevan Vasagar in Nairobi and Michela Wrong (2006), "Kenya gets $25m loan from World Bank despite corruption row", *The Guardian*, 26 January, http://www.guardian.co.uk/international/story/0,,1694912,00.html#article_continue

Other cases vary significantly in their degree of criminality and the size of loan involved. In the case of the Congo-Brazzaville, Wolfowitz personally decided that he would not authorize debt relief (in contrast to the IMF), seemingly largely as a result of the large hotel bills run up by President Denis Sassou-Nguesso during a visit to New York in September 2005. Congo was ranked 130th of 159 countries in the TI corruption index.[167]

By March 2006, the World Bank announced that no further new loans would be made to Uzbekistan. Prior loans would be honored; analytical, capacity-building and technical assistance to the government would continue. Without citing corruption as the explicit reason for the decision, Martin Reiser, the World Bank's country manager in Uzbekistan, suggested that his organization wanted to ensure that "resources are spent on projects that deliver tangible development outcomes, and we have some concerns whether in the present environment in Uzbekistan this is guaranteed."[168] The lack of transparent evidence of a precipitating cause created the impression of a relatively punitive act. Uzbekistan was ranked at joint 137th (tied with six other countries) on the TI index.

In a similar spirit, the World Bank announced that loans planned to commence in July 2006 to Yemen would be cut by over a third, because of concerns about transparency and good governance. This may have served as a warning regarding Yemen's future conduct. As the World Bank's CAS stated:

> This Country Assistance Strategy (CAS) proposes progress based on four pillars: increasing non-oil growth; improving human development outcomes; improving fiscal sustainability; and, addressing the resource sustainability crisis. The CAS also includes, under each pillar, upfront actions to improve economic governance, which need to be implemented immediately, even though the outcomes may only be visible in the medium-term.[169]

---

[167] See the Transparency International Corruption Perception Index (2005), http://www.transparency.org/policy_research/surveys_indices/cpi/2005

[168] Reisler is quoted in World Bank (2006), "World Bank Halts New Lending to Uzbekistan", 16 March, http://www.noticias.info/asp/aspComunicados.asp?nid=155865&src=0

See also Wolfowitz quoted in Radio Free Europe: Paul Wolfowitz (2006), "World Bank Says No New Loans For Uzbekistan", *Radio Free Europe Radio Liberty*, 16 March, http://www.rferl.org/featuresarticle/2006/03/9CAD79B2-B46F-4241-A165-6F279119F167.html

[169] See "Yemen Overview", http://web.worldbank.org/WBSITE/EXTERNAL/COUNTRIES/MENAEXT/YEMENEXTN/0,,menuPK:310172~pagePK:141132~piP

Clearly, country assistance and reform on corruption were henceforth to be intrinsically related. Yemen was ranked joint 103rd (with three other countries) in the TI index.[170]

Perhaps most curiously, the World Bank interrupted a project in Argentina designed to supplement the wages of poor workers, because of accusations of electoral corruption dating back to 2003 in which the government had brought charges against one senior official and fired ten others. According to Sebastian Mallaby, "The bank's Argentina team responded by building in a few corruption safeguards and pressing to resume lending. However, Wolfowitz has demanded that the safeguards be expanded further still."[171] Argentina is a rarity; a country that repaid its World Bank and IMF loans in full. Yet the project remained unauthorized and the subsequent CAS for Argentina called for extensive institutional reforms to combat corruption (while its efforts to date are limited).[172]

Argentina was ranked joint 97th (with five other states) on the 2005 TI Corruption index. It is worthwhile noting that the World Bank has several large clients whose corruption rankings are comparable to Argentina's (such as India, which then ranked one place above Argentina in TI's index). The withdrawal of such clients from borrowing from the World Bank would actually create financial problems for the Bank, and none of those countries were subject to accusations or had loans suspended at the time due to accusations of corrupt practices.

While there had been episodes of debarment during the Wolfensohn tenure, these actions were limited to a few firms in what could be regarded as high-profile cases, with sanctions not being instituted until several years after the initial decision. Nothing of this scale or scope had been implemented before, let alone in such a short a period.[173] While he shied away from internal analysis of past World Bank fraud, Wolfowitz did order "a sweeping review of what went wrong in

---

K:141121~theSitePK:310165,00.html

[170] See the Transparency International Corruption Perception Index (2005), op. cit.

[171] Sebastian Mallaby (2006), "Wolfowitz's Corruption Agenda", *The Washington Post*, 20 February, http://www.washingtonpost.com/wp-dyn/content/article/2006/02/19/AR2006021901137.html

[172] For an extensive list of suggested reforms see World Bank, "Country Assistance Strategy for the Argentine Republic, 2006–2008", p. 36, http://siteresources.worldbank.org/INTARGENTINA/Resources/1CASAr.pdf

[173] For a list of debarred firms, including their dates of debarment, see "World Bank Listing of Ineligible Firms", http://web.worldbank.org/external/default/m

the Agency for the Execution of Works in the Public Interest to Combat Unemployment Program (AGETIP), which passed Bank loans to non-governmental agencies for public-works projects in French-speaking Africa."[174]

Critics contended that the gap between discourse and practice on anti-corruption at the World Bank remained wide, and the interpretation of the meaning of corruption is open to contestation, with a question outstanding as to whether the World Bank should focus on its own complicity, stress the importance of multinational corporations (such as the OECD's or UN's initiatives), or place a greater emphasis on the activities of client states. Wolfowitz, however, was clearly unequivocal in his focus on clamping down on client states.

Not all agreed that he should look outside his own organization. Ahead of the annual 2006 spring meeting of the World Bank, Wenonah Hauter of Food and Water Watch suggested that: "The World Bank has financed many projects riddled with corruption such as the Enron power plant in Guatemala, the Chad-Cameroon oil pipeline and Shell in Nigeria. Many of these corporations are engaged in highly questionable activities, financed by the World Bank, that involve influence payments, human rights abuses, and projects with damaging social and environmental impacts. Who holds the World Bank accountable for continuing to reward corrupt behavior?"[175] Predictably, concerns about corruption dominated those meetings,[176] a development (just as predictably) praised by then Treasury Secretary John Snow.[177]

While the coincidence between the TI index and the targets of the World Bank's actions would appear to lend objectivity to Wolfowitz's decisions, it is useful to bear in mind that it is a "perception" index. Member countries of the World Bank clearly questioned the objectivity of the World Bank's choice: at the 2006 Annual Spring meeting (where

---

ain?theSitePK=84266&contentMDK=64069844&menuPK=116730&pagePK=64 148989&piPK=64148984

[174] For details see Bretton Woods Project (2005) "The World Bank weeds out corruption: Will it touch the roots?", op. cit.

[175] See Emad Mekay (2006), "IMF, World Bank and Critics Gear Up for Meetings", 21 April, http://www.commondreams.org/headlines06/0421–03.htm

[176] See Suzanne Presto (2006), "World Bank, IMF End Meetings in Washington", *Voice of America*, 24 April, http://www1.voanews.com/english/news/a-13–2006-04–24-voa7.html

[177] See John Snow quoted in "Help poor meet fuel needs", http://www.fin24. com/International/Help-poor-meet-fuel-needs-20060423

the issue of corruption dominated the proceedings) the Development Committee was worried enough by the possibly capricious nature of some of these suspension decisions to insist that the organization set up standards and criteria to guarantee objectivity (and, presumably, transparency) over future cases. As a Bretton Woods' Project report suggested, "Apparently some fairly charged statements were given by developing country representatives who are not pleased by the high-profile and apparently arbitrary way in which president Wolfowitz has approached the issue thus far."[178]

The guidelines were to be in place by the fall meeting of 2006,[179] and the World Bank initially planned to avoid any public consultation on the draft guidelines being circulated. But the draft guidelines, as mentioned earlier, were leaked and this fact, combined with public pressure from NGO groups, convinced the World Bank to solicit public commentary. Hoping to confine external input, however, the consultation period was highly abbreviated by organizational standards before presentation of a revised draft to the board. Somewhat ironically, the World Bank was accused of a lack of transparency in preparation of its anti-corruption guidelines. More generally, "To many, the Bank lacks credibility to be the leader of the fight against corruption, given its own support (past and present) for corrupt governments and the secrecy that still shrouds much of the Bank's own operations."[180]

Nonetheless, Wolfowitz pressed ahead with his efforts, making it arguable whether any chasm between rhetoric and action had been reduced under Wolfowitz. The issue of anti-corruption now dominated the agenda, its linkage to growth evident in the language of advocates, its linkage to poverty alleviation far more tenuous. The World Bank was attempting to generate a new global norm, one in which disapproving critics suggested it was defining its new role as a

---

[178] See Bretton Woods Project (2006), "Highlights of the World Bank – IMF spring meetings 2006", 22 April, http://www.brettonwoodsproject.org/article.shtml?cmd%5B126%5D=x-126–535552

[179] See Taipei Times (2006), "Wolfowitz's 'saber rattling' against corruption raises eyebrows", 13 May, http://www.odiousdebts.org/odiousdebts/index.cfm?DSP=content&ContentID=15462

[180] See (2006) "All eyes on the World Bank's development of its anti-corruption strategy", Bank Information Center, 27 July, http://www.bicusa.org/bicusa/issues/misc_resources/2911.php

"global policeman" with the issue of anti-corruption as its mandate.[181] As one report stated, "Civil society groups have voiced concern that the Bank's approach doesn't adequately recognize that anti-corruption and good governance efforts need to be driven by the public in borrowing countries, not by external actors."[182] Although some stakeholders approved of these measures, this initiative did not appear to address the primary concerns of the Global South, or the perennial NGO protestors at the gates.

The decline of the anti-corruption agenda

The circumstances surrounding the end of Wolfowitz's tenure were highly publicized and well documented. His appointment as president had been unwelcome by European governments and World Bank staff alike, in part because of his involvement in the planning of the Iraq war and in part due to their concern that the US influence at the Bank was too strong.[183] Although there was general agreement at the Bank that ending corruption in countries receiving aid was an important priority, the imperious way Wolfowitz pursued his agenda alienated Bank executives and staffers alike. They still thought poverty alleviation should be the Bank's top priority. It is, therefore, not surprising that accusations that leaked in early 2007, branding him as a man who used his position to travel widely in exercises of self-promotion, prompted little defense of Wolfowitz.[184] Doubts over his ability to generate funds for the Bank in this context were soon raised.[185] Further, his poor management skills were publicized, with one anonymous source alleging that Wolfowitz

---

[181] See Taipei Times (2006), "Wolfowitz's 'saber rattling' against corruption raises eyebrows", op. cit.

[182] See (2006) "All eyes on the World Bank's development of its anti-corruption strategy", op. cit.

[183] Steven Weisman and Peter Goodman (2007), "Wolves at The Door", *The Age*, 30 April, http://www.theage.com.au/news/in-depth/wolves-at-the-door/2007/04/29/1177787972629.html; (2007) "Focus – Paul Wolfowitz", *The Age* (Melbourne, Australia), 30 April, p. 11.

[184] Karen DeYoung (2007), "For Washington Insider, Job Was an Uneasy Fit", *The Washington Post*, 18 May, p. A01, http://www.washingtonpost.com/wp-dyn/content/article/2007/05/17/AR2007051702376.html

[185] Krissah Williams (2007), "For Wolfowitz, Slings and Arrows: World Bank Chief's Leadership Role Called into Question", *The Washington Post*, 12 April, http://www.washingtonpost.com/wp-dyn/content/article/2007/04/11/AR2007041102202.html

"couldn't run a two-car funeral."[186] Criticism increased when it was revealed that Wolfowitz's partner, Shaha Riza, was transferred to the US Department of State when he took over the Bank's helm, but continued to receive her pay from the Bank, and that her salary had increased from \$132,660 to \$193,590. This charge proved the most damaging, since the man who spearheaded the anti-corruption measures himself appeared fallible to the charge of corruption.

The ensuing ethics charges brought against Wolfowitz were, therefore, the veneer of two underlying clashes. The first was between Democrats and Republicans at home, the former seeking to damage the Bush Administration. The second was between the US and European governments concerned with the issue of the procedures by which the president would henceforth be nominated, with the Europeans seeking to reduce American domination of the World Bank.

On the US side, Democrats in Congress, such as Barney Frank (D-MA), chairman of the US House Financial Services Committee, supported the contention that with Wolfowitz at the helm funding the Bank would become difficult.[187] Highlighting its concern that the US would lose its historic position as the Bank's *de facto* leader, members of Congress (with a notable emphasis on poverty alleviation and not anti-corruption) pressed President Bush further in one letter arguing that:

> It is evident, however, that the troubles relating to Mr. Wolfowitz have thrust the Bank into an historic crisis, which is jeopardizing the Bank's ability to garner support from member countries and, by extension, the Bank's ability to perform its fundamental purpose of alleviating poverty...The Bank's Board may feel compelled to vote on the future of Mr. Wolfowitz's tenure as President, an unprecedented step. We do not believe the Bank's mission or U.S. interests would be advanced by such a vote.[188]

---

[186] Karen DeYoung (2007), "For Washington Insider, Job was an Uneasy Fit", op. cit.

[187] William McQuillen and Kevin Carmichael (2007), "Wolfowitz Support Crumbles, Putting Onus on Paulson", www.bloomberg.net, 9 May, http://www.bloomberg.com/apps/news?pid=20601085&sid=aBmHYws3Hsrk&refer=europe

[188] Harry Reid, Dick Durban, Patty Murray, and Chuck Schumer (2007), "Senate Leadership Expresses 'Grave Concern' re. Crisis at The World Bank", *Democratic Caucus's Senate Journal (Letter to President George W. Bush)*, 9 May, http://democrats.senate.gov/journal/entry.cfm?id=273846

Both US control and its legitimacy were at risk.

European representatives were just as trenchant. Although they pre-ferred to see the nomination process reformed, they soon tactically shifted as the Administration dug in its heels to protect Wolfowitz, fearing that the Bank would become embroiled in a drawn-out dis-pute that would erode its ability to raise and distribute funds.[189] The European push to change the nomination process for president at the Bank ceased, with Dutch Finance Minister Wouter Bos signaling this shift, indicating that the Europeans would support the historic prac-tice on condition that Wolfowitz resign. "Up to now the appointment procedure seems to have worked...We have a problem with the presi-dent, not the procedure."[190]

Against the backdrop of American and European jostling, Robert Wade's testimony in Congressional hearings was sobering: "While the US and European governments were fighting over President Wolfowitz's future, the African Development Bank held its annual meeting not in Africa but in Shanghai"[191] – signaling the symbolic emergence of an effective challenger to US domination.

Past popularity, future prospects

Under Wolfensohn, the World Bank's goal was to develop a reputation; that it stored and diffused "knowledge" in an attempt to define the way people thought about development and implemented policy, in an attempt to legitimate World Bank prescriptions. In that sense, in the words of Pia Riggirozzi, the World Bank under Wolfensohn sought to act as a "norm broker." Riggirozzi further argues that, "despite the lev-erage of the World Bank as a financial institution and a 'Knowledge Bank', implementation of reform programmes in developing countries is embedded in complex policy processes in which the dominance of a particular actor or paradigm *vis-à-vis* others is not simply sustained by

---

[189] Steven R. Weisman (2007), "Deal Is Offered for Chief's Exit at World Bank", *New York Times*, 8 May, http://www.nytimes.com/2007/05/08/washington/08wolfowitz.html?hp

[190] Wouter Bos, as quoted in Sheyam Ghieth and Meera Loui (2005), "Europeans Call for End to Standoff Between Wolfowitz, Directors", www.bloomberg.com, 8 May, http://www.bloomberg.com/apps/news?pid=20601087&sid=al1lYZ1bipH8&refer=home

[191] Robert H. Wade (2007), "What to do About the World Bank", *Testimony to House Financial Services Committee*, 22 May, http://www.lse.ac.uk/collections/DESTIN/pdf/testimonytocongress.pdf

coercive, disciplinary power of the lender. That is, policy change does not entail a one-way exercise of power and imposition of paradigms, but rather, its capacity to amalgamate and find compromise between the World Bank and local knowledge(s)."[192] This mission shifted with Wolfowitz's arrival, from norm broker to incipient hegemon. With his departure and Zollick's appointment, however, efforts to impose the anti-corruption norm as the greatest priority substantially subsided.

The admittedly limited data drawn from public opinion surveys presented in this chapter suggests that the World Bank was able to accomplish this feat in attempting to address the problem of poverty in the course of the 1990s and early 2000s. Despite the criticism of NGOs, and the hostility of the US government under George Bush, the general public in poor recipient countries applauded Wolfensohn's efforts. Other, comparable examples can be drawn from individual episodes that substantiate the claim that legitimate global norm-building involving the US and the World Bank is possible. Mallaby claims, for example, that the Clinton Administration was able to achieve this in the case of the rebuilding of Bosnia and during the Asian crisis.[193] However, doing so requires the broad perception that more is at stake than America's narrow interests.

The year 2005 was notable for the "Make Poverty History" campaign, in which the G8 agreed to forgive debts for many of the HIPC countries, but it was a year in which the World Bank took a countervailing shift. In the Wolfowitz era, the World Bank moved its focus away from CDF policies designed to address poverty to a narrower agenda based on anti-corruption predicated on tighter conditionality. As Jeff Powell said at the time, Wolfowitz "made corruption the defining issue of his first year at the Bank... ordered a halt on hundreds of millions in Bank lending to countries across the globe; initiated a framework to coordinate multilateral development banks' anti-corruption efforts; and ordered internal reviews of Bank programmes plagued by corruption."[194] This change responded to the preferences of Northern elite stakeholders,

---

[192] For a discussion of this point see Pia Riggirozzi (2006), "The World Bank as Conveyor and Broker of Knowledge and Funds in Argentina's Governance Reforms", in Diane Stone and Chris Wright (eds), *The World Bank and Governance: A Decade of Reform and Reaction* (New York, London: Routledge, 2006).

[193] Sebastian Mallaby (2004), *The World's Banker: A Story of Failed States, Financial Crises, and the Wealth and Poverty of Nations*, op. cit., p. 363.

[194] See Jeff Powell (2006), "Beware the big, bland wolf: The first year of Paul Wolfowitz at the World Bank", *Bretton Woods Project*, 19 June, http://www.brettonwoodsproject.org/art.shtml?x=538757

closely reflected American interests and values, and marked a shift away from the policies that enhanced its popularity among client states.

Largely in response to this new focus, the World Bank changed its role from an organization where knowledge is gathered, and the primary intent is to fight poverty, to one that emphasizes the enforcement of strict anti-corruption guidelines intended to foster growth (albeit cloaked in the language of a moral crusade). During Wolfowitz's first year in office, the World Bank identified a select list of relatively dependent egregious offenders and took action designed to remedy their transgressions. By the end of his tenure, Wolfowitz found himself on the list.

However, if Riggirozzi is correct, effective implementation requires local cooperation – and that requires that states believe that they will reap the benefits themselves. In this context, therefore, legitimacy is required before acceptance of a norm and before enforcement becomes widespread. Even the World Bank itself admitted that there was no evidence of this happening, and so continued to mix punitive punishment with a country-by-country approach, largely reliant on a mixture of threat and impositions by its country specialist teams.

With Wolfowitz's departure, a cycle of sorts was completed, with aspects of continuity and change. In his final years, Wolfensohn had returned to focusing on infrastructural development, and Wolfowitz continued that trend. That aspect generated little argument, because there was a coincidence of interest among clients and shareholders: "This return to infrastructure is being driven by the financial imperative for the Bank to maintain loan volumes in middle-income countries and from rich country interest in lucrative construction contracts."[195]

But other aspects of the cycle were more contested: from appearing to represent the broad interest of the Global South to one where the interests of Northern stakeholders predominated. The support of a relative small troupe of NGOs, even influential ones inside the Washington Beltway, who claimed that their support for this new norm was moral rather than simply technocratic, did little to enhance the legitimacy of the campaign globally. It is simply a band-aid, one unlikely to generate the sweeping domestic support needed for progress globally. The result was coercion, and a reinforcement of the claim that IFIs simply act as global conduits for imperialist American interests.

---

[195] See Jeff Powell (2006), "Beware the big, bland wolf: The first year of Paul Wolfowitz at the World Bank", op. cit.

4
The Bush Doctrine and the Norms of Preemptive and Preventive Intervention[1]

> We're working very closely with all of these organizations and with a number of NGO partners in carrying out this program of assistance ... we have achieved and benefited from an incredible level of cooperation from the United States military forces.[2]
> To date, the U.S. Agency for International Development and all U.S. federal government partners have together provided more than $450 million in support for Haiti and for its people. This has contributed to helping to launch the largest and most effective urban search and rescue effort ever conducted.[3]

---

[1] This chapter draws upon a variety of material that first appeared in several locations, including Simon Reich (2006), "The Evolution of a Doctrine: The Curious Case of Kofi Annan, George Bush and the Doctrines of Preventative and Preemptive Intervention", in William Keller and Gordon Mitchell (eds), *Hitting First: Preventive Force in U.S. Security Strategy* (Pittsburgh, PA: University of Pittsburgh Press); Simon Reich (2003), "Power, Institutions and Moral Entrepreneurs", *ZEF-Discussion Paper on Development Policy No. 65*, Center for Development Research (ZEF), Bonn, March, http://www.mafhoum.com/press7/226P3.pdf; and Simon Reich (2006), "Hand Across the Ocean: Power, Influence and the Establishment of Global Norms", a paper prepared for a workshop entitled *La préférence pour la norme: L'Europe dans le regard du monde*, presented at CERI, Sciences Po Paris, 23–24 June.

[2] Lewis Lucke (2010), 'Press conference on relief work in Haiti', *United States Government Haiti Joint Informational Center*, 10 February, 2010 http://www.state.gov/documents/organization/136866.pdf

[3] Rajiv Shah (2010), 'Haiti Earthquake Relief- One Month Later', *Foreign Press Center Briefing*, 12 February, 2010, http://fpc.state.gov/136632.htm

[Commenting upon criticism of US efforts, Italian Foreign Minister France Frattini said] With regard to this incident, the Italian government has no desire to reprimand anyone, and has not done so. And if there have been words that have appeared critical that was not our intention...Let's just roll up our sleeves and get to work, as we have done and continue to do, with the US and the UN.[4]

In March 1999, after several attempts by the United Nations Security Council to compel Serbia into abandoning its policy of violence against ethnic Albanian separatists operating in Kosovo, the United States led NATO on a 90 day bombing campaign to prevent a humanitarian catastrophe. Nearly a decade later, in August 2008, citing Kosovo as a precedent and waving the flag of humanitarian intervention, Russian troops disregarded Georgian sovereignty to prevent what they perceived to be a *genocide* in South Ossetia and Abkhazia. At an emergency meeting of the Security Council, the Russian Permanent representative stated:

There is still time to avoid further casualties, including among the civilian population. The Georgian leadership must reflect and must return to civilized means of resolving difficult issues related to a political settlement. The Russian Federation will continue its efforts to prevent any further bloodshed and to put the situation in South Ossetia back on a peaceful track.[5]

The message was clear. Russia would continue what it perceived to be a humanitarian intervention until the security of ethnic Russian civilians in Georgia could be assured.

Powerful entrepreneurial actors who promoted the norm of preventive intervention had essentially crafted such arguments in the 1990s. These ranged from the United Nations Secretary Generals Boutros Boutros-Ghali and Kofi Annan to former Australian and Algerian Foreign Ministers Gareth Evans and Mohamed Sahnoun respectively. Support from nongovernmental organizations (NGOs) such as Médicins Sans

---

[4] Franco Frattini (2010), "We don't want to reprimand, but cooperate with the US", *Interview with Minister Frattini E Polis*, 27 January, 2010, http://www.esteri.it/MAE/EN/Sala_Stampa/ArchivioNotizie/Interviste/2010/01/20100127_frattiniusabertolaso.htm?LANG=EN

[5] Vitaly Churkin (2008), Statement of Russian Permanent Representative to the United Nations, *Security Council, 5951st meeting Record Number S/PV.595>8 August*, http://daccess-dds-ny.un.org/doc/UNDOC/PRO/N08/454/58/PDF/N0845458.pdf?OpenElement

Frontières and European, Canadian, and American academia came from decades of work attempting to institutionalize the norm of preventive humanitarian intervention.[6] They shared little in common in terms of their motives or political views. Yet they all contributed – wittingly or otherwise – to the evolution of the norm of preventive intervention by arguing in favor of the reconstitution of the definition of sovereignty, contributed significantly to the erosion of its standing as the operational cornerstone of the international system, and thus provided the justification for an unprecedented large-scale military action.

In many of these cases, their goal had been to enhance the protection of civilians in the context of intrastate wars. The 1990s had reputedly been a watershed in that it was the first decade of the Twentieth Century in which intrastate wars had outnumbered interstate ones.[7] In these wars, violence was increasingly directed against civilians in conflicts between state and non-state actors instead of civilian casualties occurring as collateral damage in conflicts between states. The intended process of widespread violence against unarmed civilians that had so grotesquely reached its ultimate statement in the Nazi war against the Jews in the Holocaust now risked becoming the norm, albeit on a smaller and less effective scale, across the globe. The cry "never again" was being invoked by advocacy groups in numerous wide-ranging contexts across Africa, Asia and Europe as ethnic conflict and genocidal behavior – illustrated most vividly in Rwanda and Bosnia – threatened to spread.

The arbitrary, sometimes capricious or impotent, and even reputedly calculating response of the international community on a case-by-case basis led advocates, increasingly vocally, to demand mechanisms for anticipating, monitoring, evaluating and, if necessary, enforcing

---

[6] For the purposes of this chapter, I adopt J. L. Holzgrefe's definition of humanitarian intervention as "the threat or use of force across state borders by a state (or group of states) aimed at preventing or ending widespread and grave violations of the fundamental human rights of individuals other than its own citizens, without the permission of the state within whose territory it is applied." See J. L. Holzgrefe (2003), "The Humanitarian Intervention Debate", in J. L. Holzgrefe and Robert O. Keohane (eds), *Humanitarian Intervention* (New York: Cambridge University Press), p. 18.

[7] For details see The Human Security Report (2005), "Part I- The Changing Face of Global Violence", *Human Security Center*, http://www.humansecurityreport. info/HSR2005_PDF/Part1.pdf; and Human Security Report (2005), "Part III- The Assault on the Vulnerable", *Human Security Center*, http://www.humansecurityreport.info/HSR2005_PDF/Part3.pdf

measures to forestall the slaughter of innocent civilians. These preventive mechanisms, they insisted, would reside under the domain of the international community. One – and possibly the most provocative – variant of the argument (as described in greater detail below) was that the United Nations should develop an independent capacity to evaluate and act when sanctioned by its members. While intervention had its historic roots, which far pre-dated the late twentieth century, this period marked a demarcation in terms of both the universal character of its application and the proposed source of its implication.

Support for this initiative was uneven across UN member states, but proponents clearly had momentum on their side as they worked assiduously to garner the support of important regional actors such as Nigeria and South Africa. The US, however, was reluctant either to abjure any claims on its sovereignty or to accept the enforcement costs of a preventive intervention doctrine abroad until the Bush Administration sought to legitimize its intervention in Iraq – what subsequently became known as the Bush Doctrine – in its appeals to the UN. On that day, as US Secretary of State Colin Powell made the US case to the UN, for very different reasons and seeking to invoke the norm of intervention in very different ways, two formulations collided. The result was to strike a significant blow to the efforts to construct and enforce a global norm built on the principle of humanitarian intervention.

These seeds of discontent with the status quo, predicated on humanitarian grounds, had the unforeseen (and unintended) consequence of generating alternative justifications for preventive intervention that differed in motive and style. Of course, it is not surprising that they did so for very different reasons. These initial proponents advocated the doctrine of preventive intervention in the name of humanitarianism through multilateral action on the basis of emergent large-scale threats to civilian populations either from their own governments or from contending non-state military forces in the context of disintegrating states.[8] The version eventually advocated by the Bush administration justified the grounds for initiating unilateral military action on the basis of an emergent "clear and present" danger to American citizens and property, regardless of whether that threat was to be carried out within the US or not. Humanitarian or "enlightenment" considerations were therefore replaced by strategic ones as the basis for abrogation of the territorial

---

[8] For further details on the evolution of this debate within the United Nations and affiliated organizations, see Simon Reich (2003), "Power, Institutions and Moral Entrepreneurs", op. cit.

integrity of another state, and the possible replacement of indigenous governments.

What is striking is that, although entrepreneurial and American support existed, the American doctrine of *"preemption,"* its interchangeable use with the term *"preventive"* intervention, and the resulting actions in Iraq and elsewhere alarmed UN member states. American support for one version and the support of moral entrepreneurs for another version – epitomized by "the responsibility to protect" doctrine – ironically ensured that neither was institutionalized, though it may be argued that one consequence was the possibility for unilateral interventions by hegemonic powers within their spheres of influence, such as that carried out by Russia in Georgia. Member support for humanitarian initiatives melted away under fears that the US, other major powers or the international community itself would use a broad humanitarian doctrine to justify more selective intervention in their countries for strategic reasons. Momentum was lost, and with it the prospect of effective action to save the lives of civilians – most immediately in The Democratic Republic of the Congo and Sudan.

The guiding norm of the UN: sovereignty and peacekeeping

Although advocacy towards a norm of preventive humanitarian intervention reached its crescendo in the late 1990s and early 2000s, the gestation period took almost five decades. From the end of World War II, the presiding security principle at the UN was that of peacekeeping. According to Mats Berdal, the thirteen UN peacekeeping operations between 1948 and 1988 generated a body of principles, procedures, and practices that came to constitute a corpus of case law and customary practice. As Sir Marrack Goulding, former UN Under-Secretary General responsible for peacekeeping operations, importantly noted, "this collection of law and practice sets precedent in the UN and is the primary way in which all future activity is justified."[9] This entailed the two most essential humanitarian principles – neutrality (not taking sides with warring parties) and impartiality (nondiscrimination and

---

[9] Personal interview with Sir Marrack Goulding (2002), Zentrum für Entwicklungforschung, Bonn, Germany, 5 July.

proportionality) with the guiding intention of "doing no harm."[10] The peacekeeping approach entails a conventional view of the principle of sovereignty:

> The traditional conception of sovereignty as rights attributes to states jurisdictional exclusivity within their own borders and grants very limited and narrowly construed bases of legitimacy for other actors, whether another state or an international institution, to intervene in any form in what in their territorial locus are considered domestic affairs.[11]

According to this doctrine, intervention is only justified in extreme situations, retroactively, with the consent (if not at the initiative) of states, and thus legitimacy is predicated on the assumption that the activities of peacekeepers are by the consent of all antagonists, impartial in conduct, and their operations are transparent, nonintrusive, and minimally coercive in character. As John Ruggie notes, "peacekeeping is a device to guarantee transparency, to reassure all sides that each is carrying out its promises."[12] Elsewhere, William Zartman has termed this as a condition of "ripeness."[13] Empirically, nonintervention was the general practice. To intervene without invitation was illegitimate,[14] and this shaped state action.[15] As Finnemore succinctly states, "sovereignty and self-determination norms trumped humanitarian claims

---

[10] Thomas G. Weiss (1999), "Principles, Politics, and Humanitarian Action", *Ethics & International Affairs*, 13:1, 1–22 (especially pp.1, 3).

[11] Bruce W. Jentleson (2000), "Coercive Prevention: Normative, Political and Policy Dilemmas", *Peaceworks No. 35* (Washington, DC: United States Institute of Peace), p. 18, http://www.usip.org/files/resources/pwks35.pdf

[12] John Gerard Ruggie (1997), "The UN and the Collective Use of Force: Whither or Whether?", in Michael Pugh (ed.), *The UN, Peace and Force* (London: Frank Cass), p. 6.

[13] For a comprehensive statement, see I. William Zartman (1989), *Ripe for Resolution* (New York: Oxford University Press); I. William Zartman (2000), "Ripeness: the Hurting Stalemate and Beyond", in Paul Stern and Daniel Druckman (eds), *International Conflict Resolution after the Cold War* (Washington, DC: National Academy Press), pp. 225–50; and more recently, in a post-9/11 context, see the application of the concept in I. William Zartman, "The Attack on Humanity: Conflict and Management", *Social Science Research Council Paper*, http://www.ssrc.org/sept11/essays/zartman_text_only.htm

[14] Martha Finnemore (2003), *The Purpose of Intervention: Changing Beliefs about the Use of Force* (Ithaca, NY: Cornell University Press), p. 16.

[15] On the influence of legitimacy on state action, see Thomas M. Franck (1990), *The Power of Legitimacy among Nations* (New York: Oxford University Press).

during the Cold War."[16] Genocides in places such as Cambodia were thus carried out without the intervention of the international community. Ruggie, however, summarizes the UN peacekeepers' posture and operational assumptions concisely when he states:

> Above all, peacekeeping is predicated on the consent of the parties which, typically, have agreed to cease hostilities before a peacekeeping mission is deployed. Moreover, peacekeepers fight against neither side but play an impartial interpositionary role, monitoring a ceasefire or controlling a buffer zone. Indeed, they do not fight as such. They carry only light arms and are authorized to shoot only in self-defense and, on occasion, in the defense of their mission if they come under direct attack. Unlike fighting forces, then, peacekeepers are not intended to create the peace they are asked to keep. They accept the balance of forces on the ground and work within it. Ironically, this military weakness may be an advantage in that it reassures all parties that the peacekeeping force cannot alter the prevailing balance to their advantage. In short, peacekeeping is a device to guarantee transparency, to reassure all sides that each is carrying out its promises.[17]

John Ruggie has argued that there has not been a systematic doctrinal approach adopted towards peacekeeping at the UN. Rather, the organization's understanding has been very poor, notably when it strays into what he describes as "gray area" operations that straddle the terrain between peacekeeping (in its most limited sense) and "war fighting."[18] The term "peacekeeping," he points out, is not even mentioned in the UN Charter.[19]

Ruggie suggests that peacekeeping's operationalization as a doctrine (not a norm) is the source of the problem. But the UN's incapacity to form and implement a coherent doctrine does not detract from the notion that such a peacekeeping norm (whether explicit or not) exists

---

[16] Martha Finnemore (2003), *Purpose of Intervention: Changing Beliefs about the Use of Force*, op. cit., pp. 16–17.

[17] John Gerard Ruggie (1997), "The UN and the Collective Use of Force: Whither or Whether?", op. cit., p. 5.
Note that Ruggie draws extensively from Boutros Boutros-Ghali (1992), An Agenda for Peace (New York: United Nations), Document No. A/47/277 – S/24111, 17 June, http://www.un.org/Docs/SG/agpeace.html

[18] Ibid., pp.1–2.

[19] Ibid., p. 5.

and guides behavior. Indeed, important to the emergence of this norm over four decades was the central notion that the primary purpose of peacekeeping is to allow antagonists to end aggression in order to generate a possible agreement. Mediation is only of limited interest once both sides have exhausted their desire to fight. As Mats Berdal has suggested, it

> ... has traditionally been used to describe various forms of legitimized collective intervention aimed at avoiding the outbreak or resurgence of violent conflict between debutants. As a distinctive form of third-party intervention governed by the principles of consent and minimum force, peacekeeping operations have been expressly non-threatening and impartial.[20]

Challenging the shibboleth of peacekeeping

The turning point began in the early 1990s, when powerful and well-placed entrepreneurial actors sought to question the utility of the prevailing doctrine of peacekeeping. Those ranging from UN Secretary-General Kofi Annan to human rights activists challenged the concept of sovereignty as sacrosanct. They shared a belief that the peacekeeping doctrine was too reactive and limited in character and a reliance on the consent of all parties was a recipe for paralysis. Advocating preventive intervention in the aftermath of the Cold War challenged a historic shibboleth, that of the preeminence of the concept of sovereignty. Doing so thus facilitated a reconstitution of an international order in which sovereignty was neither emblematic of, nor a guarantor of, the status quo.[21]

---

[20] Mats R. Berdal (1993), "Whither UN Peacekeeping: an analysis of the changing military requirements of UN peacekeeping with proposals for its enhancement" (London: International Institute for Strategic Studies), p. 3.

[21] For a discussion of the nature of sovereignty see Stephen D. Krasner (1999), *Sovereignty: Organized Hypocrisy* (Princeton, NJ: Princeton University Press). He has, of course, argued that sovereignty is varied in character and was never as foundational as those who caricature realism have argued. For varied contrasting views see Daniel Philpott (2001), "Usurping the Sovereignty of Sovereignty", *World Politics*, 53, 297–324; and Daniel Philpott (2001), *Revolutions in Sovereignty: How Ideas Shaped Modern International Relations* (Princeton, NJ: Princeton University Press); Thomas J. Biersteker and Cynthia Weber (eds) (1996), *State Sovereignty as a Social Construct* (Cambridge: Cambridge

The issue of the conditions under which intervention could take place had predated the Cold War but had largely been eschewed during those five decades. Peacekeeping was the dominant interventionist response of the international community during the Cold War, one that began eroding at the end of the Cold War. Certainly, the process of simultaneous convergence and fragmentation in the last two decades of the twentieth century has been well documented and debated, and the combined accelerating effects of this process on conflict needs little elaboration here.[22] But, with the reconstitution of the international system, the initial deep and abiding wedge into the Cold War conception of sovereignty blossomed with the development of the doctrine of preventive intervention. This doctrine challenged peacekeeping as the dominant policy response. It shared with peacekeeping a focus on a humanitarian mission. Yet proponents of preventive intervention questioned the preeminence of sovereignty and the notion of territorial integrity in the limited circumstances of state disintegration and ethnic conflict. Rather, they focused extensively on the human rights of victims and the responsibilities of states to enforce those rights.[23] The shift in focus was therefore from the security of states to that of individuals, with the primary instrument being multilateral institutions attempting to employ multilateralist processes of decision-making and joint implementation within the defined parameters of the protection of civilians within failed states.[24] Imminent danger demanded preventive measures.[25]

As the notion of the abrogation of sovereignty again gained legitimacy, a key debate ensued, designed to address the question of "under

---

University Press); and J. Samuel Barkin and Bruce Cronin (1994), "The State and the Nation: Changing Norms and the Rules of International Relations", *International Organization*, 48, 107–30.

[22] For a concise but clear listing of these forces and their influences on intrastate conflict, see Fen Osler Hampson, Jean Daudelin, John B. Hay, Holly Reid and Todd Martin (eds) (2001), *Madness in the Multitude: Human Security and World Disorder* (New York: Oxford University Press).

[23] For a summary statement of this position see The International Commission on Intervention and State Sovereignty (2001), *The Responsibility to Protect* (Ottawa: International Development Research Center), p. xi, http://www.iciss.ca/pdf/Commission-Report.pdf

[24] For a concise justification of the principles legitimating intervention by just such a moral entrepreneur, see Kofi A. Annan (1999), "Two Concepts of Sovereignty", *The Economist*, 16 September, http://www.economist.com/world/middleeast-africa/displaystory.cfm?story_id=E1_PNQSJV

[25] Martha Finnemore (2003), *The Purpose of Intervention: Changing Beliefs about the Use of Force*, op. cit., pp. 135–6.

what conditions could non-consensual intervention be justified?" Martha Finnemore notes that, for more powerful states, "What has changed is when it will suit them – not the fact of intervention but its form and meaning. What has changed are state understandings about the purposes to which they can and should use force."[26]

By 1997, the authors of one major report concluded that an alternative doctrine, what some have referred to as a "peace enforcement" approach,[27] was already unfolding. As they remarked at the time, "at the moment there is no specific international legal provision against internal violence (apart from the genocide convention and more general provisions contained in international human rights instruments), nor is there any widely accepted principle that this should be prohibited."[28]

The foundations of the doctrine of preventive intervention drew from the assumption that sovereignty is conditional upon universally acceptable behavior and global norms, and that potential large-scale conflicts with dire humanitarian implications can be readily identified. Preventive intervention is intended to forestall such crises and timely coercive action to intercede can therefore be successfully undertaken.[29] Rather than being reactive, organizations like the UN must learn to be preemptive.[30] Thus, "effective preventive strategies rest on three principles: early reaction to signs of trouble; a comprehensive, balanced approach to alleviate the pressures, or risk factors, that trigger violent conflict, and an extended effort to resolve the underlying root causes of violence."[31]

Action was therefore justified by a contrasting definition of sovereignty to the one upon which peacekeeping rested. Peacekeeping focused on the rights of states. In this alternative version, states have responsibilities or obligations to their citizenry, "where a population is

---

[26] Martha Finnemore (2003), *The Purpose of Intervention: Changing Beliefs about the Use of Force*, op. cit., p. 11.

[27] Donald C. F. Daniel and Bradd C. Hayes (with Chantal de Jonge Oudraat) (1999), *Coercive Inducement and the Containment of International Crises* (Washington, DC: U.S. Institute of Peace Press), p. 19.

[28] The Carnegie Commission on Preventing Deadly Conflict (1997), *Preventing Deadly Conflict* (New York: Carnegie Corporation of New York), p. 28.

[29] For such a list of factors see, for example, Carnegie Commission on Preventing Deadly Conflict (1997), *Preventing Deadly Conflict*, op. cit. 43–4.

[30] See, for example, Kofi Annan (2001), *Prevention of Armed Conflict: Report of the Secretary-General*, UN Document A/55/985-S/2001/574, 7 June, p. 1, http://www.unhchr.ch/Huridocda/Huridoca.nsf/e06a5300f90fa0238025668700518ca4/4688bbfc70b03e4bc1256adf003fe11a/$FILE/N0140464.pdf

[31] Carnegie Commission on Preventing Deadly Conflict (1997), *Preventing Deadly Conflict*, op. cit., p. xviii.

suffering serious harm, as a result of internal war, insurgency, repression or state failure, and the state in question is unwilling or unable to halt or alter it, the principle of non-intervention yields to the international responsibility to protect."[32]

Thus sovereignty:

> Does not include any claim of the unlimited power of a state to do what it wants to its own people ... It is acknowledged that sovereignty implies a dual responsibility, externally to respect the sovereignty of other states, and internally, to respect the dignity and basic rights of all the people within the state. In international human rights covenants, in UN practice, and in state practice itself, sovereignty is now understood as embracing this dual responsibility. Sovereignty as responsibility has become the minimum content of good international citizenship.[33]

Implicitly, state authorities are responsible for protecting the safety of their citizens, as well as the promotion of their welfare; they are responsible to both the national citizenry and international community through the UN; and state officials are accountable and responsible for their acts of commission and omission. In sum, impunity is no longer a means of defense.[34] Failure to enact these responsibilities provides a "just cause" for intervention.[35]

Such claims were formulated in the context of the development of the new concept of human security, with its primary focus on the security of individuals rather than the territorial integrity of states.[36] Human security's holistic approach was consistent with the doctrine of preventive intervention in at least three different respects. First, its proponents moved beyond the precipitant causes to consider underlying ones by distinguishing between *structural* and *operational* elements of prevention. Broader structural components (such as the battle against

---

[32] International Commission on Intervention, *Responsibility to Protect*, p. xi.

[33] Ibid., p. 8. For an academic analysis in support of this view tracing a broader historical element, see Bruce Cronin (1998), "Changing Views of Sovereignty and Multilateral Intervention", in Joseph Lepgold and Thomas G. Weiss (eds), *Collective Conflict Management and Changing World Politics* (Albany, NY: SUNY Press), pp. 157–80.

[34] Ibid., pp. 13–14.

[35] Ibid., pp. 32–4. This same point is also made by Bruce W. Jentleson (2000), "Coercive Prevention: Normative, Political and Policy Dilemmas", op. cit., pp. 19–20.

[36] Ibid., p. 15.

poverty and disease) involved crucial long-term strategies to avoid the conditions that foster intrastate conflict. Operational aspects involved strategies that address the immediate or contingent precipitants of war.[37] Second, in contrast to peacekeeping, this approach did not simply focus on military intervention. Military intervention is only one form of preventive intervention. Broader strategies advocated included political and diplomatic initiatives, and economic threats or incentives, as well as the threat or use of force. Intervention included twin components of sanctions and rewards that extended beyond the threat of imminent duress.[38] Third, this approach extended "downstream" to include not only conflict resolution but "peace-building," often in the form of the reintegration and reconstruction of fragmented states. Conflict prevention, where appropriate, thus entailed an extended, indefinite commitment to a process beyond the immediate use of force and sanctions. William Odom, former director of the National Security Agency, commented that one does "recognize what successful interventions involve. Simply put, they must provide a surrogate government for a very long time, normally decades, while effective indigenous governmental institutions are created. Interventions inspired only by humanitarian impulses without a concomitant willingness and capacity to provide surrogate government are both politically and morally irresponsible."[39]

So the analysis of causes, the breadth of function, and the degree of time commitment all shifted in the context of the doctrine of preventive intervention from that of peacekeeping. While debates ensued over the timing of the introduction of forces, it was agreed by proponents that a war fighting capacity is essential to establish and sustain

---

[37] This distinction is discussed in Carnegie Commission on Preventing Deadly Conflict (1997), *Preventing Deadly Conflict,* op. cit., p. 39; and amplified in Kofi Annan (2001), *Prevention of Armed Conflict: Report of the Secretary-General,* op. cit., p. 7.

[38] This point is discussed at length in Carnegie Commission on Preventing Deadly Conflict (1997), *Preventing Deadly Conflict,* op. cit., pp. 48–63. Daniel and Hayes (with Oudraat) focus on a variety of coercive aspects to extend the notion they developed of a "coercive inducement" option that judiciously employs forceful persuasion to implement community norms or mediate in crisis, including but not limited to military force. See Donald C. F. Daniel and Bradd C. Hayes (with Chantal de Jonge Oudraat) (1999), *Coercive Inducement and the Containment of International Crises,* op. cit., pp. 21–2.

[39] William Odom (2001), "Intervention for the Long Run", *Harvard International Review,* 22:4, 48–52.

credibility, with force remaining "an appropriate" option; that its use should be "fair but firm."[40]

The appeal of this approach extended beyond the idealistic to a rationalist one. Some commentators argued that "an ounce of prevention is worth a pound of cure." Bruce Jentleson, for example, offered a rationalist riposte to traditional realist approaches by suggesting that the option of preventive intervention saves money because of the huge costs involved in individual peacekeeping operations in the 1990s compared with the estimated costs of a preventive intervention operation.[41]

Tom Farer gives a pragmatic and contemporary face to such realist arguments when he states that advocates of humanitarian intervention have:

> ...attempted to show that unremediated butchery in foreign lands adversely affects the interests of people at home. They emphasized material factors like spikes in undocumented immigration caused by persons fleeing persecution and the threat of deadly diseases or international criminal and terrorist organizations able to incubate in anarchic places.[42]

Who led the charge?

The UN's own leadership played a pivotal role in the development of this doctrine in a series of stages.[43] A succession of UN peacekeeping failures led critics to conclude that the UN then had neither the resources nor strategy to act effectively.[44] Three cases were pivotal. The first was that of the Former Yugoslav Republic of Macedonia (FYROM), a very small and otherwise undistinguished operation whose importance lay in the fact that it set a precedent by becoming the first case in which the principle of preventive intervention was used to justify

---

[40] Bruce W. Jentleson (2000), "Coercive Prevention: Normative, Political and Policy Dilemmas", op. cit., p. 5.

[41] Ibid.

[42] Tom J. Farer (2003), "Humanitarianism Intervention before and After 9/11: Legality and Legitimacy", in J. L. Holzgrefe and Robert O. Keohane (eds), *Humanitarian Intervention*, op. cit., p. 59.

[43] For an extended discussion of these events see Simon Reich (2003), "Power, Institutions and Moral Entrepreneurs", op. cit.

[44] Joel Stedman (1999), "UN Intervention in Civil Wars: Imperatives of Choice and Strategy", in Donald C. F. Daniel and Bradd C. Hayes (with Chantal de Jonge Oudraat), *Coercive Inducement and the Containment of International Crises*, pp. 40–1.

UN activities under Resolution 795.[45] The second case was Rwanda, significant because of the very size of the genocide, the clear signals of impending slaughter, the apparent capacity of the West to intervene at a relatively small cost, and its refusal to do so. More notable, therefore, for what the UN did not do, Rwanda became inextricably associated with head of UN forces Roméo Dallaire's attributed 1994 claim that the deployment of a relative small number of 5,000 mobile troops could have significantly reduced the slaughter in Rwanda, if not quelled it.[46] The third case was Somalia, where the UN significantly shifted away from the traditional peacekeeping approach towards a more coercive operation with a broader intent.

Of the three, the importance of FYROM as a historic precedent cannot be overstated. The role of the Rwandan genocide in illustrating the lack of equity and moral paucity of the West was of enormous importance in promoting the doctrine of preventive intervention. The importance of the Somalia mission, however, cannot be underestimated because of Western forces' extensive involvement and yet the failure of both the US and UN missions, which illustrated the need for a more coherent strategy (than peacekeeping) in the context of humanitarian crises.

At this time, Boutros Boutros-Ghali, then presiding Secretary-General of the UN, became the most vocal proponent of the development of a capacity for preventive intervention. In a 1992 report entitled "An Agenda for Peace" published relatively soon after Boutros-Ghali took office, he characterized preventive intervention as a new technique designed to prevent cross-border or intrastate conflict.[47] Here, he introduced the concept of "peace enforcement" as one designed to maintain cease-fires. As Edward Luck suggested, Boutros-Ghali stressed that: "low-level action, at modest cost and risk, may prevent the need

---

[45] See, for example, Alice Ackermann and Antonia Pala (1996), "From Peacekeeping to Preventive Deployment: a study of the United Nations in the former Yugoslav Republic of Macedonia", *European Security*, 5:1, 83–97; Mats Berdal (1995), "United Nations Peacekeeping in the Former Yugoslavia", in Donald C. F. Daniel and Bradd C. Hayes (eds), *Beyond Traditional Peacekeeping* (London: Palgrave), p. 232; Carnegie Commission on Preventing Deadly Conflict (1997), *Preventing Deadly Conflict*, op. cit., p. 64; Bruce W. Jentleson (2000), "Coercive Prevention: Normative, Political and Policy Dilemmas", op. cit., pp. 6, 16.

[46] For just one example of this oft-cited claim see Kofi Annan (2001), *Prevention of Armed Conflict: Report of the Secretary-General*, op. cit., p. 6.

[47] Mats R. Berdal (1993), "Whither UN Peacekeeping: an analysis of the changing military requirements of UN peacekeeping with proposals for its enhancement", op. cit., p. 18.

at a later point to choose between doing nothing and intervening forcefully."[48]

Two months later, Boutros-Ghali characterized this as a task beyond a traditional peacekeeping function, entailing deployment beyond the expressed consent of antagonists and in which the UN could use necessary force. As Daniel and Hayes point out, "in this way he sanctioned the term 'peace enforcement' and, whatever his intentions, helped advance the view that the international community now had available a continuum of options with peace enforcement in the middle"[49] – a means of enforcing a peace against all signatures to an agreement who violated its terms. "In such a conception the peace support contingent is somewhat like a policeman on the beat with authority to support community-backed norms against all comers regardless of their affiliation."[50] Further developing this idea, by 1995, Boutros-Ghali dropped the term "peace enforcement" and instead simply began to refer to "enforcement," thus further delineating between peacekeeping and enforcement in the move towards prevention.[51]

Meanwhile, in early 1993, Kofi Annan became the Undersecretary General, responsible for peacekeeping operations. Prior to this appointment, he had vocally favored adopting a new approach to peace support built on the principle of inducements founded on the principle that "inaction in the face of massive violence is morally indefensible, non-involvement an illusory option."[52] Annan was animated by his outrage at the inequity he perceived in the West's willingness to act to intervene in Bosnia, given the greater potential magnitude of the human tragedies he considered likely in Somalia, Sudan, Mozambique, and Liberia. This choice Annan considered to be motivated by the strategic location

---

[48] Edward C. Luck (1995), "The Case for Engagement: American Interests in UN Peace Operations", Donald C. F. Daniel and Bradd C. Hayes (eds), *Beyond Traditional Peacekeeping*, op. cit., p. 69.

[49] Donald C. F. Daniel and Bradd C. Hayes (with Chantal de Jonge Oudraat) (1999), *Coercive Inducement and the Containment of International Crises*, op. cit., pp. 18–19.

[50] Ibid., p. 23.

[51] Ibid., pp. 18–19.

[52] Kofi Annan (1996), "Peace Operations and the United Nations: Preparing for the Next Century" (New York: United Nations Working Paper), p. 15.

of the war in Europe, a clear if unpopular point he made during a visit to Sarajevo in 1992.[53]

Certainly, Boutros-Ghali's demands were most immediately stimulated by events in Somalia, where hundreds of thousands of victims were dying. Yet the Organization of African Unity (OAU) opposed UN intervention on the grounds that the Somali government had not requested assistance.[54] The Organization of Islamic Conference (OIC), however, did press for action, providing Boutros-Ghali with a justification to visit Somalia. In the midst of the fighting, Boutros-Ghali prevailed upon the General Assembly (GA) under resolution 733 to belatedly establish a total arms embargo, urge a cease-fire, establish a humanitarian relief effort, and issue an invitation to all parties in Somalia to attend a meeting in New York in an attempt to reach a compromise. But these efforts at reconciliation proved unsuccessful, complicated by a history of personal animosity between Boutros-Ghali and Somali warlord Mohamed Aideed.[55]

The UN and the US did eventually intervene in Somalia, an episode chronicled extensively elsewhere.[56] This intervention, however, according to critics, proved to be such a failure in large part because of the poor relationship that existed between the US and the UN. The US was initially intent on pursuing an independent policy through UNITAF with short-term goals, prioritizing the provision of immediate relief to starving Somalis. Boutros-Ghali's intent, however, was on instituting a longer-term process of nation-building that would precipitate a further

---

[53] Stephen J. Stedman (1995), "UN Intervention in Civil Wars", in Donald C. F. Daniel and Bradd C. Hayes (eds), *Beyond Traditional Peacekeeping*, op. cit., p. 47.

[54] Donald C. F. Daniel and Bradd C. Hayes (with Chantal de Jonge Oudraat) (1999), *Coercive Inducement and the Containment of International Crises*, op. cit., p. 84.

[55] Ibid., p. 86.

[56] See, for examples of an extensive literature, Mike Blakely (1999), "Somalia", in Michael E. Brown and Richard N. Rosecrane (eds), *The Costs of Conflict: Prevention and Cure in the Global Arena* (New York: Rowman and Littlefield), http://www.wilsoncenter.org/subsites/ccpdc/pubs/costs/cosfr.htm; Carnegie Commission, *Preventing Deadly Conflict*, op. cit., p.75–90; Donald C. F. Daniel and Bradd C. Hayes (with Chantal de Jonge Oudraat) (1999), *Coercive Inducement and the Containment of International Crises*, op. cit., pp. 73–112; and William J. Durch (1997), "Introduction to Anarchy: Humanitarian Intervention and 'State Building' in Somalia", in William J. Durch (ed.), *UN Peacekeeping, American Politics and the Uncivil Wars of the 1990s* (London: Palgrave MacMillan Press), pp. 311–66.

move towards preventive intervention. The Americans, according to Stephen John Stedman, were uninterested in such goals.[57] Rather, they were preparing for an independent, short-term action before handing the operation over to UN responsibility.

Commentators have suggested that the American leadership of UNITAF marked a watershed in the expansion of functions from traditional peacekeeping to broader peace operations. In contrast, it was the initial UN deployment, UNOSOM I, that constituted a classic peacekeeping operation there.[58] The UN Security Council passed resolutions 751 and 767, which sanctioned the deployment of troops, airlift of emergency supplies and the provision of an advisory team to Somalia.

The US commitment extended to the provision of UNITAF troops with the extent of stabilizing the situation and providing a secure environment for the delivery of humanitarian assistance. The UN Security Council approved this initiative, Resolution 794, in December 1992. Under the designated "Operation Restore Hope," the UNITAF force would act forcefully and without the consent of locals if necessary, allowing a greater use of all necessary force when faced with resistance, the appearance of weaponry, the construction of roadblocks, or evidence of banditry.[59] Pointedly, the Americans therefore successfully shifted outside the parameters of the traditional peacekeeping practice pushing the agenda of Boutros-Ghali's peace enforcement approach, securing the distribution of relief supplies and stemming the death of Somalis.

Boutros-Ghali then encouraged the next move towards the doctrine of preventive intervention. In the wrangling over the second UNOSOM mission, the US reiterated its unwillingness to continue its participation, pressing the UN to begin the transition towards its phased withdrawal, to be replaced by UN troops. Resolution 814 created UNOSOM II, its mandate being to provide humanitarian intervention, create a secure environment for economic assistance, and assist in the political reconstitution of a Somali government.[60]

---

[57] Stephen J. Stedman (1995), "UN Intervention in Civil Wars", op. cit., p. 48.
[58] This view is expressed by Donald C. F. Daniel and Bradd C. Hayes (with Chantal de Jonge Oudraat) (1999), *Coercive Inducement and the Containment of International Crises*, op. cit., p. 86.
[59] Ibid., p. 90.
[60] Ibid., p. 98.

Yet Boutros-Ghali recognized that only the US could effectively dis-
arm and demobilize the militias. He encouraged the US to implement a
coercive disarmament plan, extending its operations beyond the South
to throughout Somalia.

In fact, the Secretary-General did not even want to start planning for
UNOSOM II until the United States accepted this broader mandate and
began carrying it out. But, despite a change in administrations (Bush
to Clinton), the US course of limiting the geographic scope of the operation and avoiding general disarmament activities was set and would
not change. As a result, Boutros-Ghali continued to insist until late
April 1993 that it was premature and dangerous to begin planning for
a US takeover. He was so certain that UNITAF could be pressured into
implementing a "coercive disarmament" plan that the United Nations
never prepared a plan of its own.[61]

It was, therefore, Boutros-Ghali who demanded a further move away
from peacekeeping towards greater coercive preemption.[62] Indeed, par-
adoxically, as the situation in Somalia worsened (and the US introduced
a war fighting "Quick Reaction Force" to Somali in search of the warlord Mohamed Aideed), the gap between the US position and that of the
UN subsequently widened, for, counterintuitively, it was Boutros-Ghali
who advocated that the UN adopt an increasingly aggressive position,
even as the US position softened. Lobbying hard for Security Council
Resolution 837, he advocated that UN forces use all necessary means
to arrest, detain, and prosecute Somali militants who had attacked UN
forces. As Daniel and Hayes assert, the successful adoption of Resolution
837 "changed the entire premise upon which UNOSOM had been operating. The United Nations was now at war."[63] Some contingents, like the
Italians and the French, followed this new UN directive, issuing conflicting orders to their troops. Violence, however, escalated, with the US
intent on locating Aideed, while a separate UN force operated intent on
defeating Aideed's SNA forces, stabilizing the situation and embarking
on a process of nation-building.

Yet neither operation succeeded. UNOSOM failed, according to Daniel
and Hayes, because it lacked the doctrine, resources, or political backing

---

[61] Ibid., p. 99.

[62] See Gary Anderson (1995), "UNOSOM II: Not Failure, Not Success", in Daniel
and Hayes, *Beyond Traditional Peacekeeping*, op. cit., pp. 273, 278–9.

[63] Donald C.F. Daniel and Bradd C. Hayes (with Chantal de Jonge Oudraat)
(1999) *Coercive Inducement and the Containment of International Crises*, op. cit.,
p. 102.

to fight a war. According to Stephen Stedman, the US refusal to support the UN mission and the eventual US withdrawal doomed the operation to failure.[64] Edward Luck's assessment was that the US announcement of its intention to withdraw its force from Somalia and not join the UN operation was sufficient to precipitate the unraveling of the latter.[65] Nonetheless, despite the mission's evident failure, events in Somalia proved to be a watershed. They signaled the consolidation of a move away from peacekeeping to something that was broader in scope and different in character. Boutros-Ghali's efforts to bring order to Somalia and consolidate the humanitarian operation there may have failed, but laid the foundation for the idea of linking enforcement powers to a political mandate. Kofi Annan may have been correct in suggesting, in a 1994 interview, that it would be some time before the UN would support a peace enforcement mission of its own.[66] Yet the foundation had been laid for the construction of a doctrine in support of that idea,[67] with the UN the venue for such a debate.[68]

Consolidating the debate

The period between 1996 and 2001 was marked by a different kind of conflict and intervention, notably the low-level sustained presence of FYROM into 1999, and a series of events that marked the sustained NATO campaign in Kosovo as sanctioned by the UN. These were linked to the principles of preventive intervention, but neither was precipitated by the same kind of broad-based humanitarian crisis as earlier in the decade.

---

[64] Stephen J. Stedman (1995), "UN Intervention in Civil Wars", op. cit., p. 69. Gary Anderson's comments are consistent with Stedman's assessment. See Gary Anderson (1995), "UNOSOM II: Not Failure, Not Success", op. cit., p. 273.

[65] Edward C. Luck (1995), "Case for Engagement", op. cit., p. 71.

[66] Stanley Meisler (1994), "Kofi Annan: The Soft Spoken Economist who runs UN Peacekeeping Forces", *Los Angeles Times*, 21 June.

[67] An outstanding case for examination is that of Bosnia. But, I believe, doing so would support a comparable argument to that detailed in the Somalian case. Unlike in Somalia, UNPROFOR, the force provided by the UN, preceded any US involvement. It initially proved inadequate in dealing with the aggression of the Bosnian Serbs. It was only when US policy changed course, and they began air strikes against Bosnian Serb positions, that all antagonists were coerced into participating in the Dayton Peace Accords. See, for example, Joseph R. Biden (1998), "Bosnia: Why the United States Should Finish the Job", *SAIS Review*, 18:2, 1–7.

[68] Edward C. Luck, "Case for Engagement", op. cit., p. 69.

Indeed, the appointment of Kofi Annan as Secretary-General of the UN signaled its "takeoff" stage, as he emphatically promoted humanitarian intervention through the UNDP yearly reports.[69] In his cumulative statement, the UN's Millennium report entitled *We the Peoples: the Role of the United Nations in the 21st Century*, Kofi Annan expressed his views about the major challenges facing humanity in the new century, a "human-centered" approach to security focused on poverty, aids, debt relief, and conflict prevention.[70] This redefined security in terms of threats to individuals rather than to the territorial integrity and sovereignty of states.[71] In that context, Annan characterized the necessary move as being from the movement from a "culture of reaction" to a "culture of prevention."[72] According to Bruce Jentleson, Annan advocated a significant shift in order to reinterpret a series of UN Articles as being collectively threaded to justify preventive intervention. These included Article 2(7) on sovereign rights; Article 3 on rights regarding life, liberty, and personal security; Article 55 on human rights as a fundamental and universal freedom; and Article 56, which pledged membership action towards promoting these goals: "even national sovereignty can be set aside if it stands in the way of the Security Council's overriding duty to preserve international peace and security."[73]

This rhetoric was expressed in a series of UN documents issued by the Secretary-General designed to exhort the Security Council and General Assembly to accept multiple aspects of intervention as central to a "culture of intervention." In justifying a new interpretation of "sovereignty as responsibility," Annan stated that "conflict prevention is one of the primary obligations of member states set forth in the Charter of the United Nations, and United Nations efforts in conflict prevention must be in conformity with the purposes and principles

---

[69] For a perspective consistent with this, see, for example, Adam Garfinkle (2001), "Strategy and Preventive Diplomacy", *Orbis*, 45:4, 503–18.

[70] Kofi A. Annan (2000), *We the Peoples: the Role of the United Nations in the 21st Century* (New York: United Nations Department of Public Information), p. 43, http://www.un.org/millennium/sg/report/full.htm

[71] See, for example, Caroline Thomas (2000), *Global Governance, Development and Human Security: The Challenge of Poverty and Inequality* (London: Pluto Press).

[72] Although there are numerous examples of Annan offering this statement, for emphasis, see the first line of Kofi Annan (2001), *Prevention of Armed Conflict: Report of the Secretary-General*, op. cit., p. 6.

[73] See Bruce W. Jentleson (2000), "Coercive Prevention: Normative, Political and Policy Dilemmas", op. cit., p. 20.

of the Charter."[74] He suggested that "the time has come to translate the rhetoric of conflict prevention into concrete action."[75] Consistent with this theme, Annan attempted to institutionally reorganize the UN along these lines, by reorienting the 14 departments under the umbrella of the Interdepartmental Framework for Coordination in 1998 to focus the efforts of the Department of Political Affairs, primarily in order to address the issue of prevention. Furthermore, he also aggressively promoted a series of UN resolutions designed to strengthen peacekeeping and nation-building capacities.[76]

Annan was assisted in these efforts by a series of senior former politicians and high-profile UN officials. Among the members of this group were Lakhdar Brahimi, former Algerian Minister for Foreign Affairs and chair of The Report of the Panel on United Nations Peacekeeping Operations; senior Algerian Diplomat, OAU and Arab League official Brundtland Commission member, Mohamed Sahnoun; and Gareth Evans, former Australian Foreign Minister and Member of Parliament. Sahnoun and Evans served as co-chairs of the 2001 report entitled *The Responsibility to Protect*, issued by an NGO, the International Commission on Intervention and State Sovereignty. Although a former politician, Evans, importantly, also served at the time as president of the widely respected and influential International Crisis Group. This report still constitutes arguably the most comprehensive statement of the foundations of a preventive intervention doctrine almost a decade later. The mandate of the commission, funded by the Canadian government, was clearly to reinforce Annan's position.

Changing US leadership and the emergence of a rival doctrine of "Preemptive Intervention"

The second half of the decade and the turn of the millennium were notable for several cases of "indirect American intervention" (East Timor, Sierra Leone, and Liberia), and one contentious case of direct intervention in Kosovo. Critics argued that the NATO bombing in Kosovo might

---

[74] Kofi Annan (2001), *Prevention of Armed Conflict: Report of the Secretary-General*, op. cit., p. 1.

[75] Ibid., p. 3.

[76] Ibid., pp. 13–15.

have been illegal under international law[77] (albeit the bombing was purportedly justified by Belgrade's abrogation of UN Security Council Resolution 1199) because of China's and Russia's refusal to sanction the bombing campaign. Others denounced the American position as hypocritical because President Clinton claimed a moralist and collectivist impulse but was in fact unilateralist in action and motivated by self-interest.[78] Proponents of intervention, in contrast, suggested that its legality was justified by the precedent of a growing volume of humanitarian law.[79]

President Clinton's decision to articulate his "Clinton Doctrine" on 22 June 1999 did not seem to be influenced by international legal considerations. In offering a perspective consistent and congruent with the emergent norm of preventive intervention as advocated by Annan, Clinton offered "an avowal to stop mass murder everywhere despite the cost to the principle of sovereignty."[80] Sovereignty was conditional and the use of force legitimate. The key question concerned the condition under which it was applicable.

This congruence between the UN and US positions, however, was quickly eclipsed by George W. Bush's presidential election, as the new President articulated his explicit hostility to such humanitarian, preventive missions.[81] Bush indefatigably stated his position during his presidential campaign: "We should not send our troops to stop ethnic cleansing and nations outside our strategic interest."[82] Bush and his

---

[77] See, for example, Julie Mertus (2000), "Reconsidering the Legality of Humanitarian Intervention: Lessons from Kosovo", *William and Mary Law Review*, 41:5, 1743–88. Mertus does argue, however, that the intervention may indeed be justifiable according to the UN Charter.

[78] For a discussion of this issue, see Jeffrey C. Isaac and Suzanne Dovi (2001), "Hypocrisy and the Limits of Debunking it", *Polity*, 34:1, 31–40.

[79] See, for example, Klinton W. Alexander (2000), "NATO's Intervention in Kosovo: The Legal Case for Violating Yugoslavia's National Sovereignty in the Absence of Security Council Approval", *Houston Journal of International Law*, 22:3, 403–50.

For a further variety of assessments by notable legal scholars see Editorial (1999), "NATO's Kosovo Intervention", *American Journal of International Law*, 93:2, 824–62.

[80] Cited in Adam Garfinkle (2001), "Strategy and Preventive Diplomacy", op. cit., p. 507.

[81] For a sympathetic statement of this perspective see Charles Krauthammer (2001), "The New Unilateralism", *The Washington Post*, 8 June, p. A29.

[82] George W. Bush to ABC News, 23 January 2000, quoted in Adam Garfinkle (2001), "Strategy and Preventive Diplomacy", op. cit., p. 503. For supporting

advisors seemed immovable on the issue, their position echoing the sentiment expressed elsewhere that it was not the American role to prevent each tragedy (nor was it capable of doing so) and that American national interest (albeit narrowly construed) should be the basis of decision-making.[83]

Echoing and responding to the policies and events of his father's administration,[84] Bush's position was that America's objectives should be conditioned by two considerations; to avoid being bogged down in "nation-building" ("the Vietnam syndrome") and to avoid taking casualties as the foremost goal (the "zero casualties syndrome"). Humanitarian intervention, influential columnist Charles Krauthammer argued, would clearly transgress both of these goals.[85] Only later were events in Iraq to reflect how far George W. Bush reversed course on both of these issues.

American commitment to the development of the norm of preventive intervention therefore stalled. Within the White House, however, alternative views were being contested that concurred with the UN and the Clinton Administration's view that sovereignty was conditional.[86]

---

evidence see Condoleezza Rice (2000), "Campaign 2000: Promoting the National Interest", *Foreign Affairs*, January/February, 45–62.

[83] For an expression of this position see, for example, Christopher Layne (1995), "Minding Our own Business: The Case for American Non-Participation in International Peacekeeping/Peacemaking Operations", in Donald C. F. Daniel and Bradd C. Hayes (eds), *Beyond Traditional Peacekeeping*, op. cit., pp. 87–8.

[84] George W. Bush had wanted to avoid problems when initially engaging in Somalia, driven to act by a humanitarian impulse but keen to avoid the suggestion that Americans were there either to govern or to assist in forming a new government. See William Odom (2001), "Intervention for the Long Run", op. cit., pp. 48–9; Thomas G. Weiss (1999), "Principles, Politics, and Humanitarian Action", op. cit., p. 51.

[85] William Odom (2001), Intervention for the Long Run", op. cit., pp. 48–9.

[86] The first doctrine, *of integration*, was articulated by Richard Haass, who then held the post of director of the Policy Planning Staff at the US State Department. Haass dramatically outlined his views in a speech before the Foreign Policy Association. These were reflective of an imperial notion of America's role in the world. Haass spoke of the paucity of, and confusion about, both the goals and the instruments of policy. This confusion, he suggested, engulfs the way in which Americans respond to a series of transnational threats, including mass destruction, terrorism, infectious diseases, and environmental degradation. In the aftermath of September 11th, according to Haass, there was a need to develop a new doctrine that fused the "transnational and the traditional" and to provide a coherence and rationale for addressing a series of threatening situations across Latin America, Asia, and the Middle East.

Neoconservatives in the Bush White House advocated the doctrine of *preemptive* intervention (often, confusingly, referred to interchangeably as "preventive intervention" by White House staff and military advisors).[87] This variant distrusted multilateralism, regarded cooperative security as an attack on American sovereignty, and focused on the use of power for the narrowly defined purpose of national security. Military force should be used by the US quickly and at a moderate cost, consistent with supposedly historical (if in fact an inaccurate account of) American behavior.[88] The "neocons" regarded Colin Powell, the Secretary of State, as the epitome of multilateralism and seemed to be gaining the upper hand in their advocacy of a unilateral position, a trend that accelerated as a result of the events of September 11th.

All of these expressed principles and goals were subsequently belied, of course, by events in Afghanistan and Iraq. September 11th was emblematic in demonstrating that the US cannot avoid engagement. It is how the US engages the rest of the world, rather than *whether* it engages, that is key. Bush's version of the "culture of prevention" was signaled early in speaking of a possible terrorist attack, when he stated that: "If we wait for threats to fully materialize, we will have waited too long."[89]

President Bush released a revised edition of the *National Security Strategy* (NSS) on 16 March 2006. It asserted America's right to use preemptive force against terrorists and their sponsors. Notably, the 2006 conceptualization of preemptive strikes differed from the 2002 version in that it introduced a new organizing principle into American strategic doctrine – that America was "in the early years of a long struggle" in which preemptive strikes are a necessary American foreign policy tool.

While multilateralism should be encouraged to deal with threats to US security, the NSS clearly stated that: "if necessary however, under long-standing principle of self defense, we do not rule out the use of force before attacks occur, even if uncertainty remains as to the time

---

[87] In effect, there appeared to be little operational distinction in the employment of the two terms by the Bush Administration. For the purpose of clarity, however, I use the terms distinctly.

[88] William Odom (2001), "Intervention for the Long Run", op. cit., p. 48.

[89] George W. Bush (2002), "President Bush Delivers Graduation Speech at West Point", *United States Military Academy*, 1 June, http://georgewbush-whitehouse. archives.gov/news/releases/2002/06/20020601–3.html

and place of the enemy's attack."[90] The main targets of preemptive strikes would be pariah states harboring weapons of mass destruction (WMD) or knowingly providing safe haven to terrorists. The NSS drew no distinction between terrorists and the nations that harbor them. The primary goal was to protect innocent US citizens, not foreign ones.

The intent was twofold – first, to respond to a perceived imminent threat by either foreign governments or the terrorists that they purportedly harbored in order to thwart attacks against Americans, whether they were located on home or foreign soil. Countries that were considered the launching pad for terrorists were to be held culpable and could not claim immunity from hostile intervention on the grounds of sovereignty. Second, and the more extended intention of the doctrine of preemptive intervention, was to derail the efforts of foreign governments to develop new technologies to create nuclear, biological, or chemical weapons that could hold the United States strategically and seemingly permanently at bay. "Rogue states" with a nuclear bomb presented the United States with a nightmare scenario; the possibility that such countries could be used as terrorist bases and could develop WMDs, their safety guaranteed by their hosts' capacity to offer a devastating, military response.

The effect was to further dilute the concept of sovereignty. Preemptive action on the basis of a "clear and present danger" was not an innovation. Arab troops massing on the border to attack Israel in 1967 had prompted an Israeli countermeasure and the notion had gained both legitimacy and currency. It was invoked by the Bush administration, with far less clarity as to the threat, indiscriminately across the globe and into the future in order to address the concern that some countries might generate an unassailable reprisal capability that might put them beyond America's capacity to intervene. The Bush doctrine of "clear and present danger" thereby came to include the concept of the "potentially materializing danger." These accusations when applied to Iraq – that it was a haven for terrorists, that it was within striking distance of securing a military capability that would protect it from US incursion, and that it could soon pose a possible future threat to US security at home – resonated with the American public and gave the

---

[90] See (2006) "National Security Strategy of the United States of America", *White House*, March, p. 23, http://georgewbush-whitehouse.archives.gov/nsc/nss/2006/nss2006.pdf

neoconservatives within the Bush Administration a coherent doctrine upon which to found their claims.

The abandonment of the principle of preventive intervention

It is well known that Colin Powell's speech before the UN Security Council, designed to gain support for US intervention in Iraq in February of 2003, failed.[91] The Bush Administration could not get the doctrine of preemptive intervention institutionalized. Clearly this was a blow to the Bush Administration's legitimacy abroad. Skeptics were able to attack the veracity and capacity of American intelligence, a clamor that grew over time as it became abundantly clear that Iraq had neither weapons of mass destruction nor effective, credible plans to create them.

Yet, arguably, the US was essentially able to recover from the denial of this support and pursue a thinly veiled unilateralist initiative under the guise of the "coalition of the willing" composed of a large British contingent and augmented by symbolic forces from a diverse array of countries. Perhaps the most convincing evidence of this point remains the image of George W. Bush, in response to a claim made by his opponent John Kerry in a presidential debate that the US had pursued a unilateralist policy, offering an almost apologetic admonishment that we should not forget Poland's involvement in the US-led coalition.

What is less discussed is that it signaled more than a blow to the Bush administration's efforts to legitimate American action. Whether advertent or unintended, these actions stymied the prospects for the emergence of a global norm of preventive intervention predicated on humanitarian principles. As mentioned earlier, numerous small states had expressed their anxiety at the prospect of a UN preventive intervention norm built on the principles of humanitarianism. A prospective standing UN army of 10,000 troops would be larger, and in many cases better trained and equipped, than their own. So many governments felt that they risked voting into existence the potential instrument of their own demise. At least, however, there was the prospect of some transparent evidence of any claims against them, the establishment of a judicious adjudication process, and the need for some kind of consensus

---

[91] For a full version of these comments see Colin Powell (2003), "Remarks to the United Nations Security Council", 5 February, http://merln.ndu.edu/MERLN/PFIraq/archive/state/17763.pdf

acknowledging the need for intervention. Further, the UN had a chronicled history and bureaucratic culture of incremental action. The abrogation of the principle of sovereignty was therefore, operationally, not likely to have a pernicious effect on them, reserved instead, they were constantly told, for the most extreme of cases.

The same principle that would abrogate sovereignty in the name of preventive intervention would, however, do the same for preemptive intervention. In contrast, American behavior seemed capricious, narrowly self-interested, and arbitrarily driven by populist and nativist domestic American sentiments, even among some of America's traditional European allies, such as France. Efforts to institutionalize change at the UN along these lines were therefore throttled.

Ironically, having failed in their efforts to locate the purported weapons of mass destruction in Iraq, the Bush Administration subsequently resorted (as a second line of defense for their actions) to justifying the invasion on the basis of humanitarian intervention. As Ken Roth points out, the claim seemed less than credible.

> [T]he United States-led coalition forces justified the invasion of Iraq on a variety of grounds, only one of which–a comparatively minor one–was humanitarian. The Security Council did not approve the invasion, and the Iraqi government, its existence on the line, violently opposed it…To justify the extraordinary remedy of military force for preventive humanitarian purposes, there must be evidence that large-scale slaughter is in preparation and about to begin unless militarily stopped. But no one seriously claimed before the war that the Saddam Hussein government was planning imminent mass killing, and no evidence has emerged that it was.[92]

Nonetheless, in the end, the Bush Administration came full circle in support of the doctrine of intervention, resorting (however incredibly) to the same humanitarian principle as that advocated by the NGOs and Kofi Annan. Only the UN body stood in the way of its institutionalization and acceptance as a global norm.

---

[92] Ken Roth (2004), "War in Iraq: Not a Humanitarian Intervention", *Human Rights Watch World Report 2004*, January, http://www.hrw.org/legacy/wr2k4/3.htm#_Toc58744952

5
Cyberspace, the New Frontier – and the Same Old Multilateralism

Panayotis A. Yannakogeorgos

Speaking at the Newseum, Washington D.C. on Internet Freedom, US Secretary of State Hillary Rodham Clinton said "countries or individuals that engage in cyber attacks should face consequences and international condemnation."[1]

Responding to reporters, Mr. Burton said "As the President has said, he continues to be troubled by the cyber security breach that Google attributes to China. His view, and as he said even in China, he thinks that unfettered Internet access is an important value."[2]

The term "cyberspace" still elicits a sense of fundamental departure from business as usual. Depicted in the popular press as being a metaphor for a medium without geographic boundaries, the dynamic new applications using computer networking technology are the epitome of a global project that, although barely visible, has an extensive geography consisting of terrestrial, maritime, outer space, and electromagnetic elements.[3] The processes of negotiation and bargaining, as well as the endemic politics of cyberspace, are surprisingly familiar.

---

[1] Hillary Rodham Clinton (2010), "Remarks on Internet Freedom", 21 January 2010, http://www.state.gov/secretary/rm/2010/01/135519.htm
[2] White House Briefing Room (2010), "Gaggle by Deputy Press Secretary Bill Burton Aboard Air Force One en route Cleveland, Ohio", 22 January 2010, http://www.whitehouse.gov/the-press-office/gaggle-deputy-press-secretary-bill-burton-aboard-air-force-one-en-route-cleveland-o
[3] Elihu Zimet and Edward Skoudis, "A Graphical Introduction to the Structural Elements of Cyberspace", in *Cyberpower and National Security* (Washington, DC:

For the most part, however, details of the case look like ineffectual multilateralism as usual, as the US strives to lead and others fail to follow. American technological innovation in the development and maintenance of the Internet's backbone is unquestioned. But a global effort to promote regulatory reform, including the inclusion of global stakeholders in the governance of the domain name system (DNS), is a tense political issue closely linked with national cybersecurity. In sum, American "leadership" as first among equals has led to a succession of dead ends.

In this chapter we examine these processes – the competition between multinational corporations, other norm entrepreneurs and the US to dictate the terms of global cybersecurity norms; the efforts to institutionalize them at a global level; and the predictable failures in attempts at enforcement. Ironically – to use some of the jargon of the social sciences – an inability to generate a suitable global norm has only enhanced insecurity for all actors, as has the failure to agree over how to protect a non-excludable global public good. This has therefore led to a negative-sum outcome. In other words, American attempts to lead have resulted in everyone being worse off. Creating the Internet, and policing it, are two very different problems.

Conflict in cyberspace is a growing problem. Russian hacker-networks indirectly linked to the Kremlin opened a devastating cyber-front against Estonia in 2007. During Russia's 2008 war against Georgia, Russian hackers opened a front in cyberspace the night before conventional forces began their operations. The US is not exempt from this problem. Over the years, Chinese-based hacker networks alone have managed to extract 40 terabytes of information critical to US national security.[4] Many military analysts believe cyber defense and attack will be vital to future military efforts. Indeed, according to Lani Kass, director of the Air Force Cyber Task Force, "We are already at war in cyberspace," as both countries and terrorist organizations currently attempt to carry out cyber-attacks on US interests. Kass points out that "Chinese attacks on DOD (Department of Defense) networks are on the upswing,

---

National Defense University Press, 2009), pp. 91–112. See also Aharon Kelerman (1993), *Telecommunications and Geography* (New York: Belhaven Press), p. 14.

[4] Economic and Security Review Commission (2007), *Report to Congress of the U.S.-China Economic and Security Review Community*, November, http://www.uscc.gov/annual_report/2007/report_to_congress.pdf

and China is now the United States' peer competitor in cyberspace."[5] In early 2010 it was revealed that unauthorized users attributed to the Chinese government had hacked into 33 US companies, including Google e-mail accounts belonging to Chinese dissidents. The spat between Washington and Beijing brought into public view the accusations that had commonly stayed behind closed doors, rarely making material for public diplomacy.

Challenges to cyberspace security go beyond preventing the corruption of information systems and the promotion of Internet freedom. Well-executed cyber-attacks are not limited to data theft. Using the same techniques, hackers can inject false information into a system, with a number of serious consequences.[6] Recently, the CIA warned that, "cyber attackers have hacked into the computer systems of utility companies outside the United States and made demands, in at least one case causing a power outage that affected multiple cities."[7] There is circumstantial evidence that Chinese hackers may have been responsible for past power blackouts in the United States, including the notable "Northeast Blackout" of 2003. During this event, over 100 power plants were shut down, in part due to the disruption of communication lines used to manage the power grid. This disruption was attributed to a then circulating computer virus.[8] It has been noted by "one security analyst in the private sector with close ties to the intelligence community... that some senior intelligence officials believe that China played

---

[5] Levon Anderson (2006), "Countering State-Sponsored Cyber Attacks: Who Should Lead?" in Jeffrey L. Groh, David J. Smith, Cynthia E. Ayers and William O. Waddell (eds), *Information as Power: An Anthology of Selected United States Army War College Student Papers* (Carlisle Barracks, PA: US Army War College), pp. 105–122, 106, available online at http://www.csl.army.mil/usacsl/Publications/infoaspowervol2/IAP2%20-%20Section%20Two%20(Anderson).pdf

[6] The threat to the US power grid is tangible. During a DHS exercise, hackers were given the task of breaking into the information system of a power generator. They were able to physically destroy the generators by gaining remote access to those in the SCADA control system. The Aurora vulnerability, as this exploit is labeled, lends credence to the suggestion that the manipulation of computer code can be just as effective in destroying critical infrastructure as a missile would be.

[7] Ellen Nakashima and Steven Mufson (2008), "Hackers Have Attacked Foreign Utilities, CIA Analyst Says", *Washington Post*, 19 January, A04.

[8] Shane Harris (2008), "Chinese Hackers Pose a Clear and Present Danger to U.S. Government and Private-Sector Computer Networks and May be Responsible for Two Major U.S. Power Blackouts", *National Journal Magazine*, 31 May 2008, http://www.nationaljournal.com/njmagazine/cs_20080531_6948.php

a role in the 2003 blackout that is still not fully understood."[9] Further investigation of China's role is impossible due to data limitations.

Responding to any cyber-incident requires being able to attribute the origins of the attack, which is a complex task, and is often impossible if military or intelligence services are involved in the attack. Nationally based efforts are insufficient in ensuring that global cybersecurity is maintained. Collectively, the international community recognizes the dimension of this problem and has, in response, articulated the need for a global norm intended to secure cyberspace. Although the US disagrees, the majority of global stakeholders have identified the ITU as the appropriate institution through which to organize global cybersecurity efforts. Since 2002, there has been a flurry of activity under the auspices of the ITU designed to emphasize the importance of cybersecurity for maintaining the free flow of information and democratic governance structures for the Internet. Furthermore, discussions of the militarization of cyberspace and how to regulate conflict in this domain within the context of global cybersecurity have remained absent from the agenda, in part due to a US focus on cybersecurity as a criminal issue.

Cybersecurity is crucial for the success of the "Information Society" in which e-commerce, e-governance and e-learning can take place in a regulated manner. The negotiation processes of cyberpolitics generally take place at the ITU, the UN General Assembly (UNGA) and the World Summit on the Information Society (WSIS). The UNGA has recognized the importance of cyberspace as an enabling environment for the Information Society, and that international cooperation is required to assure the peaceful use of Information and Communication Technologies (ICT).[10] The WSIS *Declaration of Principles* and the *Plan of Action*, *Tunis Commitment* and the *Tunis Agenda* reaffirm a global willingness to secure the cyber-commons in order to stimulate a digital Information Society. These embryonic global protocols have sought to shift the position from one where the US has complete technical oversight into one that includes non-US representatives. The US, until recently, blocked all such related efforts.

---

[9] Shane Harris (2008), "Chinese Hackers Pose a Clear and Present Danger to U.S. Government and Private-Sector Computer Networks and May be Responsible for Two Major U.S. Power Blackouts", *National Journal Magazine*, 31 May 2008, http://www.nationaljournal.com/njmagazine/cs_20080531_6948.php

[10] UN General Assembly (2002), "Developments in the field of information and telecommunications in the context of international security", *Resolution No. A/RES/56/19, PP7*, 7 January, http://daccess-dds-ny.un.org/doc/UNDOC/GEN/N01/476/28/PDF/N0147628.pdf?OpenElement

After years of maintaining its position, in September 2009, the US National Telecommunications and Information Administration (NTIA), a bureau of the US Department of Commerce, made what appears superficially as a first step towards internationalizing the DNS. The US, however, retains the ability to shut down the Internet because of its command of network technology.[11]

US businesses currently dominate global networks as a result of their research, development, management and production of ICT, which are part of the Internet's core. This command of global network infrastructure reinforces the view that any global movement to internationalize the core technologies of the information revolution is contrary to broad US security interests, thereby leading to friction on other issues related to global cybersecurity between the US and the rest of the world. Thus, while cybersecurity norms are emerging, and are being codified and institutionalized, US support for them is lukewarm – and they are therefore weakly implemented.

Cyberspace is considered a global commonage, much like land, sea, air, and outer space.[12] The basic environmental platform of cyberspace – the electromagnetic spectrum – has existed as long as the other commons. Recent technological progress, however, has resulted in the harnessing of the spectrum's potential to facilitate social, economic,

---

[11] United States Code §606 section 47 (d) *War Powers of the President*, wherein it states: "Upon proclamation by the President that there exists war or a threat of war, or a state of public peril or disaster or other national emergency, or in order to preserve the neutrality of the United States, the President, if he deems it necessary in the interest of national security or defense, may suspend or amend, for such time as he may see fit, the rules and regulations applicable to any or all stations or devices capable of emitting electromagnetic radiations within the jurisdiction of the United States as prescribed by the Commission, and may cause the closing of any station for radio communication, or any device capable of emitting electromagnetic radiations between 10 kilocycles and 100,000 megacycles, which is suitable for use as a navigational aid beyond five miles, and the removal there from of its apparatus and equipment, or he may authorize the use or control of any such station or device and/or its apparatus and equipment, by any department of the Government under such regulations as he may prescribe upon just compensation to the owners."

[12] Greg Rattray, Chris Evans, and Jason Healey, "American Security in the Cyber Commons", in *Contested Commons: The Future of American Power in a Multipolar World*, Abraham M. Denmark and Dr James Mulvenon (eds), Center for a New American Security, 2010, pp. 137–76; Ahmad Kamal (2005), *The Law of Cyber-Space: An Invitation to the Table of Negotiations* (Geneva, Switzerland: United Nations Institute for Training and Research), http://www.un.int/kamal/ thelawofcyberspace/The%20Law%20of%20Cyber-Space.pdf

political, and military activities. Definitions of cyberspace are numerous, and fall into two categories: strategic and metaphorical.

The strategic definition is the one that is parsimonious and coherent, and has the greatest field utility. Arguably, the strategic definition as coined by the US DOD is one that will best serve the global community in international negotiations aiming to govern cyberspace. That is:

> A domain characterized by the use of electronics and the electromagnetic spectrum to store, modify and, exchange data via networked systems and associated physical infrastructure[13]

Overall, this definition may have the greatest analytical utility for the study of how this domain will be governed by a regime of global character. The strategic conceptualization is precise, internally coherent, and parsimonious, thereby offering a greater field utility and contextual range for such a study. De-emphasizing or ignoring the physical character of cyberspace does not contribute to the effort of governing this commonage.

Popular metaphorical definitions of cyberspace argue that cyberspace is nongeographical. Instead, they suggest, it is a highly malleable social construct to which the laws of physics do not apply.[14] Robert Keohane and Joseph Nye have suggested that:

> The contemporary information revolution, however, is inherently global since "cyberspace" is divided on a nongeographical basis. The addresses "edu," "org," and "com" are not geographical.[15]

Such conceptualizations define cyberspace as a social construct outside the realm of physical environment. Keohane and Nye's analysis is particularly problematic because the domain names they mention do have geographical coordinates. The Internet Corporation for Assigned Names and Numbers (ICANN) – a US-based corporation

---

[13] US Department of Defense, *The National Military Strategy for Cyberspace Operations*, November 2006, p. 3.

[14] Martin Libicki (2007), *Conquest in Cyberspace* (New York: Cambridge University Press).

[15] Robert O. Keohane and Joseph S. Nye (1999), "Power and Interdependence in the Information Age", *Democracy.com? Governance in a Networked World* (Hollis, NH: Hollis Publishing Company), pp. 197–214, especially p. 199.

whose servers are located in the US and operated under agreement with the Department of Commerce – is responsible for the administration of top-level domains such as *.com* and *.org*. The physical location of the administration is in fact the crux of the issue in global cybersecurity negotiations.

Technologically, the DNS is the element that makes the Internet user-friendly. It allows the use of Uniform Resource Locators (URLs) to communicate with other machines on the Internet. Instead of having to type in the numeric IP address of a website, a person can simply type what has become a standard address into a web browser in order to connect with the corresponding location.[16] The major domain names, such as ".com" or ".net," are maintained and updated by ICANN. The US therefore sustains (and from every indication clearly wishes to maintain) a critical hold on this technology.

Cybersecurity norm entrepreneurs

The key social actors are generally a function of the issue areas in which they operate. On most issues, however, private sector corporations and representatives of civil or social organizations tend to clash. This is evident in the case of cybersecurity, where corporate interest in control (for the sake of profit) conflicts with the goals of social norm entrepreneurs seeking to use the Internet as a democratizing tool.

Within the ITU, multinational corporations contribute to the formulation of international standards and policies regulating global information flows, including those broadcast over the Internet. The trend of forming public–private partnerships in order to strengthen the critical information infrastructure, and thereby secure cyberspace, rests on the cooperation of private companies with the state. Thus, at first glance it would appear that the most influential actors in any global cyberspace regime would be corporations such as AT&T, CISCO, and Microsoft. Yet, in international telecommunications negotiations, a state and its ICT firms share a symbiotic relationship – evident in the behavior of the state–business relationship in telecommunications meetings at the

---

[16] IP addresses thus reside on DNS databases on root servers that allow the translation of URLs into IP addresses. See Robert E. Molyneux (2003), *The Internet Under the Hood: An Introduction to Network Technologies for Information Professionals* (Westport, CT: Libraries Unlimited), pp. 85–6.

ITU.[17] This has been the case ever since the International Telegraph Union, the ITU's predecessor, was formed in the mid-nineteenth century with the intent of regulating telegraph policies.[18]

Some ICT corporations, such as CISCO or Ros Telecom, having earned the trust of ITU members over time as a result of their ownership of the physical telecommunications infrastructure and their proactive contributions to the ITU's program of work, are viewed as more legitimate actors than civil society representatives.[19] This can be attributed to the practice of the ITU in including such business entities in its program of work. Although they did not have voting rights at the WSIS, some states may have served as the mouthpiece of the businesses headquartered within their borders.

In contrast, global civil society representatives decisively lack the corporate advantage at global conferences because they do not research, develop, and deploy the enabling environment of the Information Society. Rather, they focus on ethical issues, ensuring that policymakers embrace democratic principles in implementing cybersecurity measures. It is notable, however, that (originating with the international negotiations that began at the WSIS) global civil society representatives have emerged as active participants, invited by the United Nations to contribute to the drafting of political statements (such as the outcome documents from the WSIS).

Marc Raboy and Normand Landry provide a comprehensive account of the WSIS process from the perspective of global civil society. Noting that the global media did not give the two summits prime coverage, they emphasize the importance of the WSIS, because it:

> ...has placed the governance of global communication on the world agenda, sparking a long overdue discussion that has, in turn, become

---

[17] For further information on the symbiotic relationship between the US Department of State and MNCs, see Edward A. Comor (1994), "Communication Technology and International Capitalism: The Case of DBS and U.S. Foreign Policy", in Edward A. Comor (ed.), *The Global Political Economy of Communication: Hegemony, Telecommunication and the Information Economy* (New York: St Martin's Press), pp. 83–102.

[18] Jill Hills (2002), *The Struggle for Control of Global Communications: The Formative Century* (Chicago, Ill: University of Illinois Press).

[19] Marc Raboy and Normand Landry (2005), *Civil Society Communication and Global Governance: Issues from the World Summit on the Information Society* (New York: Peter Lang Publishing), p. 26.

the spearhead of a larger re-conceptualization of the manner in which global decisions are made.[20]

Although their work does detail the Summit's structure, it focuses on the participation of global civil society and its interaction with the UN system, nation-states, and the multitude of constituent actors. They acknowledge that states were the predominant actors in negotiations taking place during the preparatory phase leading up to the actual WSIS summits. Raboy and Landry further note that the WSIS representation led to "a UN summit (that) has been given an organizational structure consisting of a number of components which bring together representatives of member states, the private sector, civil society and various UN agencies."[21] It is further noted that "the clearly expressed desire of the Summit organizer to include these actors from the beginning of the preparatory process is something new at the United Nations."[22] Their study however, focuses on civil society actors – the element that had the least overall access and impact on the outcomes of the WSIS process.[23] It appears, therefore, that NGOs had the greater number of participants but, arguably, were the least influential actors.

Indeed, closed and informal intergovernmental consultations during the preparatory phase – leading to the WSIS Geneva and Tunis phases – occurred without non-governmental actors taking a meaningful part in the decision-making process at all, despite constituting the majority of total participants. Members of civil society organizations or business entities did act, however, as advisers to national governments during the process.[24]

In relegating the participation of non-state entities to the sidelines, states effectively monopolized all authoritative decision-making through their voting rights on key decisions and texts during the Summit itself, complicating the process. Raboy and Landry contend that civil society organizations have a lot to contribute and deserve a greater role in the Internet governance debate. They have not yet, however, been trusted with voting privileges.

---

[20] Marc Raboy and Normand Landry (2005), *Civil Society Communication and Global Governance: Issues from the World Summit on the Information Society* (New York: Peter Lang Publishing), p. 1.

[21] Ibid., p. 30.

[22] Ibid.

[23] Ibid., p. 17.

[24] Ibid.

Articulating and institutionalizing a global culture of cybersecurity: the UNGA, ITU, WSIS and beyond

The importance of organizing and expanding the Information Society was recognized early by the UNGA, in that the establishment of a "global culture of cybersecurity" is key in creating a secure environment for the information society. Initiated at the UNGA with its resolution 57/239 in 2003, the processes have now been institutionalized through the global community meeting at the ITU, which is mandated as the main global institution responsible for the global culture of cybersecurity.[25]

At the UNGA, member states declared their awareness that "effective cybersecurity is not merely a matter of government or law enforcement practices, but must be addressed through prevention and supported throughout society."[26] By identifying the provisioning of cybercrime as an activity separate from government or law enforcement, they essentially created a broader cybersecurity framework in which private actors were given the task of preventing cybercrime. The UNGA stated that "technology alone cannot ensure cybersecurity," specifically "in a manner appropriate to their roles, government, business, other organizations, and individual owners and users of information technologies must be aware of relevant cybersecurity risks and preventive measures and must assume responsibility for, and take steps to enhance the security of these information technologies."[27] The trend towards a broad number of actors (including governments) all of whom are responsible for securing ICT and preventing its misuse was therefore established in a manner that relieves them of the primary responsibility for national security in the cyber-domain. Hence, a global cybersecurity norm emphasizes the role of private actors in providing cybersecurity to society writ broadly, rather than signifying their importance in *supporting* government and law enforcement efforts.

A significant component of the resolution in which global cybersecurity norms are read is the annex of resolution 57/239. This specifies nine elements that form the foundation of the global culture of cybersecurity, as summarized in Table 5.1 below.[28]

---

[25] United Nations General Assembly (2003), "Creation of a Global Culture of Cybersecurity", *Resolution No. A/RES/57/239*, 31 January, http://www.itu.int/ITU-D/cyb/cybersecurity/docs/UN_resolution_57_239.pdf

[26] Ibid., Preliminary Paragraph 5.

[27] Ibid., Preliminary Paragraph 7.

[28] Ibid., Operational Paragraph 3.

Table 5.1   Foundations of the global culture of cybersecurity

Element	Intended outcome
Awareness	All Information Society stakeholders, including individuals, should sustain a level of awareness regarding the importance of having secure information systems.
Responsibility	Stakeholders are responsible for securing their own information systems, and reviewing the policies, practices, measures, and procedures pertaining to their own cyberspace.
Response	Timely and cooperative response is achieved with stakeholders sharing information about threats, vulnerabilities, and security incidents in order to facilitate the detection of and response to the misuse of information systems. Cross-border information sharing may be required.
Ethics	The ethical basis of the GCC is founded on utilitarian grounds in that each participant is expected to respect the interests of others and to act or avoid inaction that will harm others.
Democracy	Cybersecurity regimes are guided by democratic principles, identified as the freedom of thoughts and ideas, free flow of information, confidentiality of information and communication, protection of personal information, openness and transparency.
Risk assessment	Periodic broad-based risk assessments of the security implications of technological, physical and human factors, policies, and services should be conducted in order to determine what an appropriate level of risk is, and how best to manage the risk of potential harm to information systems according to a scale based on the importance of information to the information system being assessed.
Security design and implementation	Security should be incorporated during the planning, design, development, operation, and use of an information system.
Security management	It is on the basis of dynamic risk assessment that security management occurs.
Reassessment	Given the dynamic nature of the information insecurity, in order to assure that all the above elements remain relevant, a periodic reassessment of security protocols and procedures is required.

This global culture of cybersecurity grew out of a prior process within the UNGA whereby Resolution 56/19, entitled "Developments in the field of Information and Telecommunications in the Context of International Security," highlighted several key issues pertaining to the Information

Society and the provision of its security in cyberspace. UNGA acknowledged the potential misuse of ICT in ways that will "adversely affect the
security of states in both civil and military fields."[29] Member States were
encouraged to prevent the use of information technology for criminal or
terrorist use while concurrently promoting its peaceful use. In the operational paragraphs of resolution 56/19, the UNGA called on Member States
to support and contribute to multilateral efforts whose task was to identify
and develop appropriate countermeasures to current and future threats to
international security resulting from the misuse of information technology. Cybersecurity solutions, it noted, must be "consistent with the need
to preserve the free flow of information"[30] – a challenging objective, since
security measures tend to impede the flow of information.[31]

In 2004, the UNGA addressed the importance of protecting critical
information infrastructures,[32] identified as "those used for, inter alia, the
generation, transmission and distribution of energy, air and maritime
transport, banking and financial services, e-commerce, water supply,
food distribution and public health – and the critical information infrastructures that increasingly interconnect and affect their operations."[33]
This included the DNS. Eleven elements for the enhancement of the
protection of critical information infrastructures were proposed in the
annex of this resolution. First, it was urged that emergency warning networks should be established to identify and warn of cyber-vulnerabilities,
threats, and incidents. Secondly, general awareness must be raised in
order to facilitate an understanding of the role that stakeholders play in
developing critical infrastructures. The resolution further encouraged

---

[29] Op. cit., Preliminary paragraph 8.

[30] Ibid., Operational paragraph 1.

[31] For example, when a firewall is installed on a computer network and set to
the most secure setting, the firewall makes the use of Internet applications more
difficult than beforehand. Free flow of information is preserved when the firewall is adjusted to fit the patterns of an individual's usage. Analogous problems
exist when implementing cybersecurity solutions on a larger scale. A corporate
firewall may block applications that are useful for some users, but present a
security risk for most users. However, if firewalls and anti-virus software are too
expensive, an attacker can exploit the lack of security and likewise prevent the
free flow of information. Both these examples indicate pitfalls of holding the
private sector and individuals responsible for cybersecurity.

[32] United Nations General Assembly (2003), "Creation of a global culture
of cybersecurity and the protection of critical information infrastructures",
Resolution No. A/RES/59/199, 30 January, http://www.itu.int/ITU-D/cyb/cyberse-
curity/docs/UN_resolution_58_199.pdf

[33] Ibid., Preliminary paragraph 3.

the formation of partnerships between private and public stakeholders to better prevent, investigate, and respond to threats on critical information infrastructures. Communication networks, for example, should be in place and regularly tested to assure their effective operation during a crisis situation. Correspondingly, the resolution urged States to develop adequate domestic laws and policies allowing for the investigation and prosecution of cybercrimes, as well as training personnel who would enable the investigation and prosecution of such abuses. Moreover, the annex noted that states are primarily responsible for identifying the perpetrators of an attack against critical information infrastructure, and the sharing of this information with affected states. Appropriate international cooperation should thus accord with properly crafted domestic laws to assure that critical information infrastructures are secure.

As mandated by the ITU, the WSIS and the Global Cybersecurity Agenda are the main summits where governments and all interested stakeholders debate issues and determine the objectives and principles surrounding the structure of the Global Information Society. Although the WSIS Summits in Geneva and Tunis received limited media attention, the foundational work occurring in the preparatory committees and other conferences related to the WSIS received even less attention. These conferences were the venues where the foundation for a common understanding of the Information Society at the WSIS was laid out.[34] The preparatory phases (hereafter PrepCom) were the most important, because this is where states voted on items on the Summit's agenda, on the processes and procedures of the Summit, and where the wording of the final outcome documents was finalized and presented at the Summit itself during interaction with global civil society representatives. Regional meetings were held to supplement the work during the PrepCom phases, and assure that each region could design and define its own needs and expectations regarding the Information Society.[35] By the end of the process, when the Summit's two phases commenced, the international community was willing to finalize the principles of the Information Society.

In 2002, during the lead-up preparatory phase of the WSIS, the United Nations Economic Commission for Europe reported on the challenges to the WSIS process. It noted that complexities and con-

---

[34] Marc Raboy and Normand Landry (2005), *Civil Society Communication and Global Governance: Issues from the World Summit on the Information Society*, op. cit., p. 19.
[35] Ibid., p. 20.

troversies arising from the process were not only due to technological development issues, but were also because of several key questions, including the issue of security.[36] Furthermore, it was then noted that "there is a growing sense of fatigue with global conferences and processes, and that there is no global architecture for international dialogue on knowledge of information technologies" including the Internet.[37] The WSIS emerged out of such concerns at the behest of the ITU, the main institution of global governance given the task of organizing the WSIS. A High-level Summit Organizing Committee was formed to "coordinate the efforts of the United Nations family in the preparation, organization and holding of WSIS."[38] The ITU Secretary-General served as the committee chairman and as the WSIS Executive Secretary; the ITU was led by senior ITU officials and was given the task of ensuring that the contributions of the actors participating in various conferences were comprehensively merged with the contributions from the Preparatory Committee and regional meetings, in a consensus document that would serve as the basis for the *Declaration of Principles* and *Plan of Action* of the WSIS.[39]

The Geneva Summit of the WSIS, held between 10 and 12 December 2003, gave all the relevant parties the opportunity to initiate a formal process of developing the Information Society based on trust and security. The priorities established by UNGA resolutions, notably 56/121 and 57/239, were discussed. The meeting resulted in the drafting and adoption of the *Declaration of Principles* and *Plan of Action* by "the representatives of the peoples of the world."[40] The *Declaration of Principles* decrees that the Information Society should be organized around:

> [A] common desire and commitment to build a people-centered, inclusive and development oriented Information Society, where everyone can create, access, utilize and share information and knowledge,

---

[36] United Nations Economic Commission for Europe (2002), *The Information Society in Europe and North America: Contributions from the UNECE to the WSIS Prep Com 2*, December, p. 3.

[37] Ibid.

[38] World Summit on the Information Society, *Roles of HLSOC, WSIS-ES, Host country Executive Secretariats, and ITU*, http://www.itu.int/wsis/basic/roles.html

[39] Marc Raboy and Normand Landry (2005), *Civil Society Communication and Global Governance: Issues from the World Summit on the Information Society*, op. cit., p. 21.

[40] World Summit on the Information Society (2003), *Declaration of Principles* WSIS-03/GENEVA/DOC/0004, Paragraph 1.

enabling individuals, communities and peoples to achieve their full potential in promoting sustainable development and improving their quality of life, premised on the purposes and principles of the Charter of the United Nations and respecting fully and upholding the Universal Declaration of Human Rights.[41]

The Information Society should, therefore, be based on democratic principles, according to which individuals would be guaranteed the right to freely create and transmit information and knowledge, as long as their objectives did not conflict with the principles of the *UN Charter* and the *Universal Declaration of Human Rights*.

Security forms the cornerstone of the Information Society. Paragraph Five of the *Geneva Declaration* states that users must have confidence in the Information Society. A framework of trust that includes "information security and network security, authentication, privacy and consumer protection" must be established to assure that data, privacy, access, and trade are protected.[42] Additionally, the WSIS recommends that appropriate actions at the national and international levels should be taken to secure cyberspace, so that ICT is not used "for purposes that are inconsistent with the objectives of maintaining international stability and security, and may adversely affect the integrity of the infrastructure within states."[43] In this regard, the *Declaration of Principles* calls for all interested stakeholders to have a strong commitment to the concept of "digital solidarity" with governments at the national and international level, and recognizes that new forms of partnership will be required in order to meet the goals set out in the *Declaration*.

In addition to the *Declaration of Principles*, participants at the Geneva session of the WSIS agreed upon a negotiated *Plan of Action* for achieving the goals set out. In section C5.12, the WSIS defined what actions must be taken to fulfill the objectives contained in Paragraph Five of the *Declaration of Principles*.[44] Reiterating the importance of security and its role in developing user confidence in ICT, the *Plan of Action* recommended that private–public partnerships address the prevention of, the

---

[41] World Summit on the Information Society (2003), *Declaration of Principles WSIS-03/GENEVA/DOC/0004*, Paragraph 1.

[42] Ibid., Paragraph 5.35.

[43] Ibid., Paragraph 5.36.

[44] World Summit on the Information Society (2003), *Plan of Action WSIS-03/GENEVA/DOC/0005*, Section C5.12.

detection of, and the response to cybercrime and other forms of ICT misuse. For their role, governments were mandated with the task of developing guidelines taking into account the ongoing efforts in these areas.

The main outcome of the second WSIS summit on the Information Society was the adoption of the *Tunis Commitment* and the *Tunis Agenda for the Information Society*. Significantly, the *Tunis Agenda* called on the Information Society to establish the "requisite legitimacy of its governance, based on the full participation of all stakeholders, from both developed and developing countries, within their respective roles and responsibilities."[45] Internet governance was there defined as "the development and application by government, the private sector and civil society, in their respective roles, of shared principles, norms, rules, decision-making procedures, and programs that shape the evolution and use of the Internet."[46] It did not clearly define the role of each stakeholder, governments in particular, in Internet governance, thereby allowing private actors a strong role in governing the Internet. Given that the core operators of the Internet are US based, the global consensus is that this US control is a threat to their own cybersecurity.

Furthermore, the *Tunis Agenda* stated that "the existing arrangements for Internet governance have worked effectively to make the Internet the highly robust, dynamic and geographically diverse medium that it is today, with the private sector taking the lead in day-to-day operations, and with innovation and value creation at the edges."[47] It stressed that there is:

[A] need for enhanced cooperation in the future, to enable governments, on an equal footing, to carry out their roles and responsibilities, in international public policy issues pertaining to the Internet, but not in the day-to-day technical and operational matters, that do not impact on international public policy issues.[48]

The private sector's role is therefore clearly defined by the *Tunis Agenda* as being responsible for the day-to-day operations of the Internet, and governments should play no role in these technical and operational

---

[45] World Summit on the Information Society (2003), *Tunis Agenda for the Information Society*, WSIS-05/TUNIS/DOC/6, Paragraph 31.

[46] Ibid.

[47] Ibid., Paragraph 55.

[48] Ibid., Paragraph 69.

aspects. The governmental role remains unclear, other than that it should be significant in policymaking. As will be shown in the diplomatic dispatches (in the next section), the language relating to cybercrime and Internet governance was shaped by the US insistence that ICANN was, and continues to be, a suitable mechanism regulating the day-to-day operations of the Internet. As the Internet expanded globally, the international community has come to disagree with the US position, maintaining that Internet governance mechanisms should be internationalized, a move ICANN itself made in late 2009.

The US response in the process of negotiation

Despite the domestic rhetoric within the United States, the US avoids any discussion of international law to regulate the militarization of cyberspace, focusing instead on issues of cybercrime, bridging the digital divide, promoting public–private partnerships, market liberalization, and the creation of independent regulatory agencies.[49] The US position on the freedom of information flows was apparent in its suggestions that issues such as content regulation should not be discussed since it "infringes on the right of all to freedom of expression as set forth in Article 19 of the Universal Declaration of Human Rights."[50] The focus of the EU was on clusters of e-government, e-learning and e-inclusion, and within each cluster it was "implied that security, privacy protection, and general trust are underlying conditions in order to build people's confidence on the information society."[51] Russia raised challenges to the Information Society, such as "national sovereignty and security in the information space, non-interference in internal affairs and freedom of information, and the safeguarding of human rights in global

---

[49] World Summit on the Information Society (2005), *United States Contribution document WSIS/PC-1/CONTR/9-E*, http://www.itu.int/dms_pub/itu-s/md/02/wsispc1/c/S02-WSISPC1-C-0009!!MSW-E.doc, Annex 2. It should be noted here that the US is beginning to alter its public position on issues pertaining to intra-state cyberwar. Nonetheless, fundamental differences exist between the US and Russia and resolution will be a long process. For more information on issue this see: John Markof and Andrew E. Kramer, "In Shift, US Talks to Russia on Internet Security" *The New York Times*, December 12, 2009, p.A1.

[50] Ibid.

[51] World Summit on the Information Society, *Denmark, speech on behalf of the European Union*, http://www.itu.int/wsis/docs/pc1/statements_general/denmark.doc. See also World Summit on the Information Society, *Denmark, speech on behalf of the European Union Content and Themes for the World Summit on the Information Society (WSIS)*.

telecommunication."[52] Likewise, the PRC identified security as the key to information and communications networks, arguing that:

> Communications security is directly related to the risks and losses in communications. Security guarantees may improve consumer confidence and further promote the applications of infocom technologies and networks. Security of infocom networks involves technologies as well as laws and regulations and requires international cooperation.[53]

Fighting cybercrime, they suggested, is of utmost importance in ensuring the security of communications networks. International organizations and mechanisms were essential for this purpose. They identified research and development initiatives intended to develop security technologies and "strengthening control of network security and protection of communications networks through application of laws and regulations" as areas the Summit should consider.[54] However, one Council of Europe (COE) transmission note to heads of missions to the COE described the PRC's views as "being inclined to show understanding for views expressed by developing countries."[55]

All parties supported initiatives attempting to wrestle technical control of the DNS away from the US. The EU, Russia, China and the developing world prioritized security concerns, whereas the US appeared to place the emphasis on issues pertaining to the development of the Information Society. As the WSIS process progressed, the preliminary remarks on the importance of securing cyberspace and governing the Internet were soon supplanted by the US resistance to the internationalization of the ICANN. They refused to delegate command of the network, not allowing its control of day-to-day operations

---

[52] World Summit on the Information Society (2003), *First Deputy Minister of the Russian Federation for Communications and Informatization of the Preparatory Committee for the World Summit on the Information Society, Opening Ceremony*, 10 December.

[53] World Summit on the Information Society (2002), *Statement by Chinese Ambassador Sha Zukang at the First Meeting of the Intergovernmental Preparatory Committee of the World Summit on the Information Society*, 1 July, http://www.itu.int/wsis/docs/pc1/statements_general/china.doc

[54] Ibid.

[55] Council of the European Union General Secretariat (2002), "Main Items raised at the Working Lunch at Ambassador Level between the Troika and China", 5 December, p. 3.

of the domain name system to be handed over to a more diverse group of actors possibly opposed to US interests.

The Pan-European Regional Conference, hosted by Romania on 7–9 November 2002, intended to help the Western European and Others Group (including the United States and Russia) coordinate member states' participation in the WSIS. Preparatory meetings took place leading up to the November meeting. Although other regional conferences took place prior to the second PrepCom, the Pan-European conference included a diverse number of participants from 55 countries.[56] The main outcome of the Pan-European conference was the *Final Declaration of the Pan European Regional Conference*. Principle Six eventually read:

> To realize fully the benefits of ICTs, networks and information systems should be sufficiently robust to prevent, detect and to respond appropriately to security incidents. However, effective security of information systems is not merely a matter of government and law enforcement practices, nor of technology. A global culture of cybersecurity needs to be developed – security must be addressed through prevention and supported throughout society, and be consistent with the need to preserve free flow of information. ICTs can potentially be used for purposes that are inconsistent with the objectives of maintaining international stability and security and may adversely affect the integrity of the infrastructure within States, to the detriment of their security in both civil and military fields, as well as in relation to the functioning of their economies. It is also necessary to prevent the use of information resources or technologies for criminal or terrorist purposes. In order to build confidence and security in the use of ICTs, Governments should promote awareness in their societies of cyber security risks and seek to strengthen international co-operation, including with the private sector.[57]

This language echoed the UNGA resolutions on the establishment of a global culture of cybersecurity, that would not expand beyond

---

[56] Other regional conferences held in preparation of the second PrepCom were held in Bamako for Africa (28–30 May 2002), Tokyo for Asia (13–15 January 2002), Santo Domingo for Latin America and Caribbean countries (29–31 January 2003), and Cairo for Middle Eastern countries (June 2003).

[57] World Summit on the Information Society (2002), *Final Declaration of the Pan European Regional Conference*, 7–9 November, http://www.itu.int/dms_pub/itu-s/md/03/wsispc2/doc/S03-WSISPC2-DOC-0005!!PDF-E.pdf

preexisting diplomatic language. The text of Principle Six is straight-forward – effective security of information systems extends beyond the responsibility of government and law enforcement practices.[58] The militarization of cyberspace, however, was not included as an item of concern.

The process of negotiating this final draft, however, was conflict-ual. Comparing the final version of Principle Six with the revisions suggested by the US, EU and Russia indicates that the US preferred to exclude its mention. To safeguard their position, the US led a coalition against the Russians, who were concerned with the issue of cyberspace militarization. The contrast is informative. The Russians proposed the following language for Principle Six:

> Development of ICTs should take into account new challenges and threats in the field of security. There is concern that ICTs can poten-tially be used for purposes that are inconsistent with the objectives of maintaining international stability and security and may adversely affect the security of states in both civil and military fields... It is also considered necessary to prevent the use of information resources or technologies for criminal or terrorist purposes... This suggests the need for a greater awareness and understanding of security issues and the need to develop a "culture of security"... One key element of protection of ICTs against illegal use is the strengthening of informa-tion and communication networks security.[59]

The US disagreed with some of the Russians' language, and offered the following revisions:

> Development of ICTs should take into account <u>the need to defend against the wide variety and increasing number of threats to infor-mation systems and networks</u> ~~offer new challenges and threats in the field of security. There is concern that~~ ICTs can potentially be used for purposes that are inconsistent with the objectives of maintain-ing international stability and security and may adversely affect the <u>infrastructure of states to the detriment of their security in</u> ~~security of states in~~ both civil and military fields... It is also considered neces-

---

[58] World Summit on the Information Society (2002), *Final Declaration of the Pan European Regional Conference*, 7–9 November, http://www.itu.int/dms_pub/itu-s/md/03/wsispc2/doc/S03-WSISPC2-DOC-0005!!PDF-E.pdf
[59] Russian Federation proposal for the text of Principle VI.

sary to prevent the use of information resources or technologies for criminal or terrorist purposes...This suggests the need for a greater awareness and understanding of security issues and the need to develop a "culture of security"...One key element of protection of ICTs against <u>unauthorized</u> ~~illegal~~ use is the strengthening of information and communication networks security.[60]

The US revisions were guided by the global norms set out in the UNGA resolution on the *Global Culture of Cybersecurity*, which the US also wanted the EU to reflect in its declaration on Principle Six.[61] Furthermore, the US argued that the language the Russians proposed was "too narrow" and not inclusive of the wide variety of threats to computer systems,[62] focusing on the security of civil and military cyber *infrastructures* of states. The securitization of the issue was thus diluted. The US maintained that its proposed language more precisely reflected the true nature of the threat – suggesting that the US believed, as a core operator of the global cyber-infrastructure, it better understood the nature of the problem. Furthermore, the removal of the word *illegal*, and replacement with the word *unauthorized*, was an attempt to avoid the inclusion of language that would challenge any US intelligence or military activities in cyberspace as illegal. The word *unauthorized*, rather, implies that the US is simply acting without the authority of the operator of an information system. Much open source documentation provides evidence that the US successfully uses cyberspace as a medium for espionage, targeting several countries, including Russia. Branding such activity as "illegal" would therefore put both the US government and business entities cooperating with US intelligence in such operations at risk. One factor, therefore, clearly motivating the US in its refusal to accept language constraining state behavior in cyberspace was its ability to collect information traveling through network infrastructures created by CISCO Systems, IDT, and Microsoft – US-based multinational corporations with close ties to the intelligence community.[63]

---

[60] United States Revision to the Russian Proposal. Markings duplicated here as they appear on the original document.
[61] US comments on the Russian text for Principle VI, received October 29.
[62] Ibid.
[63] James Bamford (2009), *The Shadow Factory: The Ultra-Secret NSA from 9/11 to the Eavesdropping on America* (New York, Anchor Books, 2009).

While noting the importance of private enterprises and civil society to the Information Society, the Economic Commission for Latin America and the Caribbean (ECLAC) countries indicated that states should lead the process.[64] Furthermore, they declared that the strengthening of international cooperation in all aspects of the Information Society was important, given the global nature of the problem.[65] In the field of cybersecurity, consistent with the general framework of the other declarations, the *Bavaro Declaration* noted the importance of the priority issues of:

> Establishing appropriate national legislative frameworks that safeguard the public and general interest and intellectual property and that foster electronic communications and transactions. Protection from civil and criminal offences ("cybercrime"), settlement and clearance issues, network security and assurance of the confidentiality of personal information are essential in order to build trust in information networks. Multilateral, transparent and democratic Internet governance should form part of this effort, taking into account the needs of the public and private sectors, as well as those of civil society.[66]

Latin America, led by Brazil, implicitly criticized the US dominance of ICANN with the inclusion of language emphasizing the importance of making Internet governance mechanisms transparent and open to more actors, as a critical component of securing cyberspace. Throughout the ensuing WSIS process, and continuing in other forums discussing Internet governance and global cybersecurity, Brazil has continued to be a vocal opponent to the US position on ICANN. In the period immediately prior to PrepCom 2 in Geneva, in February 2003, the WSIS President suggested that a legally binding *Charter for the Information Society* be instituted in the Tunis phase – an idea attractive to the representatives. However, it was made clear that "a legally binding document

---

[64] World Summit on the Information Society (2003), *Bavaro Declaration*, Paragraph 1.h, http://www.itu.int/dms_pub/itu-s/md/03/wsispc2/doc/S03-WSISPC2-DOC-0007!!PDF-E.pdf

[65] World Summit on the Information Society Asia-Pacific Regional Conference, *The Tokyo Declaration- The Asia-Pacific Perspective to the WSIS*, Paragraph 1.i, p. 3.

[66] World Summit on the Information Society (2003), *Bavaro Declaration*, op. cit., Paragraph 2.g.

would be a non-starter",[67] reflective of a US hesitancy to adopt a formal body of international law governing the Information Society and cyberspace.

The main objective of PrepCom-2 was participant agreement on the substance of the text of the Geneva *Declaration* and *Plan of Action*. While disagreement prevailed, participants did compile a draft declaration of principles and plan of action based on input from the regional conferences:

> Recognizing that confidence, trust and security are essential to the full functioning of the Information Society, guarantees should be provided to users of media, communication and information networks against cybercrime and child pornography as well as protection of privacy and confidentiality.[68]

As a result of slow momentum during PrepCom-2, the WSIS called for an intercessional meeting, subsequently held in Paris from 15 to 18 July 2003. This meeting was called to discuss the *Plan of Action* in order to align it with the text of the draft *Declaration of Principles*.[69] The deliberations of the ad hoc group dealing with confidence and security issues of the Information Society noted that the US, Brazil, Iran, and India agreed on the part of the draft text prepared by the EU. Russia, however, insisted on the inclusion of language on the security of civil and military cyber-infrastructures, and on the inclusion of clauses on cybercrime and terrorism. Others, however, rejected these clauses.[70] Furthermore, other areas of controversy arose during ad hoc committee discussions on Internet governance. Although there was general agreement on the role of the private sector (mainly ICANN) in governing the Internet, some countries, including China, argued for the transformation of this Internet governance mechanism from a private entity to an international governance mechanism.[71] The US strongly opposed this position.

---

[67] World Summit on Information Society, Transcript of Ambassadorial meeting in Geneva regarding latest developments on the WSIS process.

[68] World Summit on Information Society (2003), *Report of the Second Meeting of the Preparatory Committee*, 17–28 February, http://www.itu.int/dms_pub/itu-s/md/03/wsispc2/doc/S03-WSISPC2-DOC-0012!R1!PDF-E.pdf, Paragraph B.20.

[69] World Summit on the Information Society (2003), *Note by the President*, 18 July.

[70] Diplomatic note on the theme of the Paris intercessional meeting.

[71] Ibid.

In the lead-up to the intercessional panel, disagreements emerged within the EU delegation regarding how the Internet should be governed. France, in particular, diverged from the common EU stance, arguing that the issues of management of Internet governance, "notably, those concerning the integrity and the coherence of the system (standardization and subsidiarity), as well as the sovereignty of states in their management of national domain names, must be entrusted to an inter-governmental organization"[72] – a view in support of the position that the US should internationalize ICANN.[73] Russia and the US, meanwhile, continued to disagree over the language of the *Draft Declaration of Principles* in the area of building confidence, trust, and security in the use of ICT at the third PrepCom.[74] Although Russia had been isolated in meetings prior to PrepCom-3, over its insistence on the use of language "in both civil and military fields" when referring to cybersecurity threats, the PRC supported Russia on the inclusion of this language in exchange for Russian support on two items – "consistent with the need to preserve the free flow of information" and "in accordance with the legal system of each country" in reference to cybersecurity issues.[75] This language, however, remained unchanged in other drafts prepared during PrepCom-3.[76]

The issue of Internet governance, therefore, proved to be one of the most contentious issues during PrepCom-3. The US insistence that language referring to the coordination of the international management of the Internet should be removed from the draft was the main sticking point on this issue. In paragraph 40, the US objected to language referring to a "technical level" of private sector involvement in the Internet:

> The management of the Internet encompasses both technical and policy issues. The private sector has had and will continue to have

---

[72] Draft Declaration of Principles refined in April 22/23, Paragraph 18.

[73] However, the dispute between France and other EU members was resolved prior to the intercessional mechanism during negotiations at the Deputy Representative level in the Committee of Permanent Representatives (COREPER-1). (Diplomatic dispatch dated 16 May 2003 on the results of the EU Commissions meeting at the level of delegate–expert).

[74] World Summit on the Information Society (2003), *Draft Declaration of Principles WSIS/PC-3/DT/1-E*, 19 September.

[75] Ibid., Paragraph 28.

[76] World Summit on the Information Society (2003), *Draft Declaration of Principles WSIS/PC-3/DT/1(rev.2B)-E*, 26 September, Paragraph 28.

an important role in the development of the Internet <u>at the techni-</u>
<u>cal level.</u>[77]

The US did agree to the addition of a new paragraph (42) in which
"Internet issues of an international nature related to public policies
should be coordinated between government and other interested
parties."[78] However, less developed countries preferred alternative language referring to coordination "through/by appropriate intergovernmental organization under the UN framework" or "as appropriate on
an intergovernmental basis."[79] Thus, it is clear that the US remained
hesitant to relinquish its informal control over ICANN, while other
participants were resolute that ICANN should be transferred to an
intergovernmental organization, preferably within the UN framework. In a second draft prepared during PrepCom-3, an alternative
paragraph 40 was introduced, which included language regarding the
important role the private sector should play at "the technical and
commercial levels."[80] With only a few months until the WSIS's main
event in Geneva, the international community continued to wrangle
over the text of the document in an effort to bridge the North–South
divide, including the issue of US dominance over ICANN.[81]

The second phase of the WSIS focused on the practical issues of
implementing the *Geneva Plan of Action*, addressing two significant
open questions that remained unanswered after the Geneva phase of
the WSIS. These questions centered on how the Internet was to be governed, and how the *Plan of Action* would be financed.[82] Both of these
were major areas of contention between North and South. To resolve
them, the UN Secretary General established two working groups. In
an effort to avoid the pitfalls of intergovernmental negotiations, these

---

[77] World Summit on the Information Society, *Draft Declaration of Principles*, 19
September, op. cit., Paragraph 40.

[78] Ibid., Paragraph 42.

[79] Ibid., Paragraph. 42, Alternatives b and c.

[80] World Summit on the Information Society (2003), *Draft Declaration of
Principles WSIS/PC-3/DT/1(rev.2B)-E*, 26 September, Alternative Paragraph 40.

[81] The main issues of contention were not related to cybersecurity, but rather
to human security and human rights. In an effort to bridge this divide with
Southern concerns, see Office of the United Nations High Commissioner for
Human Rights (2003),"*Background Note on the Information Society and Human
Rights*", October.

[82] European Commission Working Party on Telecommunications and
Information Society (2004), *Preparation of the Transport/Telecommunications and
Energy Council of 1/10* (6423/04 TELECOM 30 DEVGEN 37 CONUN 6).

working groups included multiple stakeholders under the independent auspices of the UN. The working definition and scope of Internet governance was generally agreed to be:

> ...the global coordination of the Internet's Domain Name System, consisting of the technical management of core resources of the Internet, namely domain names and IP addresses, and the root server system. The WGIG [Working Group on Internet Governance] should firstly concentrate on these issues. A second focal point of WGIG's work should be issues with direct impact on the Internet's stability, dependability and robustness, in particular spam.[83]

WGIG deliberations sought to resolve political issues prior to the main Summit meeting in Tunisia. These deliberations contributed largely to the Internet governance section of the *Tunis Commitment* and *Tunis Agenda for the Information Society*.

Prior to the commencement of the WGIG's program of work, the UN's ICT Task Force hosted a Global Forum on Internet Governance in March 2004.[84] At the forum, the clashes dating from the first phase of the WSIS reemerged. Marc Furrer, Director of the Swiss Federal Office of Communications, representing Switzerland at the meeting, noted that the issue of adjusting or replacing ICANN – a system that is working and improving – deflected attention from more important issues related to cybersecurity that were of greater concern to the Information Society.[85] In contrast, Brazilian and South African delegates opposed this argument. Brazilian delegate Maria Luiza Viotti claimed that Internet governance needed to be reformed, since it excluded developing countries, and appeared to be under the ownership of one group of stakeholders.[86] Lyndall Shope-Mafole, Chairperson of South Africa's National Commission, spoke

---

[83] European Commission Working Party on Telecommunications and Information Society (2004), *World Summit on Information Society (WSIS): Internet Governance-Guidelines for Discussions in the WSIS Framework*, 7 October, Paragraph 4.2.

[84] (2004) "U.N. ICT Task Force Global Forum on Internet Governance to be Held in March", http://portal.unesco.org/ci/en/ev.php-URL_ID=14347&URL_DO=DO_PRINTPAGE&URL_SECTION=201.html

[85] United Nations Press Release (2004), "Global Internet Governance System is Working But Needs to Be More Inclusive, U.N. Forum on Internet Governance Told", 26 March, PI/1568, http://www.un.org/News/Press/docs/2004/pi1568.doc.htm

[86] Ibid.

along similar lines, arguing that the legitimacy of ICANN's processes, rather than its functions, was of greatest concern to developing countries.[87] After rigorous talks, it was concluded, on the basis of concerns from the developing world, that ICANN required further reform.

An assessment of the WSIS process at the conclusion of its first phase was presented at a meeting between ITU Secretary General Yoshio Utsumi and EU Heads of Mission.[88] Utsumi stressed the importance of making the current Internet governance structure more democratic, adding that this was more of a technical problem, which had been transformed into a political issue during the Geneva phase of the Summit.[89] His expectation was that all the problems of Internet governance, especially top-level domain names, would not be resolved in Tunisia, and that discussions there should be viewed as part of a longer process.

The EU identified security as an area where horizontal cooperation would be useful in addressing the issues of cybersecurity.[90] It advocated closer global cooperation, while recognizing that many initiatives would require fine-tuning at the local level. The role of the WSIS, as envisioned by the EU, was of raising awareness of the need for effective legislation, international cooperation on enforcement and the need for best technical practices by industry, and user-level awareness of security issues.[91] Finally, the EU suggested that ICANN could improve its performance and structure through a process of internationalizing itself by opening participation to non-American companies and stakeholders.[92]

---

[87] Ibid.

[88] Transmission Note for the Attention of EU Heads of Mission (2004), *WSIS: Information Exchange of Views Between E.U. Heads of Mission and the ITU Secretary General, Mr. Utsumi,* 17 November. See also World Summit on the Information Society, Tunis Phase, 16–18 November (2004), *Letter from Yoshio Utsumi,* 2 June.

[89] Transmission Note for the Attention of EU Heads of Mission (2004), op. cit.

[90] Communication from the Commission to the Council, The European Parliament, The European Economic and Social Committee and the Committee of the Regions (2004), "Toward a Global Partnership in the Information Society: Translating the Geneva Principles into Actions: Commission Proposals for the Second Phase of the World Summit on Information Society (WSIS)", 13 July 2004.

[91] Ibid. Toward a Global Partnership in the Information Society.

[92] Council of the European Union Working Party on Telecommunication and Information Society (2004), *World Summit on Information Society (WSIS): Internet Governance- Guidelines for Discussions in the WSIS Framework,* 7 October, Paragraph 4.4.

The US position at the first PrepCom was indicative of its strategy in dealing with the ICANN issue. In its published comments, the US focused on its efforts to bridge the digital divide, an issue far more important to the developing world than Internet governance.[93] Although cybersecurity was mentioned, it was not within the context of Internet governance. This position starkly contrasted with the position of the EU, which noted its intention to actively contribute to the dialogue on Internet governance as well as issues aiming at bridging the digital divide during the Tunis phase of the WSIS.[94] Thus, the fact that the US refrained from mentioning Internet governance in its position paper is indicative of its attitude toward this issue throughout this and other international discussions and negotiations.

PrepCom-2 took place in February 2005 in Geneva, Switzerland. Between the two PrepComs, Europe continued its trend of working on issues of Internet governance in order to better inform the WGIG. Internal debates included a suggestion by France that:

> The new cooperation model should be based on a combination of the current bottom-up public-private partnership, with a light, fast-reacting and flexible oversight entity. This entity would provide a platform for policy dialogue in the interest of all governments.[95]

A suggestion that a formal entity should be established (implicitly replacing ICANN) went beyond the EU's language, which stuck to the WSIS position of creating a transparent multi-stakeholder framework based on democratic principles. In its final report, the EU argued that existing mechanisms and institutions should not be replaced, but should be built on the current structures of Internet governance, whereby public-policy issues of Internet governance could be dealt with in a multilateral environment.[96]

---

[93] *United States Position on Phase II of the World Summit on the Information Society*, http://www.itu.int/wsis/docs2/pc1/contributions/us.pdf

[94] *Preliminary E.U. Views on the Preparatory Process for the Tunis Phase of the Summit*, http://www.itu.int/wsis/docs2/pc1/contributions/eutext.pdf

[95] Presidency of the Council of the European Union (2005), *World Summit for the Information Society- Guidelines for the Exchange of Views at the Council*, 20 June.

[96] Communication from the Commission to the Council, the European Parliament, the European Economic and Social Committee and the Committee of the Regions (2005), *Towards a Global Partnership in the Information Society: The*

Subsequent to this declaration, the US National Telecommunications and Information Administration (NTIA) issued a statement affirming its position that the US would not relinquish command and control of ICANN and the DNS system. While recognizing that country-level domain names should be controlled at the national level, the US reiterated the principle that:

> ICANN is the appropriate technical manager of the Internet DNS. The United States continues to support the ongoing work of ICANN as the technical manager of the DNS and related technical operations and recognizes the progress it has made to date. The United States will continue to provide oversight so that ICANN maintains its focus and meets its core technical mission.[97]

The statement concluded by emphasizing that the "United States will continue to support market-based approaches and private sector leadership in Internet development broadly."[98] Thus, the US then – as today – refused to relinquish its control of ICANN, and, as part of its negotiating tactic, shifted its attention to the issue of bridging the digital divide.

On 26 June 2008, the High Level Experts Group (HLEG) for the Global Cybersecurity Agenda (GCA) met at ITU headquarters in Geneva to discuss its recommendations for the ITU Secretary General in the group's five work areas. The GCA is important, since the ITU institutionalized and operationalized this concept at the International Multilateral Partnership against Cyber Threats (IMPACT) hosted in Cyberjaya, Malaysia.

The working group on legal issues was unable to reach an agreement on the contentious issue of the DNS. The US, Canada, and the corporations based in these countries (i.e., Cisco Systems, AT&T, and Microsoft) contended that the ITU was not mandated to regulate and manage systems such as DNS. They argued that the recommendation that included language specific to DNS and identity management should be omitted from any recommendations submitted to the ITU Secretary General.

Contribution of the European Union to the Second Phase of the World Summit on the Information Society (WSIS), 6 February.

[97] National Telecommunications and Information Administration (2005), *Domain Names: U.S. Principles on the Internet's Domain Name and Addressing System*, 30 June, http://www.ntia.doc.gov/ntiahome/domainname/USDNSprinciples_06302005.htm

[98] Ibid.

Syria, Saudi Arabia, and Brazil opposed this view. They felt that their country-level top-level domain names (ccTLD, e.g., .gr) would not be guaranteed protection, given that ICANN, which is controlled by the US, could delete the ccTLD at any time. Despite the intervention of the ITU Secretary General, who advised meeting participants that they were there in a personal capacity and not as representatives of their respective nation-states, no compromise could be found. In the end, the members agreed to submit their recommendations to the Secretary General via the HLEG Chairman in the form of a "Chairman's report." This report would describe the opposing positions of the two parties.

The remaining points mainly centered on the objections of the US government and US corporate representatives that certain aspects of the recommendations were not part of the ITU's mandate. These elements include the ITU conducting a study of the structure of the Internet, including DNS, and organizing international conferences on cybersecurity. The main response, voiced mainly by Saudi Arabia and Syria, was that, if the ITU's mandate were conservatively interpreted, there should be no HLEG or other cybersecurity talk within ITU, since it is primarily a telecommunications organization. The United States and Canada were constantly reminded that it is the job of Member States, and not HLEG, to review the ITU mandate.

Conclusion

The US currently maintains control of a large percentage of the Internet and other elements of cyberspace. Evolving Internet patterns, however, indicate an incremental decrease in traffic passing through the US.[99] The advanced level of Russian radio-electronic warfare capabilities is clearly an emergent challenge to US national security, partially explaining the US stance at international conferences, where they object to discussions on the use of cyberspace for military or espionage purposes. Decisions have been made on the importance of raising awareness of the cybersecurity policy issue, the need to harmonize domestic laws, and the need for cooperation between private industry and government in securing information infrastructures. The main areas of disagreement are between the US and most of the rest of the world on the issue of Internet governance, specifically as it relates to the expansion of authority of DNS and ICANN to a group of international stakeholders.

---

[99] John Markoff (2008), "Internet traffic begins to bypass the U.S.", *New York Times*, 31 August.

The US objected to this until 2009 on the grounds that the configuration system was highly functional. Even with the apparent shift in this policy, however, the US still retains the technical control that other states maintain breaches their own cybersecurity. Furthermore, the US objects to the inclusion of certain legalistic language, as well as to the idea of drafting an international convention for regulating conflict in cyberspace. Rather than focusing on cyber-weapons, the US focuses on criminal misuse of this domain. The Russians, on the other hand, are eager to bring the world to the negotiating table for a treaty on cyberspace.

Overall, cyber-attacks and cyber-espionage linked to either US, Russian, or Chinese interests will continue their upward trend. As more and more people gain access to advanced ICT and enter the digital Information Society, the consequences of how states direct and respond to cyber-attacks targeting their national critical information infrastructures and other systems are unclear due to the lack of an international law regulating information warfare in cyberspace. US technical control of the global networks, and the Internet in particular, gives it a distinct advantage over other countries, albeit likely a temporary one. Its decade-long reluctance to treat the security concerns of states relating to US control of the domain name system, and hesitation to discuss the military uses of cyberspace, continue to create a sense of cyber-anarchy. This information dominance may have a long-term cost: an international convention for cyberspace addressing the militarization of cyberspace is likely necessary to protect US networks from attacks originating in private-computer networks that are not under US technical control, but, as potential competitors increase their cyber-warfare capabilities, they may no longer be as willing to negotiate as they are today. The short-term cost is more apparent: the self-interested focus of the US position, even if pursued through a multilateral strategy, has stifled the development of a global norm.

6
George W. Bush and the Sponsorship of the Anti-trafficking Norm: A Rare Success Story

> The enactment of the Trafficking Victims Protection Reauthorization Act of 2008 (TVPRA of 2008) strengthened the U.S. Government's criminal statute on forced labor...The act now explicitly provides a detailed explanation of "abuse or threatened abuse of law or legal process," a prohibited means of coercion under both the forced labor and sex trafficking statutes.
>
> The minimum standards in the TVPA call on foreign governments to prohibit all forms of trafficking, to prescribe penalties that are sufficiently stringent to deter the crime and that adequately reflect the heinous nature of the crime, and to vigorously punish offenders convicted of these crimes.
>
> In response to a Congressional mandate, [there are] actions taken by the United Nations (UN), the North Atlantic Treaty Organization (NATO), and the Organization for Security and Cooperation in Europe (OSCE) to prevent trafficking in persons or the exploitation of victims of trafficking.[1]

The words "George W. Bush" and "foreign policy success" are rarely either uttered in the same sentence, or written in the same paragraph. In the aftermath of his presidency, a shrinking ideological circle of

---

[1] Office to Monitor and Combat Trafficking in Persons (2009), "Trafficking in Persons Report 2009", *US Department of State*, pp. 26, 27, 316, http://www.state.gov/documents/organization/123357.pdf

Republicans did focus on the claim that certain aspects of his foreign policy – such as the promotion of democracy in the Middle East – would prove effective and successful in the long term.[2] None, however, was brazen enough to claim that any aspect of Bush's foreign policy was successful during the limited duration of his administration. As discussed in the opening chapters, by no metric could the wars in Iraq or Afghanistan be adjudged to be successful in policy terms, and at the onset of the global financial crisis in 2008 newspaper headlines were dominated by stories of how a reckless US economic policy had wreaked havoc abroad.

Yet, in addition to the acceleration of global flows of money since the collapse of the Soviet Union, other kinds of flows have exponentially grown – one notable example being the flow of humans within and across borders. Compared with arms and money, the media is generally less inclined to report stories of how human capital – which constitutes the materials in the supply-chain for the burgeoning human trafficking industry – has grown, often in proportion to the global recession, and with it unemployment and poverty rates. In this regard, the financial crisis of 2008 proved to be a predictable stimulus for global trade in humans.[3]

Human trafficking is generally regarded as a subcomponent of the more general phenomenon of slavery. Minimal estimates suggest that there were reputedly 27 million slaves globally at the start of the twenty-first century, consisting of adults of both genders as well as children,[4] although UNESCO claims that the number is upwards of an order of a magnitude greater.[5] Variants of slavery include bonded labor, migrant workers, and trafficked individuals (often, although not exclusively,

---

[2] See Paul Wolfowitz interviewed in *Business Week* (2002), "Wolfowitz on Democracy in the Mideast", *Business Week*, 23 December, http://www.businessweek.com/magazine/content/02_51/b3813030.htm

[3] US Department of State (2009), "Financial Crisis and Human Trafficking", *Trafficking in Persons Report 2009*, http://www.state.gov/g/tip/rls/tiprpt/2009/124798.htm

[4] Kevin Bales cited in Christien van den Anker (2004), "Contemporary Slavery, Global Justice and Globalization", in Christien van den Anker (ed.), *The Political Economy of New Slavery* (Basingstoke and New York, NY: Palgrave Macmillan), p. 19.

[5] See UNESCO Brochure (2004) *Struggles Against Slavery: International Year to Commemorate the Struggle against Slavery and its Abolition*, p. 48, http://unesdoc.unesco.org/images/0013/001337/133738e.pdf

for the sex trade).[6] Yet the dominant conceptualization of human trafficking focuses on trafficking of women for sexual exploitation rather than on other forms of trafficking that target women, such as unlicensed mail order bride companies, maid schemes, and illicit domestic servants.[7] In this selective formulation, men and children who work in slave-like conditions, or those from whom organs are harvested, have therefore largely been left out of the human trafficking agenda.[8] This focus has been justified by the claim that 75 percent of all victims of human trafficking are trafficked for sexual exploitation, although this claim is without significant empirical substantiation.[9] The data on illicit human flows is as problematic as it is for finance and arms, based largely on guesstimates using questionable assumptions and contingent on the definition of terms like "smuggling," "trafficking," "forced," and "voluntary." As a result, estimates vary widely, dependent on assumptions underlying the formula used in their calculation.

The popular vision of human trafficking begins with the forced abduction of a woman or child from a village or town somewhere in the Global South, or of a girl responding to an advert promising innocuous employment in the West. Regardless, these popular depictions often end with a girl working in the sex industry. The facts, inevitably, are far more complex. The scope is broader, the means of recruitment more

---

[6] Christien van den Anker (ed.) (2004), *The Political Economy of New Slavery*, op. cit., pp. 25–7. It should be noted that such statistics are not reliable, as is discussed in Clare M. Ribano (2007), "Trafficking in Persons: U.S. Policy Issues for Congress", *CRS Report for Congress* (Washington DC: Congressional Research Service), http://www.fas.org/sgp/crs/misc/RL30545.pdf

[7] Amy O'Neill Richard (2000), *International Trafficking in Women to the United States: A Contemporary Manifestation of Slavery and Organized Crime* (Central Intelligence Agency: Center for the Study of Intelligence), p. 27, https://www.cia.gov/library/center-for-the-study-of-intelligence/csi-publications/books-and-monographs/trafficking.pdf

[8] See, for example, Rachel Williams (2008), "Police raid farms in human trafficking inquiry", *The Guardian*, 19 November, p. 17, http://www.guardian.co.uk/world/2008/nov/19/human-trafficking-lincolnshire. Ian Traynor (2008), "Former war crimes prosecutor alleges Kosovan army harvested organs from Serb prisoners", 12 April, p. 16, http://www.guardian.co.uk/world/2008/apr/12/warcrimes.kosovo. It should be noted that efforts in 2009, including "The Declaration of Istanbul on Organ Trafficking and Transplant Tourism", are slowly putting the issues of non-sexual forms of trafficking on the agenda.

[9] See Office to Monitor and Combat Trafficking in Persons (2005), "UN Commission on the Status of Women Adopts U.S. Human Trafficking Resolution", *US Department of State*, 18 March, http://2001–2009.state.gov/g/tip/rls/fs/2005/43630.htm

varied. Illicit behavior extends beyond criminal private actors to include corrupt and complicit government officials; beyond the sex industry to several other sectors including agriculture, fisheries, and manufacturing; and, of course, beyond women and children to include men. What they all share is an emphasis on the use of force, and a reliance on an illicit process often inconsistent with public mores. Conventions and laws exist but these have historically been more notable for being breached than enforced.

Sponsorship in practice

NGOs, both within and outside the US, have worked effectively to cultivate the anti-trafficking agenda. Such policies enjoy passionate and widespread support from a broad array of civic constituents. Within the US, drawing from the political Left and Right, anti-trafficking lobbies have opposed trafficking on moralistic, criminal, and national-security grounds. Bringing together Feminists and Evangelicals, anti-trafficking is "as American as apple pie."[10]

Outside the US, the anti-trafficking lobby draws just as passionate support from various domestic and transnational NGOs in both the global north and south. Among northern representatives, for example, anti-trafficking efforts are spearheaded by an umbrella organization entitled the Polaris Project.[11] A major, notable counterpart in the Global South is the Global Alliance Against Traffic in Women (GAATW) – another umbrella organization composed of over 90 NGOs primarily based and staffed by local Southern representatives.[12] Each is, therefore, justifiably regarded as representative of global public opinion. Financial support for their campaigns is extensive, flowing from a variety of

---

[10] For a discussion of the evangelical position, see, for example, "World Evangelical Alliance creates human trafficking taskforce", *Christian Today*, 12 August 2009, http://www.christiantoday.com/article/world.evangelical. alliance.creates.human.trafficking.taskforce/23965.htm. As an example of the feminist position, see, Equality Now's commentary on female trafficking in "Campaign Against Sex Tourism/Trafficking", *Equality Now*, http://www.equalitynow.org/english/campaigns/sextourism-trafficking/sextourism-trafficking_en.html. For a discussion of this relationship between these two groups see Alani Price, "Elizabeth Bernstein's 'The Sexual Politics of "New Abolitionism"',: Imagery and Activism in Contemporary Anti-Trafficking", March 2008, http://www.csw.ucla.edu/Newsletter/Mar08/Mar08_price.pdf.
[11] For details visit http://www.polarisproject.org/
[12] For details visit http://www.gaatw.org/

actors, state and non-state alike (and extending to the United Nations as well). Advocates for action can (and do) augment their arguments about the failure of human rights with those that (similarly to their US counterparts) focus on the rhetoric of anti-crime and even, occasionally, global security.[13] It is, in large part, the focus of these civil society actors on sexual exploitation of women and children, both historically and today, which has defined the narrow focus of the anti-trafficking policy agenda.

The product, therefore, is entrepreneurial sponsorship of a norm that appears to be the result of "bottom-up" pressure from stakeholders, not a "top-down" pressure from the United States or other northern governments. It is a norm that has the necessary endorsement from a broad selection of an increasingly supportive civil society needed to establish its legitimacy.

The UN has largely adopted the agenda of these groups, reflected in a series of protocols and conventions that have galvanized action among its members. The UN's solutions have focused on the "Three P" approach: "protection, punishment and prevention."[14] Notably, US policy has not remained impassive in this regard. Rather, the US focus is consistent in sponsoring the position of NGOs, with an emphasis on the sexual exploitation of women and children, being victim-centered and adopting a predictable "zero tolerance" towards trafficking. Just as significantly, from the perspective of the framework offered in the introductory chapters of this book, these US views on trafficking have proven concordant with the efforts to coordinate the problem at the intergovernmental level of the UN. American activity appears *legitimately responsive and reactive* in sponsoring these initiatives rather than *imperialist and proactive*. Enforcement mechanisms designed to counteract resistance have been created and effectively utilized by the US as part of this sponsorship strategy.

All the rudiments for the successful development of a global norm apply, therefore, in the case of anti-trafficking. Norm entrepreneurs, seen as representative of broad swaths of civil society, have propagated the need for action based on an explicit theory of social justice result-

---

[13] For a thorough treatment of the subject of the crime-trafficking nexus, see Richard Friman and Simon Reich (2007), *Human Trafficking, Human Security, and the Balkans* (Pittsburgh, PA: University of Pittsburgh Press).

[14] LeRoy G. Potts Jr (2003), "Global Trafficking in Human Beings: Assessing the Success of the United National Protocol to Prevent Trafficking in Persons", in *The George Washington International Law Review*, 35, 227–49.

ing in widespread support of the evolution of an anti-trafficking norm. These views have been codified in a global organization (notably in the UN). Finally, in tandem, these processes have generated enough support for the anti-trafficking norm to result in effective and legitimate US regulatory policy enforcement on a global basis, through the mechanism of the Department of State's "Trafficking in Persons" report, backed by the threat of sanctions and often insistent on local intervention. Local civil society actors (albeit often implicitly) collaborate with the US by monitoring and publicly lobbying against the governments not in compliance with UN protocols and US standards. While a huge trafficking problem persists, the result has been that, over time, fewer countries abrogate the requirements laid out in the Trafficking in Persons (TIP) report, at least according to the reporting of the metric laid out by the US State Department described below.

Despite the explicit coercive elements adopted by the US, few have complained of the abrogation of national sovereignty, even among the countries that have been the focus of American policymakers. None can – or do – argue that there is a moral or material justification for trafficking, even in the face of resistance. A global norm has taken root.

The outcome of these efforts is, inevitably, not as effective as proponents had hoped. Halting the flow of human trafficking is akin to turning back the tide. Trafficking remains a serious problem and, by whatever measure, trade is booming. I argue, however, that the result is a series of policies that generate popular support and are effective to the extent that the complexities of the problem allow.

The global norm of anti-trafficking

The UN's "Three P" approach is not novel to the post-Cold War period but is, rather, a continuation of efforts that began in the late nineteenth century (although the issue was neglected, like many human rights issues, by the international community between the late 1940s and the 1990s in favor of classical Cold War issues). Indeed, movements that started in the late nineteenth century against trafficking of human beings formed the basis for current strategies designed to combat the problem.

International diplomatic initiatives designed to deal with this issue originated at the London Conference of 1899, when France was selected to coordinate the response to the trafficking of women. The increased visibility of non-European street prostitutes, in part due to advances in transportation technology and new conflicts in Asia, led several entrepreneurial forces in the Victorian era to encourage governments to take action against what they deemed an immoral phenomenon.[15] Then, as now, states were prodded into action by entrepreneurial actors, notably the Anti-Slavery Society, a London-based NGO founded in 1839, historically the most forceful actor in the field of anti-slavery. The diplomatic dialogues that were initiated at the Paris Conference of 1902, and its successor conferences, were intended to harmonize the laws dealing with human traffickers and their victims.[16] Interestingly, the American Social Hygiene Association, rather than a component of the Federal Government, served as the primary US representative at such conferences.[17]

These efforts culminated in the *International Agreement for the Suppression of the White Slave Traffic* (1904), in which the "Three P" approach of protection, punishment, and prevention was apparent in the elements of the treaty. The 1904 protocol included three major components. First, contracting governments and signatories were required to create a new domestic central authority designed to document cases of tracking and identifying victims and criminals with the intent of prosecution. Second, monitoring and surveillance was to be stepped up at all ports of entry as a form of enhanced border control. Finally, assistance, including repatriation where appropriate, was to be provided for sex trafficking victims.[18] Yet the United States did not accede to the Agreement until 1908, in part because it did not want to highlight the concept of a "white slave trade," preferring to deal with the issue through an expansion of its own domestic procedures to deal with the problem.[19]

---

[15] Eileen Scully (2001), "Pre-Cold War Traffic in Sexual Labor and its Foes: Some Contemporary Lessons", in David Kyle and Ray Koslowski (eds), *Global Human Smuggling* (Baltimore, MD: John Hopkins University Press), pp. 83–9.

[16] Alain Corbin (1990), *Women for Hire: Prostitution and Sexuality in France after 1850* (Cambridge, MA: Harvard University Press), pp. 294–5.

[17] Eileen Scully (2001), "Pre-Cold War Traffic in Sexual Labor and its Foes: Some Contemporary Lessons", op. cit., pp. 83–9.

[18] Voluntary compliance with the Agreement by non-signatories was encouraged. The contracting governments were: United Kingdom, Germany, Belgium, Denmark, Spain, France, Italy, Netherlands, Portugal, Russia, Sweden and Norway, and Switzerland.

[19] Eileen Scully (2001), "Pre-Cold War Traffic in Sexual Labor and its Foes: Some Contemporary Lessons", op. cit., p. 295.

Throughout the early part of the twentieth century, spurred along by entrepreneurial actors, the states continued to deal with the issue of sex trafficking in conferences aimed at creating a common global understanding about what the guiding norms for dealing with the issue of trafficking should be. A succession of negotiated treaties followed, including the *International Convention for the Suppression of the White Slave Traffic* (1910), *International Convention for the Suppression of the Traffic in Women and Children* (1921), and the *International Convention for the Suppression of the Traffic in Women of Full Age* (1933). Each of these conventions resulted in a global expansion of the contracting parties beyond Europe.

In the postwar period, signing the *Convention for the Suppression of the Traffic in Persons and of the Exploitation of the Prostitution of Others* was one of the first acts of the newly formed UN. It was intended as an extension of these prior treaties designed to curb human trafficking, stating that the "evil of the traffic in persons for purpose of prostitution are incompatible with the dignity and worth of the human person and endanger the welfare of the individual, the family and the community."[20]

In sum, the early historical focus was on trafficking of women and children for sexual exploitation. The underlying theme was prevention of trafficking, protection of victims, and punishment of the criminals – and was adopted unanimously by the global community as a result of moral entrepreneurs raising awareness of a need to solve a global problem at the state level through international cooperation. Enforcement mechanisms, despite these agreements, remained domestic in character, and – as the slew of protocols might suggest – weak as states sought consensus on their implementation.

The reemergence and institutionalization of the anti-trafficking norm at the UN

As they had done in the late Victorian era of the late nineteenth and early twentieth centuries, northern NGOs associated with the dominant countries effectively led the process of lobbying against human trafficking for the duration of the Cold War. Notably, however, when anti-trafficking reemerged as a top priority on the global policy agenda later in the twentieth century, it was the emergence of

---

[20] See United Nations (1950), "Preamble", *Convention for the Suppression of the Traffic in Persons and of the Exploitation of the Prostitution of Others*, 21 March, http://www2.ohchr.org/english/law/trafficpersons.htm

entrepreneurial forces of a distinctly Southern character, such as the Global Alliance Against the Trafficking of Women (GAATW) in the 1990s, that was important in raising state awareness regarding the problem. Indeed, they joined their northern counterparts in playing a key role in the institutionalization of the norm at the UN. While the US has added material resources to enforce anti-trafficking initiatives, it is NGOs that have generated awareness of the issue, as well as providing victim services in partnership with national governments and corporate supporters.

Both changes to and continuities with the campaign almost a century earlier were evident. The agenda's focus continued – and eventually consolidated in the 1990s – on the issue of sexual slavery of women, even though some claim that "less then half of all trafficking victims are part of the sex trade."[21] But a major difference, as is noted below, has been addition of security and anti-crime to the moral and social justice frameworks established in the previous century.

During the Cold War, the Anti-Slavery Society remained a robust actor in a period when the global policymakers were not focused on dealing with human trafficking.[22] Affiliated with the UN in a consultative status, the Society had as its main objective that the UN should act on the issue by creating a committee to monitor a nation's compliance with international laws that prohibited slavery. It collected and collated much of the evidence used in UN reports on modern-day slavery, and supplemented that work with questionnaires given to national governments. The Society identified efforts by national governments to minimize the extent of the problems in their countries.[23] They published pamphlets citing instances of slavery in at least 26 countries and recruited speakers to speak on behalf of the society at the Human Rights Committee's meeting as their major strategies intended to bring the issue to the attention of the UN. This prompted the UN Human Rights Commission to take up the issue as part of its agenda when deliberating on elements of *International Covenant on Civil and Political Rights*.

---

[21] David A. Feingold (2005), "Human Trafficking", *Foreign Policy*, 150, 26–32.

[22] Paul P. Kennedy (1966), "Group Urging U.N. to Halt Slavery", *New York Times*, 4 December, p. 166, http://select.nytimes.com/gst/abstract.html?res=F10B13FB 3D5812718DDDAD0894DA415B868AF1D3&scp=1&sq=Group%20Urging%20 U.N.%20to%20Halt%20Slavery"&st=cse

[23] Sam Pope Brewer (1966), "Slavery Remains Issue, U.N. Finds", *New York Times*, 17 April, p. 2, http://select.nytimes.com/gst/abstract.html?res=F00E13 FB3A5A117B93C5A8178FD85F428685F9&scp=1&sq=Slavery%20Remains%20 Issue,%20U.N.%20Finds&st=cse

The Society's efforts proved fruitful, as the Covenant was adopted to include language stating: "No one shall be held in slavery; slavery and the slave-trade in all their forms shall be prohibited."[24] However, in March 1967 the Human Rights Commission deferred the issue of the abolition of slavery to the Sub-Commission on Prevention of Discrimination and Protection of Minorities. In the view of the Anti-Slavery Society, this was inadequate, since the Sub-Commission would not deal effectively with the issue, with the accusation that "the members of the commission, in voting, knew that this is what will happen."[25] Thus, without sufficient support from the UN to enforce international norms, the Anti-Slavery Society continued its work of raising awareness about the international community on the issue in the Sub-Commission.

From 1970, through the 1980s, the Society continued to identify cases of slavery around the world.[26] This included appealing for intervention of the then UN Secretary General Kurt Waldheim in the case of two Asian sisters who filed a six million dollar lawsuit in the US against two high-ranking UN officers who had forced the women to work in involuntary servitude.[27] In the early 1980s, there was a renewed push for bringing the issue of slavery and human trafficking to the UN.[28] The Anti-Slavery Society continued its awareness-raising campaign, bringing the existence of 100,000 slaves in Mauritania to the Human Rights Commission's attention. The Commission initiated a local study of the situation in order to verify and expand on the NGO's initial reports.[29]

It was not until the 1990s that the issue of human trafficking became of prime concern to the policy community's agenda. This shift was as

[24] See United Nations (1966), "International Covenant on Civil and Political Rights", *Office of the United Nations High Commissioner on Human Rights*, 16 December, Article 8.
[25] Col. Patrick Montgomery in Thomas J. Hamilton (1967), "U.N. Unit Sends Slavery Issue to Subcommittee; Human Rights Group Asserts Lack of Time Barred Action–Downgrading Seen", *New York Times,* 22 March, p. 6.
[26] New York Times (1972), "Forced Marriages In Zanzibar Studied By U.N. Commission", 9 April, p. 14.
[27] New York Times (1977), "Sisters Bring A Lawsuit Against 2 U.N. Officials", 12 August, p. A4.
[28] See, for example, "Commission on Human Rights resolutions 1982/20" of 10 March 1982; on the question of slavery, 1982/20 of 4 May 1982 and 1983/30 of 26 May 1983; on "The suppression of the traffic in persons and of the exploitation of the prostitution of others", 1988/34 of 27 May 1988 and 1989/74.
[29] Bernard D. Nossiter (1981), "U.N. Gets a Report On African Slaves", *New York Times*, 26 August, p. A11, http://www.nytimes.com/1981/08/26/world/un-gets-a-report-on-african-slaves.html

a result of a combination of three interrelated factors: the emergence of new southern NGOs through the expansion of funding; reframing of trafficking as a gender, human rights, and criminal issue; and new US engagement in the aftermath of the Cold War.

Although the Anti-Slavery Society had been raising awareness at the UN for nearly half a century about the issue of slavery, it was not until funding was extended to other groups and human trafficking was reframed in terms of women's rights that the issue began to gain a wider audience at the UN.[30] In December 1991, the UN General Assembly created a Voluntary Trust Fund on Contemporary Forms of Slavery in response to the global concern over modern manifestations of slavery.[31] This proved to be a watershed. The fund was designed to "assist representatives of non-governmental organizations from differing regions, dealing with issues of contemporary forms of slavery, to participate in the deliberation of the Working Group on Contemporary Forms of Slavery by providing them with financial assistance, and secondly, to extend through established channels of assistance, humanitarian, legal and financial aid to individuals whose human rights have been severely violated as a result of contemporary forms of slavery."[32] Until then, the Anti-Slavery Society had been funded by private donations and membership dues and had operated without UN funding. Its name and stature gave it legitimacy, but other NGOs could not operate globally and had no effective input at the UN. Thus, creation of the Voluntary Trust Fund proved a significant step in creating the mechanisms for inclusion of a global civil society in UN processes in support of a global norm of anti-trafficking and anti-slavery.[33]

In the same period, Human Rights Watch (HRW) began to inform the US Congress about the extent of human trafficking globally through its own awareness-raising initiatives. In one presentation to the Subcommittee on International Security, International Organizations, and Human Rights of the Committee on Foreign Affairs, House of Representatives, HRW suggested that:

---

[30] See Charlotte Bunch (1990), "Women's Rights as Human Rights: Toward a Re-Vision of Human Rights", *Human Rights Quarterly*, 12, pp.486–98.

[31] UN General Assembly (1991), "Resolution 46/122 United Nations Voluntary Trust Fund on Contemporary Forms of Slavery", *OHCHR Resolution 46/122*, 17 December, http://www.un.org/documents/ga/res/46/a46r122.htm

[32] Ibid.

[33] The areas of interest to the Voluntary Trust Fund are: trafficking, sexual slavery, child labor and child servitude, debt bondage, serfdom, forced labor, forced marriage, and sale of wives.

Trafficking in women who are either duped or coerced into prostitution is rampant in Asia and elsewhere. For example, our most
recent human rights report noted the sex trade in Thailand involves
thousands of women and children, many of whom are forced or
tricked into prostitution and are held as virtual captives by brothel
operators.[34]

Further emphasizing the need for policy change in Washington,
HRW noted the following in its publication *A Modern Form of Slavery:
Trafficking of Burmese Women and Girls into Brothels in Thailand*:

To our knowledge, until this year, the U.S. has not made either the
traffic in women and girls or forced prostitution in Thailand an issue
in decisions regarding official aid to Thailand. In contrast to the $4
million allocated by the U.S. in fiscal year 1993 to Thailand to control the traffic in narcotics, no U.S. aid is targeted to stop the traffic in
women and girls. The U.S. Agency for International Development's
Thailand mission has no program that specifically assists victims of
sex trafficking or forced prostitution.[35]

Subsequently, as a part of its aid to Thailand, the US Congress called
on the Thai government to begin prosecuting human traffickers. The
year 1994 thus marked the first concrete steps taken by the US government towards the eventual enforcement that would appear with the TIP
report of the early twenty-first century.[36]

In the same year, the UN's General Assembly adopted resolution
48/104, entitled the *Declaration on the Elimination of Violence Against
Women*, which included language on "trafficking in women and forced

---

[34] Human Rights Watch, "Human rights abuses against women: hearings before
the Subcommittee on International Security, International Organizations, and
Human Rights of the Committee on Foreign Affairs, House of Representatives,
One Hundred Third Congress, first and second sessions, September 28 and 19,
1993; October 20, 1993; and March 22, 1994."
[35] Asia Watch and the Women's Rights Project (1993), "Trafficking of Burmese
Women and Girls into Brothels in Thailand", *Human Rights Watch*, http://www.
hrw.org/legacy/reports/1993/thailand/#_1_62
[36] Office to Monitor and Combat Trafficking in Persons (2001), "Trafficking in
Persons Report, 2001", *US Department of State*, July, http://www.state.gov/g/tip/
rls/tiprpt/2001/index.htm

prostitution."[37] Further, in the same year, the Secretary General issued a report prior to the Annual Meeting of the General Assembly calling attention to the issue of trafficking in women.[38] In the GA's *Report of the Committee on the Elimination of Discrimination Against Women*, the involvement of the Women's Affairs Bureau was identified as having "been largely responsible for preparation of the report."[39] These developments created the impetus for hosting conferences at which those local NGOs and civil society organizations that had previously not been deeply integrated in the UN system could share their experiences and help prod their national governments and the UN into action. With the financial support of the Voluntary Trust Fund, the situation had now changed – from one where the Anti-Slavery Society monopolized a position at the UN to one where representation was more evenly distributed.

This shift, not surprisingly, took place in stages. Although the work of local NGOs grew in importance, it was the larger northern NGOs that that were initially able to project themselves globally and aid the anti-trafficking initiatives. At the UN's Fourth World Conference on Women held in Beijing, China in 1995, HRW presented its *Global Report on Women's Human Rights,* which dealt in part with the issue of trafficking in women. With this report, HRW brought pressure to bear on state-sponsored acts of violence against women, such as: "rape during armed conflicts is regularly dismissed as 'spoils of war', domestic violence and trafficking of women into prostitution are regarded as private matters and police, border guards and prison officers go unpunished for sexual assaults against female prisoners and refugees."[40] Certainly, the terms of the debate had decisively changed.

By then, it was becoming clear that intergovernmental coordination was needed to address the problem, which had transcended national boundaries and lacked updated international legal regimes designed to

---

[37] United Nations General Assembly (1993), "Declaration on the Elimination of Violence Against Women", *General Assembly Resolution 48/104*, 20 December, http://www.unhchr.ch/huridocda/huridoca.nsf/%28symbol%29/a. res.48.104.en

[38] United Nations General Assembly (1996), "Advancement of Women: Violence Against Women Migrant Workers", *Report of the Secretary General Resolution A/51/325*, 16 September, http://www.un.org/documents/ga/docs/51/plenary/a51–325.htm

[39] United Nations General Assembly (1993), "Declaration on the Elimination of Violence Against Women", *General Assembly Resolution 48/104*, 20 December, http://www.unhchr.ch/huridocda/huridoca.nsf/%28symbol%29/a. res.48.104.en

[40] Human Rights Watch (1995), "Governments Contribute to Violence Against Women", *Deutsche Presse-Agentur*, 3 September.

address the issue. In response to this need, the United Nations General Assembly resolved in Resolution 53/111 on *Transnational Organized Crime* to form an intergovernmental ad hoc committee to elaborate on establishment of an international convention for transnational organized crime, and discuss the development of "international instruments addressing trafficking in women and children, and illegal trafficking in and transporting of migrants, including by sea."[41] The work of this committee led the Convention against Transnational Organized Crime to draft the protocols and conventions signed eventually in 2000.

In the Economic and Social Council, NGOs were encouraged to participate in events hosted by the UN-financed Voluntary Trust Fund on Contemporary Forms of Slavery.[42]

In January 1999 the Global Alliance Against Traffic in Women (GAATW), an NGO alliance founded in Thailand in 1994, with primarily Southern membership, first published its landmark *Human Rights Standards for the Treatment of Trafficked Persons*. The Alliance identified eight key principles that should guide states in preventing trafficking,

---

[41] United Nations General Assembly (1999), "Transnational Organized Crime", *Resolution Adopted by the General Assembly, 53rd Session, A/RES/53/111*, 20 January.

[42] United Nations (1999), "Report of the Working Group on Contemporary Forms of Slavery", *United Nations High Commissioner for Human Rights E/CN.4/Sub.2/1999/17*, 20 July, http://www.unhchr.ch/huridocda/huridoca.nsf/%28Symbol%29/E.CN.4.Sub.2.1999.17.En?Opendocument. The following nongovernmental organizations in consultative status with the Economic and Social Council were represented by observers: AntiSlavery International, Coalition Against Trafficking in Women, International Council of Women, Federation International Terre des Hommes, International Fellowship of Reconciliation, International Movement Against All Forms of Discrimination and Racism, International Service for Human Rights, and World Federation of Methodists and Uniting Church Women. The following nongovernmental organizations were also represented by observers: African Bureau of Educational Sciences, Casa Alianza, Comité contre l'Esclavage moderne, Centre for Indonesian Migrant Workers, Foundation of Japanese Honorary Debts, Global Alliance against Traffic in Women, International Bureau for Children's Rights, Japan Federation of Publishing Workers' Union, Mouvement pour l'abolition de la prostitution et de la pornographie (MAPP), Network North Against Prostitution and Violence, Network of Sex Workers Projects, NGO Association World Citizen, NGO Group for the Convention on the Rights of the Child Focal Point on Sexual Exploitation of Children, NGO Liaison Committee on Wartime Sex Slavery and Forced Labour by Japan during World War II for the United Nations, Project Mala and Sanlaap.

providing assistance to trafficked women, and aiding in prosecution of traffickers. These were the principles of:

- Nondiscrimination
- Safety and fair treatment
- Access to justice
- Access to private action and reparations
- Presumptive residential status
- Access to health and other services
- Repatriation and reintegration
- The importance of state cooperation.[43]

These eight points became the foundation for trafficking protocols of the UN's subsequent Palermo Convention held in 2000, in which the *UN Convention on Transnational Organized Crime* was signed – thus guiding the UN and US agendas in their anti-trafficking efforts. Of significance was the Convention's supplementary *Protocol to Prevent, Suppress and Punish Trafficking in Persons, Especially Women and Children* (2000). In this document, the Palermo Convention created an international instrument institutionalizing framework for the "Three P" approach to combating human trafficking, defined as the following:

(a) "Trafficking in persons" shall mean the recruitment, transportation, transfer, harbouring or receipt of persons, by means of the threat or use of force or other forms of coercion, of abduction, of fraud, of deception, of the abuse of power or of a position of vulnerability or of the giving or receiving of payments or benefits to achieve the consent of a person having control over another person, for the purpose of exploitation. Exploitation shall include, at a minimum, the exploitation of the prostitution of others or other forms of sexual exploitation, forced labour or services, slavery or practices similar to slavery, servitude or the removal of organs;

(b) The consent of a victim of trafficking in persons to the intended exploitation set forth in subparagraph (a) of this article shall be

---

[43] Global Action Against Trafficking in Women, "Human Rights Standard for the Treatment of Trafficked Persons", www.gaatw.org, January 1999, http://gaatw.org/books_pdf/hrs_eng2.pdf

irrelevant where any of the means set forth in subparagraph (a) have been used;

(c) The recruitment, transportation, transfer, harbouring or receipt of a child for the purpose of exploitation shall be considered "trafficking in persons" even if this does not involve any of the means set forth in subparagraph (a) of this article.

The Protocol identified two root elements of human trafficking. Describing common means of organized crime groups that transport slave cargo across borders, it recognized that means short of actually handling the human cargo may be used by criminal organizations as key supply points. Corruption in all countries involved in a trafficking chain, for example, creates an environment that allows criminals to act in contravention of the global norm.[44] Another important form of non-direct involvement is the misuse of cyberspace, including the Internet, by slave traders to communicate and coordinate their actions in a secure fashion. Implementing preventive anti-corruption or cyber-security measures targeting actions abetting traffickers is thus identified in the Protocol as an important element in curbing illicit flow of trafficked humans across borders.

The inclusion of the anti-trafficking protocol in the *UN Convention on Transnational Organized Crime* marked a key stage in institutionalizing the global norm of anti-trafficking. The lobbying by civil society actors of their governments on the need to address the problem resulted in near-universal condemnation of the phenomenon by member states.

US sponsorship of the global anti-trafficking initiative

Norm entrepreneurs in both the North and the South enhanced public awareness and promoted creation of private–public partnerships (P3). How has the US responded? Both the public and private sectors have embraced this approach. The US government has enthusiastically supported these entrepreneurial efforts to forge the anti-trafficking norm, providing a significant amount of material resources to aid the global anti-trafficking initiative. One focus of these partnerships has been to provide victim services. The US government both engages NGOs for

---

[44] United Nations (2000), "United Nations Convention Against Transnational Organized Crime and the Protocols Thereto", *United Nations Office on Drugs and Crime*, December, http://www.unodc.org/documents/treaties/UNTOC/Publications/TOC%20Convention/TOCebook-e.pdf

counseling on policy initiatives and uses them for service delivery in collaboration with the US Missions abroad.[45] USAID is the main resource for US-led efforts to support international NGO programs focusing on anti-trafficking measures. This substantial support was formally initiated in 2003, when President Bush allocated $50 million to NGOs to "protect victims, prosecute traffickers, and increase public awareness" of human trafficking.[46]

This government support has been complemented by the private sector in these efforts. US Corporations have partnered with and supported NGOs in their efforts to combat trafficking. Wyndham Hotel Group's partnership with the Washington-headquartered NGO Polaris Project provides hundreds of hotel rooms available free of charge to trafficking victims. Microsoft's support of its partners includes provision of technical assistance to law-enforcement personnel involved in computer crime that is related to the sexual exploitation of children.[47]

Clearly, NGO partnerships have proven critical to the successful implementation of the P3 approach to ending human trafficking. However, entrepreneurial support and institutionalization are not enough for anti-trafficking measures to be effective. The norm may be articulate, but without US support there would be limited implementation.

The United States' failure to support varied components of the broad human security agenda (such as opposition to the use of child soldiers under the age of 18 or the complete eradication of landmines) makes its bipartisan, enthusiastic, and wholehearted embrace of the anti-trafficking agenda all the more notable. Indeed, successive Democratic and Republican administrations have been aggressively active in promoting initiatives to combat human trafficking. Fighting human

---

[45] Francis T. Miko (2005), "Trafficking in Persons: The U.S. and International Response", *Congressional Research Service Report*, 24 June, http://fpc.state.gov/documents/organization/50256.pdf. See also US Department of State (2005), "Working for Women Worldwide: The US Commitment 2005", pp. 53–8, http://www.america.gov/st/pubs-english/2005/December/20051219114126AMakteB0.447262.html

[46] Office to Monitor and Combat Trafficking in Persons (2008), "Fact Sheet: The President's $50 million Initiative to Combat Trafficking in Persons", *US Department of State*, 15 October, http://2001–2009.state.gov/g/tip/rls/fs/08/111406.htm

[47] Office to Monitor and Combat Trafficking in Persons (2009), "Topics of Special Interest: Trafficking in Persons Report, 2009", *US Department of State*, 16 June, http://www.state.gov/g/tip/rls/tiprpt/2009/123128.htm

trafficking received widespread support in both the Clinton and Bush eras, a pattern that seemed likely to be maintained as the first decade of the twenty-first century drew to a close.

Why has the US been so supportive? The American differentiation of the anti-trafficking issue from other aspects of the human security agenda can be explained by four components. The first reason for this US support is that it is the product of the distinct character of American history. The relatively late use of race-based slavery (among modern advanced industrial states) into the mid-nineteenth century, its violent and abrupt cessation, and continued debates about legacies of its effects on US politics, all combine to make Americans sensitive to the issue – of which trafficking is a widespread modern form.

The second is a product of the distinct character of contemporary American politics. Post-Cold War politics in the United States has been noteworthy for its radical ethical tone – whether originating from the political correctness of the Left or the focus on religious values emphasized by the Right. Only in a few policy areas do these partisan opponents converge: the religious Right's opposition to stem cell research or abortion is as passionate as the Left's concern about pornography or gender discrimination. Yet one of the few areas of agreement is that of trafficking. It offends the Left's emphasis on human rights and the Right's focus on sanctity of the family structure and opposition to sexual depravity (often towards minors), which trafficking often entails. Trafficking is one of those few foreign policy areas where opposition is relatively noncontroversial; there are no interest groups railing against American measures in support of anti-trafficking.

A third, more instrumental explanation for bipartisan American administrations' support for anti-trafficking is their resolute promotion of measures enhancing the rule of law globally – of which anti-trafficking constitutes a central component in the fight against government corruption.[48] A series of American initiatives that appear superficially as crusades designed to address injustices have had the benefit of consolidating law and order and, with that, increasing the likelihood that both capitalism and liberal democracy will take firmer root.[49] Embedded in

---

[48] Office to Monitor and Combat Trafficking in Persons (2005), "Trafficking in Persons Report, 2005- Fueling Organized Crime and Erosion of Government Authority", *US Department of State*, 3 June, pp. 13–14, http://www.state.gov/documents/organization/47255.pdf

[49] In Stuart Eizenstat's memoirs, for example, he characterizes the Clinton Administration's zealous efforts on behalf of Jews who had had their property

anti-trafficking, therefore, is a clear element consistent with, if not critical to, broader American geostrategic goals.[50]

Finally, trafficking allows America to conduct foreign policy and pursue a moral crusade (thus assuaging their consciences that they are promoting human rights) while not risking American lives. Rather, anti-trafficking entails some resource cost coupled with a judicious use of coercive powers. It is foreign policy with limited risk, respecting a "zero tolerance" for losing American lives.

In tandem, these four components perhaps make anti-trafficking an attractive policy area for American administrations. It is little surprise, therefore, that in the second Clinton administration, and the successive Bush administrations, there was a zealous advocacy for anti-trafficking measures at a time when American soft power was dwindling globally. Both pursued an activist agenda on the issue. Indeed, George W. Bush reaffirmed the centrality of human trafficking to the agenda of US foreign policy by calling for its "total abolition" in the 2006 version of *The National Security Strategy of the United States of America*.[51]

In line with the global norm, American policy provisions generally (although not exclusively) link trafficking in particular to females and children as victims, and to prostitution as "forced labor," rather than opting to focus on other forms of forced labor. The preferred approach entails criminalizing the customer, because the provider of sex is forced to do so, a stance common to other countries where prostitution (unlike in the US) is legal. As John Miller, former Ambassador-at-large for trafficking, stated, the US deals "with the demand side of the equation" by going after those who exploit women and children for prostitution.[52]

Although this chapter focuses on the most important policy initiatives of both the Clinton and Bush administrations as evidence of the

---

stolen by Nazis and then Communists not as a moral issue, worthy in its own right, but rather because "property restitution was to be part of a broader U.S. policy to encourage the rule of law, respect for property rights, tolerance towards minorities, and the creation of nonpolitical administrative and judicial processes in the former Communist countries." Stuart E. Eizenstat (2003), *Imperfect Justice: Looted Assets, Slave Labor, and the Unfinished Business* (New York: Public Affairs Books), pp. 23–4.

[50] ARSIS (2004), "Human Trafficking-Newsletter", *Association for the Social Support of Youth (ARSIS)*, 1, 6, http://www.arsis.gr/traffickingenglish.pdf

[51] US President (2006), *The National Security Strategy of the United States of America*, March, p. 12,

[52] US Department of State (2005), "Working for Women Worldwide: The US Commitment 2005", op. cit.

activism of both, it should be noted that – within the span of a decade – the US introduced 14 assorted pieces of legislation, strategic plans, strategic statements, and directives as listed below:

- PDD/NSC-9, Alien Smuggling, 18 June 1993;
- Presidential Memorandum on Deterring Illegal Immigration, 7 February 1995;
- PDD/NSC-35, Intelligence Priorities, 2 March 1995;
- PDD/NSC-42, International Organized Crime, 21 October 1995;
- Presidential Executive Memorandum on Steps to Combat Violence Against Women and Trafficking in Women and Girls, 11 March 1998;
- President's International Crime Control Strategy, May 1998;
- Victims of Trafficking and Violence Protection Act of 2000, Pub.L. 106–386;
- Presidential Statement of 15 December 2000;
- Homeland Security Presidential Directive – 2, 29 October 2001;
- President's National Security Strategy, September 2002;
- National Security Presidential Directive on Combating Trafficking in Persons (NSPD-22), December 2002;
- National Strategy for Combating Terrorism, February 2003; and
- Trafficking Victims Protection Reauthorization Act of 2003, Pub.L. 108–193.

Of these, the first significant initiative undertaken by the US government was the establishment of the President Interagency Council on Women (PICW) in 1995, intended to oversee and implement the *Platform of Action* adopted at the Fourth World Conference on Women sponsored by the UN.[53]

Nineteen-ninety-eight proved to be the hallmark year for US government initiatives against human trafficking. That March, President Clinton mandated the PICW "to coordinate the United States Government response on trafficking in women and girls, in consultation with nongovernmental groups."[54] Additionally, Clinton's memorandum directed both the Attorney General to review the adequacy

---

[53] US Department of State (2010), "Welcome to the President's Interagency Council on Women", 8 January, http://secretary.state.gov/www/picw/index.html

[54] William J. Clinton (1998), "Memorandum on Steps To Combat Violence Against Women and Trafficking in Women and Girls", *Administration of William*

of US laws in the prevention of trafficking and the Department of State to develop strategies with source and destination countries to combat the problem of trafficking.[55]

In the same year, the International Crime Control Strategy – an inter-agency body first mandated by Presidential Directive 42 – was introduced. Intended by its framers to deal with broader international organized crime, it was also used to address the international crime implications of trafficking. A slew of directives, initiatives, and legislation followed. First, President Clinton issued a directive for a government-wide anti-TIP strategy centered on prosecution, protection, and prevention. Simultaneously, the Departments of Justice and Labor co-chaired a "Worker's Exploitation Task Force" intended to investigate and prosecute cases of exploitation and trafficking. A subsequent task force was then introduced, composed of a senior governmental working group on trafficking, designed to examine worldwide anti-trafficking strategies.

Clinton followed up on these initiatives by signing the Victims of Trafficking and Violence Protection Act (TVPA) of 2000 (P.L.106-386), a landmark legislation providing health care, cash assistance, and housing services for trafficked victims.[56] Coupled with victim assistance, the United States generally uses diplomatic pressure to engender domestic reforms and stimulate enforcement by governments in individual countries.

Critically, to add some coercive capacity, the TVPA created the Trafficking in Persons (TIP) Report issued annually by the Department of State. It is designed to grade the efforts of individual countries with the intent of "naming and shaming" (and potentially sanctioning) states adjudged to be wavering in their efforts. Based on a three-tier scale, the intent of the process is to coerce the worst transgressors (Tier 3 countries) through the threat of a variety of sanctions (as described below). Once placed on the Tier 3 watch list by the annual TIP report, the President must make a determination whether to place (or maintain) sanctions on Tier 3 countries every 90 days.[57]

J. Clinton, GPO, 11 March, p. 413, http://www.gpo.gov/fdsys/pkg/WCPD-1998-03-16/pdf/WCPD-1998-03-16-Pg412.pdf

[55] Ibid.

[56] To receive such benefits, however, a victim must be "willing to assist in every reasonable way in the investigation and prosecution." See US Department of Justice (2005), "Assessment of US Government Efforts to Combat Trafficking in Persons in Fiscal Year 2004", September, p. 5, http://www.justice.gov/archive/ag/annualreports/tr2005/assessmentofustipactivities.pdf

[57] Ibid., p. 2.

A Republican-controlled Congress subsequently strengthened the TPVA in 2002 with National Security Presidential Directive-22. This directive included several new components, including new provisions designed to assist local NGOs; provide hotlines and shelters for victims and education programs for those most at risk; and a new authorization increasing appropriations for FY 2003 to fund these new programs.

The following year President Bush signed, and the US Congress enacted, the Trafficking Victims Protection Re-authorization Act (P.L.108-193). New provisions refined and expanded the "minimum standards" for foreign governments; increased their responsibility for provision of data; created a new "Watch List" category; and, again, substantially increased funding for anti-trafficking programs for FY 2004 and 2005 to over $80 million for each fiscal year.[58] According to US government sources, by the end of February 2006, the Bush administration had provided more than $295 million to support anti-trafficking programs in more than 120 countries.[59]

In April 2003, Bush signed the PROTECT Act, which granted the US extraterritoriality in the prosecution of US citizens engaged in child sex tourism. In January 2006 President Bush signed H.R. 972, Trafficking Victims Protection Reauthorization Act. This amended the TVPA further by increasing assistance to foreign victims trafficked to the US; increasing the focus on children; and directing relevant US agencies to develop anti-trafficking strategies for post-conflict and humanitarian crisis areas. It also extended US extraterritoriality for US government workers and contractors who are "involved in acts of trafficking," addressing the problems of peacekeepers and aid personnel who are "complicit" in trafficking.[60] Further, section 7202 of the *Intelligence Reform and Terrorism Prevention Act of 2004* established the Human Smuggling and Trafficking Center (HSTC) "to improve the effectiveness of ongoing interagency efforts, particularly in supporting the conversion of intelligence into appropriate enforcement and other response

---

[58] Office to Monitor and Combat Trafficking in Persons (2005), "Trafficking in Persons Report, 2005- Fueling Organized Crime and Erosion of Government Authority", *US Department of State*, 3 June, http://www.state.gov/documents/organization/47255.pdf

[59] US Department of State (2005), "Working for Women Worldwide: The US Commitment 2005", op. cit.

[60] US Department of Justice (2005), "Assessment of US Government Efforts to Combat Trafficking in Persons in Fiscal Year 2004", op. cit., pp. 13–14, http://www.justice.gov/archive/ag/annualreports/tr2005/assessmentofustipactivities.pdf

actions [and]...to achieve greater integration and overall effectiveness in U.S. Government enforcement and other response efforts and to promote intensified efforts by foreign governments and international organizations to combat these problems."[61]

Current US policy links the Clinton, Bush, and Obama administrations. Indeed, Obama indicated his intent to pursue a vigorous policy, consistent with his predecessors, with the appointment of Lou De Baca, notable for his crusading commitment to the issue. As one commentator suggested: "If you are a human trafficker or someone who profits from the modern-day slave trade, and you come up against Lou de Baca: God help you.... Saying that de Baca has a vigorous attitude about slave traders is like saying Killer Whales have an affinity for seals. Since 1994, stripping traffickers of their freedom, and restoring that of their victims, has been more than de Baca's job; it's been his passion."[62] As Obama's Secretary of State, Hilary Clinton has made anti-trafficking a priority, with the first TIP report issued by the Obama administration increasing the number of countries on the Tier 3 list to 17.[63]

Clearly, anti-trafficking has become a bipartisan issue and one in which the US has been willing to pursue an aggressive policy. In part, the US has dealt directly with individual governments on the issue – one that has met with surprisingly little criticism.[64] As a part of US global anti-trafficking policy, US programs also sponsor visits by foreign governments and NGO officials in order to discuss effective prevention and protection measures.

Furthermore, the US has created and funded international enforcement programs. In addition to the TIP program's potential sanctions, the Department of Justice, as well as the FBI's International Criminal Investigative Training and Assistance Program, provides training and

[61] US Department of State (2004), "Human Smuggling and Trafficking Center (HSTC) Charter and Amendments", September, http://www.state.gov/m/ds/hstcenter/41444.htm

[62] E. Benjamin Skinner (2009), "Obama"s Abolitionist", *The Huffington Post*, 25 March, http://www.huffingtonpost.com/ben-skinner/obamas-abolitionist_b_178781.html

[63] David Gollust (2009), "Clinton says Combating Human Trafficking 'Critical'", *Voice of America*, 16 June, http://www.voanews.com/english/archive/2009–06/2009 –06-16-voa38.cfm?CFID=308591312&CFTOKEN=6599 0060&jsessionid=66302adeb4d6fd0915855363202773373b13

[64] US Department of State (2005), "Working for Women Worldwide: The US Commitment 2005", *US Department of State*, op. cit.

logistical support to other states, while the Department of Labor holds prevention and awareness-raising programs abroad.

The first US effort is designed to persuade foreign governments to enact laws against trafficking. It has, at the same time, aggressively pursued regional and multilateral initiatives. By March 2005, the US was an instrumental force in the UN Commission on the Status of Women's adoption of a trafficking resolution. The adopted resolution, entitled *Eliminating Demand for Trafficked Women and Girls for All Forms of Exploitation*, attracted more than 50 nations as co-sponsors.[65] By July, 117 countries had signed the original protocol of 2000 on trafficking formulated at Palermo, of which 85 had ratified it.[66] In December 2003, the US finally signed on as an official party to the UN Protocol "To Prevent, Suppress and Punish Trafficking in Persons, especially Women and Children" – a supplement to the 2000 Convention Against Transnational Organized Crime – which by then had been ratified by 114 nations. Bush State Department officials significantly (given the general bilateral thrust of US foreign policy at the time) described it as "an important multilateral component of the worldwide effort to combat modern-day slavery."[67] By contrast, a modest 23 members, out of a total of 46, had signed the Council of Europe convention around the same date, and the enforcement mechanisms were not immediately evident.[68]

To give these initiatives a coercive capacity, the US uses its annual TIP Report and these UN initiatives to go beyond "naming and shaming." Tier 3 countries can be subject to sanctions on "non-humanitarian, non-trade related foreign assistance" from the US. "Countries listed on Tier 3 can avoid sanctions by taking swift action within three months of

---

[65] See Office to Monitor and Combat Trafficking in Persons (2005), "UN Commission on the Status of Women Adopts U.S. Human Trafficking Resolution", op. cit.

[66] Irena Omelaniuk (2005), "Trafficking in Human Beings", *United Nations Expert Group Meeting on International Migration and Development*, 8 July, p. 7, http://www.un.org/esa/population/meetings/ittmigdev2005/P15_IOmelaniuk. pdf

[67] See US Department of State (2005), "United States Joins U.N. Anti-Trafficking Protocol", December, http://www.america.gov/st/washfile-english/2005/Decem ber/20051201162702cmretrop0.8572657.html

[68] See Directorate General of Human Rights Equality Division (2005), "The Council of Europe Convention on Action against Trafficking in Human Beings", *Council of Europe*, August, http://www.coe.int/T/E/human_rights/trafficking/ PDF_FS_TrafConv_E.pdf

the report's release."[69] Similarly, the US has threatened to withdraw its support for loans from international financial institutions, such as the IMF and World Bank, for countries that either do not pass requisite laws or do not enforce them.[70] As George W. Bush stated, nations profiting from sanctions face potential loss of US military and economic assistance as well as World Bank and IMF support.[71] As the largest depositor at the World Bank and IMF, the issue of US support has substantial implications for countries seeking loans.

The US has been just as aggressive on a regional level in organizations such as the Organization for Security and Co-operation in Europe (OSCE) and Southeast European Cooperative Initiative (SECI). The EU, for example, has supported "bottom up" initiatives in the Balkans, consistent with EU accession requirements (as a carrot held out to prospective members). These do include security elements such as strengthening and coordinating law enforcement capacities at a region-wide level and tightening external borders and visa controls. EU policy also extends to supporting human rights groups in exposing the issue; providing humanitarian, legal, and social assistance to victims of trafficking; and, finally, improving the social and economic conditions of women within and beyond EU borders.[72] Beyond denying membership to prospective accession countries (a threat that the EU never subsequently enforced), the EU initiatives have clearly lacked the coercive sanctions of the American initiative. The US, in contrast, has remained more focused on criminality and victim support than prevention, and is the driving force in SECI in organizing a regional enforcement body.[73]

---

[69] US Department of State (2005), "Combating Violence Against Women", *Working for Women Worldwide: The US Commitment*, http://library2.parliament.go.th/ebook/content-eb/women.pdf, p. 52.

[70] Francis T. Miko (2005), "Trafficking in Persons: The U.S. and International Response", op. cit.

[71] (2005) "America Will not tolerate Slave Traders, Bush says", *America in Context*, 9, 6, http://www.uspolicy.be/context/pdf/Context9_May05.pdf

[72] Press Release (2001), "Trafficking in Women- The Misery Behind the Fantasy: From Poverty to Sex Slavery a Comprehensive European Strategy", *European Union, Reference MEMO/01/64*, 3 June, http://europa.eu/rapid/pressReleasesAction.do?reference=MEMO/01/64&format=HTML&aged=0&language=EN&guiLanguage=en

[73] Andrea Bertone and Julie Mertis (2007), "The National and Regional Implications of International Efforts to Combat Trafficking in Women in the Western Balkans", in Richard Friman and Simon Reich (eds), *Human Trafficking, Human Security, and the Balkans*, op. cit. The SECI law enforcement initiatives

Assessing results

It is inevitably difficult to measure the results of all these efforts. Trafficking has flourished on a global basis as poverty and violence have worsened in many countries in the new century, complicated by a series of natural disasters and intrastate wars. The resulting commodification of humans ensures that the success of the norm cannot be measured in terms of a reduction in the incidence of trafficking. But, if measured in terms of the governmental adoption and enforcement of the global norm, there is plenty of evidence to support the view that it has been a success. According to the formula offered in the first US TIP report, published in 2001, there were 23 countries listed as "Tier 3" offenders. In the following years that number had fallen to 19, with the respective figures being 15 in 2003 and ten in 2004.

This reduced number has not been sustained: this figure of Tier 3 increased to 14 in 2005 and 17 by 2009. Yet there are two points of note. First, the composition of the "hard core" offenders group is clearly consolidating, while the remainder appears "situational." Overwhelmingly, the same countries appear on the list every year: Bolivia, Cuba, Ecuador, and Venezuela in Latin America; Burma (Myanmar) and North Korea in Asia; Sudan in Africa; and Kuwait, Saudi Arabia, and the United Arab Emirates from the Middle East (suggesting that inclusion in this group is not simply politically motivated, because some are US allies). The situation in other countries changes and appears temporary – wrought by war and famine – such as Sierra Leone in 2004 or Togo in 2005. Second, and perhaps more importantly, the number of Tier 2 countries is consistently shrinking. In 2004 there were 54 on the list. By 2005 this number had reduced by 50 percent to 27. Legislation and enactment, at least according to the TIP formula, had gained ground.

However, this decrease in the number of Tier 3 countries is in part due to the introduction of an innovative, aggressive Tier 2 "watch list," on which appear countries whose governments do not fully comply with the TVPA's minimum standards, but are making significant efforts to bring themselves into compliance with those standards. The qualification for membership of this group applies to countries where

---

have purportedly come from the US in collaboration between local forces and the FBI. See Gabriela Konevska (2007), "Policy Responses to Trafficking in Balkan Countries", in Richard Friman and Simon Reich (eds), *Human Trafficking, Human Security, and the Balkans*, op. cit.

the absolute number of victims of severe forms of trafficking is very significant or is significantly increasing; or, second, where there is a failure to provide evidence of increasing efforts to combat severe forms of trafficking in persons from the previous year; or, finally, where there is a determination that a country is making significant efforts to bring itself into compliance with the minimum standards, based on commitments by that country to take additional steps in the ensuing 12 months.

Of note is the fact that this list has been populated by many countries, formerly part of the Tier 3 list, who are – again – US allies, such as Israel.[74] Being listed as a Tier 3 member poses a threat to foreign assistance if the claims are subsequently deemed substantial and the problem is sustained. Thus an adjustment was needed that preserved the legitimacy of the list without having friends and allies alienated due to possible freezing of direct US foreign aid. Hence, an underlying reason for the introduction of a watch list was that the US could continue to emphasize the need for its friends and allies to address trafficking issues within their own borders, and at the same time have the Tier 3 list, through which sanctions could be introduced on the grounds of taking insufficient steps to end human trafficking.

The presiding question remains: how do we know when we have developed a global norm? Presumably, there is no single litmus test. Notably, even those countries that dissent from the norm have remained largely silent on the issue, unlike in other policy areas where they have appealed to principles of sovereignty (such as in assorted other cases of human rights violations such as child soldiering) or self-protection (the development of weapons of mass destruction). The legitimacy of anti-trafficking is now uncontested.

Yet, as outlined in the opening two chapters, it is not simply that a norm is advocated by NGOs, or that it is institutionalized at a global organization such as the UN. These are requisite but ultimately insufficient. Enforcement mechanisms with coercive measures that extend beyond "naming and shaming" to influence the behavior of authoritative actors are required. In this case, all states, except a few

---

[74] Janine Zacharia (2001), "US: Israel Among States Lax on Human Trafficking", *Jerusalem Post*, 13 July, p. 06.A, http://pqasb.pqarchiver.com/jpost/access/75434606.html?dids=75434606:75434606&FMT=ABS&FMTS=ABS:FT&date=Jul+13%2C+2001&author=JANINE+ZACHARIA&pub=Jerusalem+Post&edition=&startpage=06.A&desc=US%3A+Israel+among+states+lax+on+human+trafficking

that repeatedly demonstrate that they regard themselves as beyond the jurisdiction of the international community (such as Iran, Myanmar, North Korea, and Sudan), have responded to this globally sanctioned, US-sponsored initiative. While trafficking continues unabated, just as is the case with other forms of criminality such as drug or gun smuggling, the legitimacy of doing so has now been indisputably challenged – and the responsibility of states to act against it firmly established.

7
Sponsoring Global Norms: Emerging Patterns and Policy Options in Global Politics

"And today I'd like to announce that, in the context of a strong accord in which all major economies stand behind meaningful mitigation actions and provide full transparency as to their implementation, the United States is prepared to work with other countries toward a goal of jointly mobilizing $100 billion a year by 2020 to address the climate change needs of developing countries. We expect this funding will come from a wide variety of sources, public and private, bilateral and multilateral, including alternative sources of finance. This will include a significant focus on forestry and adaptation, particularly, again I repeat, for the poorest and most vulnerable among us."[1]

As the first decade of the twenty-first century drew to a close, American policymakers and pundits were less than sanguine in their assessment of either how America had fared since the turn of the century or President Barack Obama's first year in office.[2] The anniversaries carried

---

[1] Hillary Rodham Clinton (2009), "Remarks at the United Nations Framework Convention on Climate Change", 17 December 2009, http://www.state.gov/secretary/rm/2009a/12/133734.htm

[2] For a critical assessment of President Obama's accomplishments in foreign policy in his first year, see Eliot Cohen (2010), "Taking the Measure of Obama's Foreign Policy", *Wall Street Journal*, 11 January, http://online.wsj.com/article/SB10001424052748703481004574646080636258614.html; for a countervailing view see Michael E. O'Hanlon (2010), "Obama's Solid First year on

a similar theme: one of overstated and unreasonably bloated expectations followed by (under the circumstances) inevitable disappoint-
ment. America's "unipolar moment" had clearly passed, and the first
decade was one in which Chinese, Indian, and Brazilian growth rates
boomed compared with the US.[3] Stock markets in developing economies experienced unprecedented growth, while American investors
were no better off in January 2010 than they had been a decade earlier.
On 10 January 2010, it was reported that the PRC had surpassed the
Federal Republic of Germany as the world's largest exporter[4] and was
about to overtake Japan as the world's second largest economy.[5] The
PRC had clearly experienced a period of unparalleled growth in the
modern era.

Such contrasting data yielded a slew of predictions reminiscent of
those made two decades earlier, when commentators warned that the
US was about to be overtaken by Japan as the world's largest economy.
The result, we were warned at the time, would be that a rising hegemon
(in this case Japan) and the declining one (the US) would inevitably
fight over conflicting interests.[6] Of course, Japanese growth was subsequently stymied by a decade of depression while the American economy benefited from substantial growth.

No solace should be taken from the hollow nature of such past
prognostications regarding US decline. I harbor no illusions that the
US economic position is anything other than precarious. The PRC
is vaster than Japan was then. It is more focused on strategic goals
(without the limitations to decision-making presented by a democratic polity) and is far less concerned with international opinion,
as it pursues a single-minded mercantilist approach, particularly in
regards to natural resource procurement. Unlike Japan, China has a
vast domestic market, comparable in size to its global market, with
an embryonic middle class that is willing to spend. The PRC, for
example, became the world's largest auto market in 2009, as car sales

---

Foreign Policy", Brookings Institution, 1 January, http://www.brookings.edu/
opinions/2010/0101_obama_foreign-_policy_ohanlon.aspx

[3] See BBC News (2010), "China economy sees strong growth", 21 January,
http://news.bbc.co.uk/2/hi/business/8471613.stm

[4] For details see *New York Times* (2010), "China Becomes World's No. 1 Exporter,
Passing Germany", 11 January, http://mobile.nytimes.com/article;jsessionid=E8
42EC71D67E9BF4EE3460512E16F989.w5?a=528697&f=111

[5] See "China economy sees strong growth", op. cit.

[6] See George Friedman and Meredith Lebard (1991), *The Coming War with Japan*
(New York: St Martin's Press).

surged by over 40 percent in the midst of a global recession. Estimates suggest that:

> Purchases in China will also continue to be buoyed by rising household disposable income and a low penetration rate. China has less than 40 vehicles per 1,000 people compared with a G7 average of more than 600 vehicles. Per capita incomes have been advancing by 9% per annum over the past decade, and are now at US$3,600 – a level that typically leads to an extended period of rapid growth in car sales. For example, purchases in South Korea expanded by 27% per annum from 1980 through the mid-1990s – roughly 4 times the pace of per capita income growth – until incomes reached US$10,000 per person.[7]

In sum, the task facing the US in maintaining its sole superpower status is enormous. Power, it would seem, will have to be shared, whether this happens a decade or two away.

Of course, linear forecasting is consistently problematic. For example, we were told that technological innovation had put an end to the traditional business cycle;[8] that global recession was a thing of the past; and that history – defined in terms of a global struggle – had ended.[9] None of these things, in retrospect, proved to be true. So any propensity towards forecasting imminent US decline should probably be offset by humility in recognizing that we have little understanding of how a combination of factors – such as the implosion of asset bubbles, prospective ethnic tensions, leadership crises, natural disasters, global overcapacity, or political demands for democratic reform made by an emergent middle class – will play themselves out in the PRC. Still, a framework that emphasizes the significance of US sponsorship would be naïve to ignore the fact that the US is challenged by both the vagaries of its domestic economic policies and the potential rapid emergence of a new superpower.

---

[7] See Global Auto Report (2009), "On The Road To Recovery In 2010- Double-digit gains in emerging markets and the U.S. will drive a 5% increase", *Scotia Economics (Global Economic Report)*, 29 December, *Global Auto* Report – December 29, *2009*.pub

[8] Steven Weber (1997), "The End of the Business Cycle?", *Foreign Affairs*, 76: pp. 465–82.

[9] On this last point, for a short version of the argument see Francis Fukuyama (1989), "The End of History?", *The National Interest*, Summer, pp. 3–17.

Nonetheless, recent evidence reinforces the view that America continues to be willing to pay a variety of enforcement costs even as it becomes less capable of doing so. In the midst of a continued US recession, while some of the largest European economies had emerged from recession and accelerated growth in the PRC resumed, it was the US that continued to try and assume a central global role – with attendant financial costs. Specifically, as the quote at the outset of this closing chapter notes, the US stepped forward in attempting to lead when offering to underwrite the costs of a proposed agreement at Copenhagen; it disproportionately assisted the United Nations (UN) in the early aftermath of the Haitian earthquake; and it has sustained the majority of the costs in fighting insurgents in Afghanistan, Pakistan, and, increasingly, in Yemen. The PRC, despite its ability to support these initiatives, did not do so. The obvious historical parallel may lie in Charles Kindleberger's description of the interwar period that emergent hegemons must be both willing *and* able to pay the costs of assuming a global role. The US may be decreasingly able to underwrite costs, but the PRC is, at least as yet, unwilling to do so.[10]

If the US is indeed likely to maintain its propensity towards sponsorship through the payment of enforcement costs, then it suggests that the varied configurations identified in the two opening chapters and illustrated in the four case studies may have an enduring character – with predictable policy consequences. Multilateralist strategies characterized by American leadership as a "first among equals," with its reliance on burden-sharing, may prove as elusive in achieving the US policy goals as attempts to impose US preferences through imperialist or (loose) unilateralist strategies. Reliance on global norms, with the US playing a less aggressive leadership role, may actually result in preferred policy outcomes.

Global governance and global norms

Of course, this is a controversial claim. Making any such assertion must come from being able to demonstrate that we have identified a regular pattern in the interaction between the US and the international community, and that the four case studies in the prior chapters are actually reflective of an emergent pattern in global politics. The section that follows offers two mini-cases, attempting to demonstrate that the strategy, policy, and outcome are consistent with the configuration laid out

---

[10] Charles P. Kindleberger (1973), *The World in Depression, 1929–1939* (Berkeley and London: University of California Press).

in the prior pages of this book. By way of illustration, I briefly compare a weak multilateralist attempt at global governance – the banning of landmines – with a more successful case of the sponsorship of a global norm – counter-piracy. Consistently with the spirit of this book, I recognize that the discussion is more heuristic than conclusive. It does, however, add credence to the view that there is an emergent pattern to global politics.

Landmines, global governance, and failed US multilateralism

Proponents of the view that a pattern of global governance is emerging in which the United States is increasingly marginal are plentiful. They generally emphasize the role of NGOs and global institutions, focusing on protocols and ignoring behavioral outcomes or critical countervailing evidence. That pattern is ably demonstrated in the case of landmines. In terms of the schemata laid out in this book, it is a case both of global governance without US enforcement and of failed US attempts to formulate an alternative multilateral position.

Despite persistent and significant pressure from NGO groups and allied governments, and attempts to institutionalize, codify, and enforce a global norm dating from the 1980s, the United States has steadfastly refused to support the total ban on landmines. The basis of this refusal is the distinction the US draws between what are commonly termed "dumb" mines or persistent mines, which do not self-deactivate, and non-persistent mines (often known as "smart mines"), which either self-destruct or self-deactivate. The US has persistently argued that persistent mines constitute the root cause of human suffering and opposes any general ban.[11]

Efforts to eradicate landmine use date back to the Treaty of Versailles of 1919, which banned the use of "indiscriminate weapons," subsequently followed by the Geneva Protocol banning the use of a broad swath of weapons.[12] But what might be termed the "current period" of the campaign to ban landmines dates from the efforts of the

---

[11] See US Department of State (2004), "US Landmine Policy", 27 February, http://www.state.gov/t/pm/wra/c11735.htm

[12] Richard A Matthew, Bryan McDonald and Kenneth R. Rutherford (2004), *Landmines and Human Security: International Politics and War's Hidden Legacy* (New York: State University of New York Press); and Maxwell Cameron, Robert Lawson and Brian Tomlin (1998), *To Walk without Fear: The Global Movement to Ban Landmines* (Oxford: Oxford University Press), p. 81.

International Committee of the Red Cross (ICRC) to institute Protocol I to the1949 Geneva Convention legal work of convention weapons in 1979. The following year their efforts, in part, led to the Convention on Conventional Weapons (CCW), also known as UN Convention on Inhumane Weapons. This second protocol specifically mentions restrictions on landmines,[13] being ratified in 1983 with the signature of the twentieth state.

While much of the rest of the decade was notable for the ICRC's efforts to promote a wider ban, the process accelerated in the 1990s, prompted by the establishment in 1992 of two new organizations, *The International Campaign to Ban Landmines* (ICBL) and its counterpart, *The US Campaign to Ban Landmines*. Both were composed of a variety of NGOs, including most importantly (in political terms) the Vietnam Veterans of America Foundation.[14]

The US responded to these developments in 1992 by enacting Congressional legislation, the Leahy–Evans Landmine Moratorium, placing a moratorium on exports. The US was the first country to do so, and called for ratification of CCW – giving enormous impetus to the campaign.[15] France followed suit in prohibiting exports, encouraging the US to advocate, successfully, a moratorium before the General Assembly of the UN the following year. The resolution was passed unanimously. The US therefore became the leader in instituting limits on the sale of landmines.

The Swedish government, however, pressured by the Swedish Save the Children NGO, offered a more radical proposal in 1994, declaring that "an international total ban against anti-personnel mines is the only real solution to the humanitarian problem the use of mines causes."[16] The following year, Belgium and Norway became the first and second countries, respectively, to ban the use, production, trade, and stockpiling of landmines. By 1996, Canadian Foreign Minister Lloyd Axworthy announced that his country would host a "fast-track" diplomatic initiative intended to lead to a global agreement to abolish landmines, subsequently named the "Ottawa Process."

---

[13] CCW Reference Texts, http://www.ccwtreaty.com/keydocs.html

[14] For a list see "Campaign History", *International Campaign to Ban Landmines*, http://www.icbl.org/index.php/icbl/About-Us/History

[15] See Maxwell Cameron, Robert Lawson and Brian Tomlin (1998), *To Walk without Fear: The Global Movement to Ban Landmines*, op. cit., p. 218.

[16] Ibid., p. 27.

The American response was incredulity. In opposition, they attempted to develop a different venue for discussion, the Conference on Disarmament (CD). Despite the stated effort of the US to lead a global campaign, it failed to either influence the Ottawa Process or attract widespread participation in the CD. The Ottawa Treaty was signed in 1999, outlining a series of restrictions on landmine use.[17]

The Treaty was hailed as an achievement of enormous significance, notably for "middle power multilateralism," the power of moral entrepreneurs drawn from the NGO community, and the diplomatic support of the UN leadership. Kofi Annan, after its signing, declared:

> We have gathered today in a spirit of celebration, at a time of hope, to mark a historic victory for the weak and vulnerable of our world ... Your success is a welcome reminder that one does not have to be a global super-power to affect the future of international peace and security ... The Ottawa Convention is a landmark step in the history of disarmament. About this, there can be no doubt. I am confident that it will provide the final impetus for a universal ban, encompassing all mine-producing and mine-affected countries.[18]

The ICBL was awarded the Nobel Peace Prize in 1997 in recognition of the importance of its contribution to the signing of the Treaty. Within three years, 137 countries had signed the agreement, 96 subsequently ratifying it. Lloyd Axworthy boasted of the reduction in the number of countries producing and exporting landmines, and of the reduction in fatalities and casualties in individual conflicts.[19]

The US, however, refused to sign the Treaty and thereby join the convention. As a State Department document subsequently summarized the US position, the terms of the Treaty would have required the US

---

[17] For the text of the Ottawa Treaty, see International Campaign to Ban Landmines "Convention on the Prohibition of the Use, Stockpiling, Production and Transfer of Anti-Personnel Mines and on Their Destruction", http://www. icbl.org/treaty/text/english

[18] Electronic Mine Information Network (1997), "Statement of the Secretary-General: Welcomes Convention Banning Landmines as 'Landmark Step in History of Disarmament'", 3 December, http://www.mineaction. org/docs/615_.asp. See also http://www.fas.org/asmp/campaigns/landmines/ FactSheet_NewUSPolicy_2-27-04.htm

[19] Department of Foreign Affairs and International Trade (2000), "Notes for an Address by the Honorable Lloyd Axworthy, Minister for Foreign Affairs, on Human Rights and Humanitarian Intervention", 16 June.

"to give up a needed military capability."[20] The effect of the US refusal to sign was, on reflection, rather sobering. Fen Osler Hampson offers a balanced assessment in suggesting that:

> On the one hand, the failure of the United States (along with Russia, China, and India) to block the successful conclusion of the Ottawa process can be seen in some respects as a victory for cosmopolitan/middle-power multilateralism and a defeat for great-power "minilateralism". On the other hand, the victory may be a hollow one given the importance of the above states to the worldwide production and trade in landmines. In the long run, the co-operation of these countries is clearly essential if the mechanisms set in place at Ottawa are to work and the scourge of landmines is to be eradicated from the face of the planet.[21]

In the early years following the signing of the Treaty, advocates pointed to the implicit implementation of some its major components by the US as an evidence of its success. In 1998, the year following the Treaty's signing, the US spent over $48 million on humanitarian mine removal.[22] That figure then grew precipitously, from $63.1 million in 1999 to $82.4 million in 2000.[23] Indeed, by 2004, the US government spent a total of $109.3 million on humanitarian mine action programs in 31 countries, with about two-thirds of that amount being spent outside Iraq.[24] It also emerged as one of the major financial contributors to the global campaign to eliminate landmines.

---

[20] See State Department Fact Sheet (2004), "New United States Policy on Landmines: Reducing Humanitarian Risk and Saving Lives of United States Soldiers", 27 February, http://www.fas.org/asmp/campaigns/landmines/FactSheet_NewUSPolicy_2–27–04.htm

[21] Fen Osler Hampson, Jean Daudelin, John B. Hay, Todd Martin and Holly Reid (2002), *Madness in the Multitude: Human Security and World Disorder* (Ontario, CA: Oxford University Press), p. 80.

[22] See Landmine Monitor (1999), "Major Mine Action Donors", *Landmine Monitor Report 1999*, http://www.the-monitor.org/index.php/publications/display?url=lm/2005/intro/funding.html

[23] See USG Historical Chart containing data for FY 2004, from Angela L. Jeffries (2005), Financial Management Specialist, US Department of State, Bureau of Political–Military Affairs, cited in *Landmine Monitor Report 2005*, 20 July, http://www.icbl.org/lm/2005/intro/funding.html#Heading213

[24] See Landmine Monitor (2005), *Landmine Monitor Report 2005*, http://www.icbl.org/lm/2005/usa.html

Yet the refusal of the US to sign the Treaty had a damaging effect on its adoption at a global level. For example, Rae McGrath, a co-laureate of the 1997 Nobel Peace Prize, felt the absence of the US in particular to be a considerable weakness because: "The problem with major countries such as the US not participating in the treaty is that it allows other non-signatories to point to the US and justify their own non-participation."[25]

Other countries were certainly given the excuse to claim extenuating or special circumstances in also refusing to sign, and this problem was compounded by the lack of political or economic pressure that the US could exert in other issue areas. The PRC reportedly has a stockpile of over 100 million landmines in places such as its border with Vietnam, citing the "legitimate self-defense needs of sovereign states;"[26] Russia reputedly has over 25 million landmines, although it ratified the CCW Amended Protocol II on 2 March 2005 and began a process of demining some parts of Chechnya; and numerous smaller batteries of weapons remain in effect in other countries. In sum:

> Forty countries, with a combined stockpile of some 160 million antipersonnel mines, remain outside of the Mine Ban Treaty. They include three of the five permanent members of the UN Security Council (China, Russia and the United States), most of the Middle East, most of the former Soviet republics, and many Asian states.[27]

Even if the US did contribute toward the mine clearance and prohibited the production of dumb mines, it lacked the legitimacy to cajole, coerce, or co-opt others to do the same – mired in the complexities of the ethical distinction between smart and dumb mines. Stephen Goose, the executive director of the arms control division of Human Rights Watch at the time, accurately stated that: "we have a great deal of momentum everywhere else around the world. The US is the only country in NATO that hasn't banned this weapon. We have a situation where the US is

---

[25] UN Office for the Coordination of Humanitarian Affairs (2004), "In depth: Laying Landmines to Rest? Humanitarian Mine Action", *Humanitarian News and Analysis*, November, http://www.irinnews.org/webspecials/hma/feaott.asp

[26] Landmine Monitor (2005), "China", *Landmine Monitor Report 2005*, http://www.icbl.org/lm/2005/china

[27] Landmine Monitor (2005), "Toward a Mine-Free World", *Landmine Monitor Report 2005*, http://www.icbl.org/lm/2005/findings.html

undermining the international norm against this weapon."[28] Many countries might have eradicated, reduced, or changed the form of mine they produced. But, measured in terms of output, no global norm had been generated. US leadership, ostensibly, resulted in noncompliance by key states.

Global counterpiracy efforts

Establishing norms of good conduct on the seas has continually ranked high on the policy agenda. Initial comprehensive efforts to codify a law to regulate behavior on the seas are evident in Justinian's Code and the Rhodesian Sea Law. Both established the rules and regulations for the use of the Eastern Roman Empire's sea space for trade and exploitation of its resources. These texts set the basis of customary international law to deal with the problem of piracy. Consistent with this perspective, the United States has brought its resources to bear on pirates around the world since the early days of the Republic.[29]

Today, the UN Law of the Sea codifies past customary international laws. It defines the boundaries, and governs behavior in a state's sovereign territorial waters, exclusive economic zones, and the high seas. Addressing piracy, the United Nations Convention on the Law of the Sea includes a definition of piracy, which is:

(a) any illegal acts of violence or detention, or any act of depredation, committed for private ends by the crew or passengers of a private ship or a private aircraft, and directed:
   i. on the high seas, against another ship or aircraft, or against persons or property on board such ship or aircraft;
   ii. against a ship, aircraft, persons or property in a place outside the jurisdiction of any State;
(b) any act of voluntary participation in the operation of a ship or of an aircraft with knowledge of facts making it a pirate ship or aircraft;

---

[28] News Max Wires (2004), "Bush Limits Landmines but Won't Sign Treaty", 27 February, http://www.newsmax.com/archives/articles/2004/2/27/113517. shtml

[29] In 1805, when 308 Americans were held hostage for ransom by the so-called Barbary Pirates, American Marines, in a joint operation with Greek mercenaries, mounted an attack on a stronghold of the Pasha of Tripoli, who in his practice of piracy did not expect a swift response from the US. For a longer term view of piracy see K. Zou (2005), "Seeking Effectiveness for the Crackdown of Piracy at Sea", *Journal of Internal Affairs*, 59:1, pp. 117–34.

(c) any act inciting or of intentionally facilitating an act described in subparagraph (a) or (b).[30]

This definition has severe practical limitations because it addresses piracy on the high seas, while most acts of piracy occur within a state's sovereign territorial waters.[31] The International Maritime Bureau (IMB) has adopted a more general definition:

> Piracy is an act of boarding any vessel with the intent to commit theft or any other crime and with the intent or capability to use force in furtherance of that act.[32]

International organizations such as the International Maritime Organization (IMO) and private organizations such as the IMB, together with states, have undertaken efforts to address the problem of piracy. The IMO and IMB have been key in defining the antipiracy agenda at global forums, including those of the UN Security Council. They provide data, coordinate communications systems, and have developed piracy response protocols.[33] Shipping insurance companies pressure individual state governments into taking actions against pirates operating in their territory. Private sector actors have performed the role of norm entrepreneurs. For example, the Joint War Committee (JWC) of Lloyd's Market Association declared up to 250 nautical miles from the coast of Somalia as an area of high activity for strikes, terrorism, and related perils, effectively raising the cost of insurance premiums.[34]

---

[30] United Nations (1982), "Preamble to the United Nations Convention on the Law of the Sea, Article 101", http://www.un.org/Depts/los/convention_agreements/texts/unclos/part7.htm

[31] Richard O'Meara (2007), "Maritime Piracy in the 21st Century: A Short Course for U.S. Policymakers", *Journal of Global Change and Governance*, Winter.

[32] Council for Security Cooperation in the Asia-Pacific "Co-operation for Law & Order at Sea", *CSCAP Memorandum 5*, p. 14, http://www.cscap.org/uploads/docs/Memorandums/CSCAP%20Memorandum%20No%205%20-%20Cooperation%20for%20Law%20and%20Order%20at%20Sea.pdf

[33] See International Maritime Organization, "Measures to Enhance Maritime Security: Interim Guidelines for the Authorization of Recognized Security Organizations Acting on Behalf of the Administration and/or Designated Authority of a Contracting Government", *Safety of Life at Sea Convention (1974)*, 10 June, http://www.imo.org/includes/blastDataOnly.asp/data_id%3D7501/1074.pdf; International Maritime Organization (1988), *Convention for the Suppression of Unlawful Acts Against the Safety of Maritime Navigation*, 10 March, http://www.imo.org/Conventions/mainframe.asp?topic_id=259&doc_id=686

[34] See, for example, Joint War Committee, *JWC Hull War, Strikes, Terrorism and Related Perils Listed Areas* (25 November 2009).

Private sector actors, however, are constrained by issues of sovereignty enshrined in the UN Law of the Sea and the UN Charters. Further, they lack the resources required to tackle the issue. Well aware of these limitations, in a 2008 statement the IMO President called "upon states interested in the safety and environmentally sound function of shipping activities, that have the capacity to do so, to take part actively in the fight against piracy and armed robbery against ships (including 'mother ships') off the coast of Somalia and in the Gulf of Aden."[35] Thus, norm entrepreneurs can only lobby for action, keeping it on the policy agenda, and bringing financial pressure to bear on states ineffectively dealing with pirates. Only states have the resources to interdict pirates and criminalize their activities.

In 2008, the UN Security Council agreed to act on the issue of maritime piracy in the Gulf of Aden. It defined Somalia, a failed state, as the epicenter of piracy as a result of its Transitional Federal Government's (TFG) incapacity to interdict pirates and secure both its territorial waters and international sea-lanes off its coast. The Security Council, acting under Chapter Seven of the *U.N. Charter*, authorized navies with the relevant resources to "use, within the territorial waters of Somalia, in a manner consistent with action permitted on the high seas with respect to piracy under relevant international law, all necessary means to repress acts of piracy and armed robbery."[36] This effectively denied Somalia's sovereign rights because it was not in a position to guarantee safe passage to the vessels in its territorial waters. Foreign militaries were thus permitted to send military forces into Somali sea and airspace to interdict pirates.

The UN authorized a multinational naval presence to patrol and interdict pirates off the coast of Somalia, including the European Union's Operation (Atalanta) and a US-led force (Combined Task Force 150 or CTF 150). Both assist the US-led force operating in the area since Operation Enduring Freedom.

Although the command of CTF 150 rotated among members, the US navy constituted the most significant element. The total multinational force has usually been comprised of fourteen or fifteen vessels.[37] As of

---

[35] United Nations (2008), "Statement by Efthimios E. Mitropoulos, Secretary-General of the International Maritime Organization", *6020th Meeting of the United Nations Security Council*, 20 November.

[36] United Nations (2008), *UN Security Council Resolution 1816 (2008)*, Article 7b, 2 June, http://www.consilium.europa.eu/uedocs/cmsUpload/N0836177.pdf

[37] Donna Miles (2009), "Latest Ship Seizures Broaden Counter-Piracy Challenge", *American Forces Press Service*, 27 March, http://www.navy.mil/search/

30 January 2010, the US contribution to all maritime security operations in the Fifth Fleet's Area of Responsibility (AOR) consisted of two Carrier Strike Groups (CSG), USS Dwight D. Eisenhower and Nimitz, and one big deck amphibious warship, which resembles an aircraft carrier (USS Bonhomme Richard).[38] A single CSG consists of a carrier, two guided missile cruisers, a guided missile destroyer, a destroyer, a frigate, two attack submarines, and a logistics supply ship.[39]

The US government has declared this issue to be a priority,[40] and it supported the creation of a successor, CTF 151, under US command, for which the USS Boxer became the flagship for the force. CTF-151 is based in Djibouti, and coordinated with, and has incorporated vessels of, the US Navy's Fifth Fleet, under the Combined Forces Maritime Component Commander/Commander US Naval Forces Central Command in Bahrain. The US Naval presence in the multinational area of operations is therefore far superior in terms of available air and sea power relative to the contributions of the other multinational forces.

This commitment is indicative of Washington's increasing frustration with the problem of maritime piracy, and its intent to enforce measures aimed at combating it. In addition to its military presence off the coast of Somalia, the US has also brought its law enforcement agencies to bear, with the FBI indicting those suspected of engaging in piracy.[41] While the private sector therefore raised awareness of the problem, and the UN responded to it by codifying and institutionalizing protocols and sanctioning the use of a multinational force, it is the US participation and enforcement of the antipiracy agenda that largely enforces this effort to address the problem of piracy.

---

display.asp?story_id=43830

[38] Information based on available open source information compiled from a variety of US Navy websites.

[39] Global Security "Carrier Strike Group", http://www.globalsecurity.org/military/agency/navy/csg-intro.htm

[40] Robyn Dixon (2009), "Obama vows to fight piracy", *Chicago Tribune*, 14 April, http://www.chicagotribune.com/news/nationworld/chi-pirates_14apr14,0,2942506.story. For a summary of the US plan, see the report of the National Security Council (2008), "Countering Piracy off the Horn of Africa: Partnership and Action Plan", December, http://www.globalsecurity.org/military/library/policy/national/0812_nsc_counter-piracy-action-plan.pdf

[41] Chad Bray (2010), "U.S. Files More Charges in Piracy Case", *The Wall Street Journal*, 12 January.

Critics contend that piracy is, in fact, a land-based problem.[42] Clearly, however, the US has been unwilling to address the broader problem of Somali governance, content to enforce aspects of a global norm legitimated by the international community.

Further cases

There are several other examples that reflect the distinction I have drawn between ineffectual global governance subverted by US efforts to lead and, alternatively, the development of global norms. From the failure to ratify the Convention on Children Rights in 1987 to the US refusal to sign the Kyoto Protocol, the results have been comparable: lack of American sponsorship has given these initiatives few teeth or resources to support their efforts.

Child soldiering in many ways typifies the problem. In response to the lobbying of an umbrella organization, the Coalition to Stop the Use of Child Soldiers (CSUCS),[43] a series of international protocols and Security Council resolutions have been issued in an attempt to eliminate the recruitment of minors.[44] The major impetus has been to institutionalize an Optional Protocol to the Convention on the Rights of the Child relating to the participation of children in armed conflict. By 2008, according to the CSUCS global report, 120 countries had ratified the optional protocol.[45] In some regards, the United States has

---

[42] See Martin Murphy (2009), "Somali piracy: not just a naval problem", Center for Strategic and Budgetary Assessments, 16 April, http:// www.csbao line. org/4Publications/PubLibrary/B.20090417.Somali_Piracy/B.20090417.Somali_Piracy.pdf

[43] The Coalition is headed by a Steering Committee of six NGOs consisting of Amnesty International, Human Rights Watch, International Federation Terre des Hommes, International Save the Children Alliance, Jesuit Refugee Service, the Quaker United Nations Office-Geneva, and World Vision International.

[44] Among the more important international conventions and protocols related to recruitment of children in armed conflicts are the *Geneva Convention, Additional Protocol I (API)* (relating to international armed conflicts), Article 77(2); *Additional Protocol II (APII)* (relating to noninternational armed conflicts), Article 4(3)c; *Convention on the Rights of the Child (CRC)*, Article 38; *Rome Statute for an International Criminal Court (ICC)*, Article 8 (on War Crimes), section 2 b) (xxvi); *Optional Protocol to the Convention on the Rights of the Child on the Involvement of Children in Armed Conflict* (OP-CRC-CAC), Article 4(1) and (2); the *African Charter on the Rights and Welfare of the Child (ACRWC)*; the *Paris Principles and Guidelines on Children Associated with Armed Forces or Armed Groups*.

[45] Coalition to Stop the Use of Child Soldiers (2008), *Child Soldiers Global Report 2008* (London, UK: CSUCS), p. 13.

been supportive of this initiative. In October 2007, the Child Soldier Accountability Act was introduced into the US Congress, amending the US criminal code to allow the prosecution of individuals who have recruited or used child soldiers, whether in the United States or elsewhere. The Child Soldier Prevention Act, also of 2007, was signed into law by George W. Bush, sanctioning cuts in US military assistance to those countries that continue to enlist or force children into their ranks.

Yet efforts at US leadership have been undermined by several factors: first, its refusal to either ratify the Optional Protocol, or accept any obligations, even as it signed it. Although sovereignty and federalism are raised as obstacles, part of the problem is that the US recruits 17-year-old children for the military, under the specified minimum age of 18. The US defends this position on the grounds that these recruits are not assigned or deployed outside the United States. The 2008 CSUCS report notes that "in the year ending 30 September 2005, 13,793 recruits aged 17 joined the US armed forces – 6,780 into the active armed forces (5,387 boys and 1,393 girls), representing 4.46 percent of all new active duty recruits, and 7,013 into the reserve forces (5,013 boys and 2,000 girls), representing 15.3 percent of the total reserves ... approximately 1,500 soldiers each year were still 17 when they completed their basic training and were ready for operational assignment."[46] Yet, although the US consistently denies that 17-year-olds are deployed, US military officials have admitted that 17-year-olds have fought in both Afghanistan and Iraq.[47]

Furthermore, the US detained suspected child soldiers as enemy combatants at Guantanamo. As the CSUCS reports:

> Omar Ahmed Khadr, a Canadian national, was taken into US custody in Afghanistan in late July 2002 when he was 15 years old and subsequently transferred to Guantánamo. In November 2005 he was charged for trial by military commission under a military order signed by President George W. Bush in November 2001. The military commission system was replaced by a revised system under the 2006 Military Commissions Act (MCA). In April 2007 Omar Khadr was charged for trial under the MCA with murder and

---

[46] Coalition to Stop the Use of Child Soldiers (2008), *Child Soldiers Global Report 2008* (London, UK: CSUCS), p. 359.

[47] Sean J. Byrne, Brigadier General, US Army, Director of Military Personnel Policy (2004), *Letter to Human Rights Watch*, 2 April.

attempted murder in violation of the law of war, conspiracy, providing material support for terrorism and spying. In June 2007 a military judge dismissed the charges against Khadr on a jurisdictional question. On 24 September 2007 a newly established Court of Military Commission Review overturned the ruling, allowing proceedings against Khadr to continue. On 11 October 2007 another Guantánamo detainee, Mohammad Jawad, was charged with attempted murder for allegedly throwing a grenade at a US military vehicle. He was 17 at the time of the attack.[48]

The detention of under-18s is as aberrant as is their recruitment in Western Europe and elsewhere in North America.

Finally, the US has steadfastly refused to participate in the ICC initiative in trying leaders of groups who use child soldiers, citing the ICC as a potentially threat to abrogate US sovereignty. Nor has it participated in the Security Council's Working Group on Children and Armed Conflict, whose major initiative has focused on the monitoring and reporting of what it terms "grave abuses" as war crimes (UN resolution 1612).[49] In sum, this global initiative has generally fallen short of its prescribed goals, in large part due to a lack of US support and enforcement.

These various initiatives – from landmines to child soldiers – are often discussed in various literatures under the rubric of "global governance", a term I have myself consciously avoided using routinely in this book because it obfuscates the issue of enforcement. But, clearly, they all represent examples of NGO-backed and UN institutionalized efforts where US sponsorship has been lacking, and enforcement problematic.

Other initiatives do appear to more closely approximate a movement towards the development of global norms. Not surprisingly, discussions concerning the norms of airline security provide one example of this process. The safety and security of international civil aviation have been promoted by the aviation industry, institutionalized at the International Civil Aviation Organization (ICAO), and supported by the US.

---

[48] Coalition to Stop the Use of Child Soldiers (2008), *Child Soldiers Global Report*, op. cit., pp. 360–1.

[49] For details see Office of the Special Representative of the Secretary General for Children and Armed Conflict, *Security Council Working Group*, http://www.un.org/children/conflict/english/securitycouncilwg.html

While the foundation of the global norm of protecting civilian air transport was laid in the mid-twentieth century with the Convention on International Civil Aviation (1944), the trend in the late 1960s and early 1970s, which saw global terrorist organizations hijacking airliners to further their political agenda, served as a catalyst for the institutionalization of uniform airline security standards.[50] Realizing that it could not protect itself against the threat without global cooperation, the aviation industry favored normalized airline security standards. The Airports Council International (ACI), the International Air Transport Association (IATA), the International Federation of Airlines Pilots Association (IFALPA), and the International Criminal Police Organization (INTERPOL) supported the creation of these standards. Enunciating this view, the UN Security Council Resolution 286, adopted on 9 September 1970, called upon "states to take all possible legal steps to prevent further hijackings or any other interference with international civil air travel."[51]

The US plays a significant role in enforcing the international standards of global airport security. In support of these standards, the Federal Aviation Administration (FAA) and the US Department of State are the most influential arms of the US federal government in assuring that states, not individual carriers, abide by global airline security norms. The FAA's International Aviation Safety Assessments (IASA) program examines whether or not a state is complying with ICAO airline safety and security standards. If it is not, the FAA may recommend to the US Department of Transportation "that carriers from that country do not have an acceptable level of safety oversight and will recommend that DOT revoke or suspend its carrier's economic operating authority."[52] Furthermore, the Department of State may issue travel warnings on a country that does not meet the FAA's IASA standards.

These measures, taken by the US, have garnered support with the members of IATA and the International Civil Aviation Organization (ICAO), who have been lobbying for Transportation Security Administration (TSA) and Department of Homeland Security (DHS) involvement in the

---

[50] For a list of conventions regarding aviation security, see *Convention on Offences and Certain Other Acts Committed on Board Aircraft* (1963), *Convention for the Suppression of Unlawful Seizure of Aircraft* (1970), and *Convention for the Suppression of Unlawful Acts against the Safety of Civil Aviation* (1971).

[51] United Nations (1970), "The situation created by increasing incidents involving the hijacking of commercial aircraft", *UN Security Council Resolution 286*, 9 September.

[52] International Aviation Safety Assessments (IASA) Program, http://www.faa.gov/about/initiatives/iasa/more/

development of consensus on aviation security standards and the enforcement of rules.[53] Those standards, notably, are to be set by the UN.[54]

Final reflections: the future of global politics

American power has waxed and waned for nearly a century, and with it America's role as the underwriter of the global system. Certainly, the combination of US economic turmoil and the meteoric rise of the Chinese economy has led to questions about the ability of the US to sustain a hegemonic role. Yet many American commentators have historically conflated the ideas of leadership and sponsorship, while critics of American power have focused on the notion that such power is becoming increasingly dispensable. In this book, I have argued that there is a category of emergent global norms that remain reliant on enforcement mechanisms if they are to be effective – and only the US is willing to pay the cost of underwriting them. Indeed, what remains surprising in a period of fiscal retrenchment is the lack of public debate over the size of the enormous American defense budget. This situation is certain not to last, but, while it does, it offers the prospect of global convergence in a select group of policy areas that are consistent with American interests and values – areas where the US is willing to provide sponsorship.

If my analysis is correct, then it potentially offers both theoretical and policy-oriented insights. Theoretically, it suggests that current debates about the future direction of global politics are misplaced. First, they distinguish between a world of American hegemony (conflating leadership and sponsorship) and one of global governance where American power is largely irrelevant. Setting the agenda, or a lack thereof, I have suggested, is not the true litmus test of the essential role of the US in any new pattern of world politics. Rather, what we may be witnessing is a world in which American leadership – either through domination or as a "first among equals" – has given way to one in which societal actors do play a greater role in formulating agendas, yet are reliant on American acquiescence in the implementation of policies predicated on the values

---

[53] See, for example, Department of Homeland Security (2010), "Secretary Napolitano Meets with Global Airline Industry Leaders in Geneva to Strengthen Aviation Security Standards", 22 January, http://www.dhs.gov/ynews/releases/pr_1264178353596.shtm

[54] See Andrew Beatty (2010), "US looks to UN for new airline security standards", *AFP*, 26 January, reprinted at http://www.google.com/hostednews/afp/article/ALeqM5gqLgt_pywpJyhVxgPyQUO7snIBfA

they advocate. Social and material forms of power, therefore, consequentially become equally important in the expansion of norms.

When it comes to applying theory to policy, theoreticians embedded in disciplinary departments have traditionally rejected any linkage to the policy implications of their work, considering it both intellectually less honorable and normative in character. The concept of "praxis," the process by which a theory lesson or skill is enacted or practiced, has long since gone out of vogue. Perhaps such reluctance is explained by its initial Marxist roots[55] or alternatively by the evident failure of mainstream American political scientists in their efforts at social engineering through modernization theory in the 1960s and 1970s.[56]

In this book, I have attempted to reclaim the idea in bridging the gap between theory and policy. Certainly, I suggest, there are elements of this argument that may be modestly prescriptive. Specifically, American policymakers in the postwar era have defined policy choices as lying between unilateralism and multilateralism (with imperialism as an unacknowledged but ever-present option), largely contingent on their ideological persuasion. America's role in terms of leadership – defined as the formulation of policy – has remained unquestioned. Such an approach lacks a degree of sophistication and is increasingly dysfunctional and self-defeating in a world where the countervailing forces are not simply other states but a variety of transnational actors. The relative simplicity of the bipolar world has been usurped by one in which enemies are decreasingly visible and the number of "veto players" have proliferated. In that sense, letting others formulate the agenda, and enforcing those of which the US approves, may be a more effective policy than efforts at persuasion or dominance. In that sense, Steven Lukes' third dimension of power, in which the agenda is not overtly controlled,[57] may have more to say to American policymakers than recurrent debates about unilateralism and multilateralism in American foreign policy.

---

[55] For a discussion of Antonio Gramsci's use of the term praxis, see Bruno Gulli (2002), "Praxis and the Danger: The Insurgent Ontology of Antonio Gramsci", *Cultural Logic*, http://clogic.eserver.org/2002/gulli.html

[56] Perhaps the most notable example of this conservative genre is that of Walt Rostow (1960), *The Stages of Economic Growth: A Non-Communist Manifesto* (Cambridge: Cambridge University Press). He attempts to show the factors needed for a country to reach the path to modernization. Rostow served as Deputy Special Assistant to the President for National Security Affairs and as counselor of the Department of State and Chairman of the Policy Planning Council, and as Special Assistant for National Security Affairs in the Kennedy and Johnson Administrations.

[57] Steven Lukes (1974), *Power: A Radical View* (London: Macmillan Press), p. 25.

Index